What Your Colleagues Are Saying

"In *Write From the Beginning*, Rebecca G. Harper clearly values teachers by answering common questions they pose and offering choices! This book will be your go-to professional text to develop a writing curriculum that meets students where they are and provides the practice needed to move them forward. Filled with practical lessons to help students learn through writing, find their voices and their stories, and persuade others, Harper has crafted a book that supports *all* students!"

—**Laura Robb**, Author of *Read Talk Write: 35 Lessons That Teach Students to Analyze Fiction and Nonfiction*

"*Write From the Beginning* is a must-read for elementary writing teachers. From anchor text recommendations and lesson ideas to quick tips and extensions, this book is a treasure trove for teachers who want to bolster students' confidence and independence in writing."

—**Julie Wright**, Educational Consultant and Author

"If you're looking for a strategy-packed resource to enhance your writing instruction, Rebecca G. Harper has you covered! *Write From the Beginning: 43 Joyful Lessons to Foster Skilled Writers Every Day* offers adaptable lessons to suit the developmental stages and abilities of your students. Organized by instructional goals, each chapter provides engaging techniques, student samples, and practical tips to support your teaching. Whether you're focusing on storytelling, descriptive writing, research, voice, or persuasive writing, you will find that this book provides the tools and inspiration to nurture capable, confident writers."

—**Maria Walther**, Literacy Consultant and Author of *The Ramped-Up Read Aloud, Shake Up Shared Reading,* and *More Ramped-Up Read Alouds*

"Harper's tone throughout the book is encouraging, and her passion for writing is evident. The extensions are clearly written, making them easy to follow, with a list of materials and step-by-step instructions for implementing the writing activities. The book is filled with examples of children's writing, recommended children's literature for each writing type, and clearly outlined extensions that teachers can apply in their classrooms. It is a valuable resource for both new and experienced teachers!"

—**Julia López-Robertson**, Professor, University of South Carolina

"Rebecca G. Harper's *Write From the Beginning* is a gift to the profession. One of the challenges of becoming a good writing teacher is developing a well-rounded repertoire of writing lessons. Rebecca's book will be an invaluable resource for teachers, with truly joyful lessons on teaching children how to write texts in a wide variety of genres in which they elaborate beautifully and bring their own unique voices into their writing."

—**Carl Anderson**, K–12 Writing Consultant, Author of *Teaching Fantasy Writing: Lessons That Inspire Student Engagement and Creativity, Grades K–6* and Coauthor of *How to Become a Better Writing Teacher* (with Matt Glover)

Write From the Beginning, Grades K–5

Dedication

For my best friend from way back, Will C. Franklin, AKA Chill Will.

Thanks for being there for me from the beginning and forever. I love you to infinity and beyond.

Write From the Beginning, Grades K–5

43 Joyful Lessons to Foster Skilled Writers Every Day

Rebecca G. Harper

FOR INFORMATION:

Corwin
A SAGE Company
2455 Teller Road
Thousand Oaks, California 91320
(800) 233-9936
www.corwin.com

SAGE Publications Ltd.
1 Oliver's Yard
55 City Road
London EC1Y 1SP
United Kingdom

SAGE Publications India Pvt. Ltd.
Unit No 323-333, Third Floor, F-Block
International Trade Tower Nehru Place
New Delhi 110 019
India

SAGE Publications Asia-Pacific Pte. Ltd.
18 Cross Street #10-10/11/12
China Square Central
Singapore 048423

Vice President and Editorial Director: Monica Eckman
Senior Acquisitions Editor: Liz Gildea
Content Development Editor: Sarah Ross
Product Associate: Zachary Vann
Production Editor: Tori Mirsadjadi
Copy Editor: Diane DiMura
Typesetter: C&M Digitals (P) Ltd.
Cover Designer: Scott Van Atta
Marketing Manager: Margaret O'Connor

Printed and bound by CPI Group (UK) Ltd, Croydon, CR0 4YY

LCCN 2024051627

This book is printed on acid-free paper.

25 26 27 28 29 10 9 8 7 6 5 4 3 2 1

CONTENTS

Visit the companion website at
https://companion.corwin.com/courses/writefromthebeginning
for downloadable resources.

Note From the Publisher: The author has provided links to web content throughout the book that is available to you through QR (quick response) codes. To read a QR code, you must have a smartphone or tablet with a camera. We recommend that you download a QR code reader app that is made specifically for your phone or tablet brand.

Links may also be accessed at https://companion.corwin.com/courses/writefromthebeginning

ACKNOWLEDGMENTS

As I write these acknowledgments, I am sitting in an airport after dropping off my oldest daughter, Amelia, for her freshman year at Vanderbilt University in Nashville. Talk about time flying. And while I made it through the move-in day without being a complete mess, I did cry at the ticket counter to a random American Airlines attendant. Thank you, whoever you are, for recognizing that this momma needed a minute.

It is altogether fitting that these acknowledgments begin with thanks to my three children. Amelia, Macy Belle, and Vin—you remain my three best and brightest accomplishments. I hope you three know that the title I wear most proudly is Mom. While you are each at different stages and places in your lives, know that no matter where you are, when you need me, I will be there.

Amelia—Do your thing in Nashville. Study hard. Stay strong. Swim fast. Leave the bar early. And call your mother.

Macy Belle—Thank you for always bringing the laughs, the best stories, and the brightest smile wherever you go. You keep being that force of nature that knocks the world off its axis, but please, try not to fall out of your desk in class.

Vin—Thank you for the hugs, the movie nights, and for schooling me on whatever this new language is that you keep speaking. I won't be the last woman you love, but I was the first. No cap.

I will love you three forever.

These past few months have been a whirlwind, and in some cases a tornado, with life swirling around me, uprooting items and completely changing the landscape of my life. I heard someone once say that the only one who likes a change is a baby, and I am pretty sure that is the God's honest truth. Regardless, change is inevitable, and I am most grateful for those who stand by me no matter the circumstances. There are so many people who have been in my corner from jump and whose kindness I will never forget.

Thank you to

Sabina Jokulis
Minda Jokulis
Melissa Hofstetter
Eric Hofstetter
Nicole Cain
Carissa Parrish
Brandi Reynolds
Jenna Gurley
Laura Carr
Shelly Tanner
Elaina Leonard
LE Johnson
Mark Epps
Connie Rule

My AU doctoral students, with a special shout-out to Cohorts 8, 9, and 10.

You will never know how much you all mean to me.

Writing a book always involves more than just me, though sometimes it feels like a lonely existence with deadlines looming (I missed every single one on this book). There are so many people who have helped contribute to this manuscript either through student samples, feedback, or classroom implementation. Without them, this book would have never been completed.

I am so grateful to the teachers and young people who provided writing samples for this book. Thank you to

Jared Allison
Tre Cain
Skylar Clay
Damien Groves
Fulton Groves
John David Groves
Amelia Harper
Macy Belle Harper
Vin Harper
Nickolas Jokulis
Mickolas Jokulis
Alysha Mooney
Shelly Tanner

Much thanks is owed to my developmental editor, Sara Johnson. I met Sara almost a decade ago at a reading conference in some city I have forgotten, where I was presenting during the last session on the last day of the conference. Truthfully, I expected no one to be in attendance, but my session was packed. Sara stayed after and asked if I had ever considered writing a book. Thanks to her, I got my first book contract. We reconnected when I started writing for Corwin and what a full circle moment that was. Sara has been an absolute angel this go-round as I have missed **every single deadline** and never once did she get angry or fuss at me, though she most definitely should have. Instead, she asked me how she could support me. Sara, thank you. Thank you for giving me an opportunity years ago and for the grace you extended to me during this latest work.

And lastly, to that local author who helped me find my wings—you changed my life. That I can call. #78

With a full and grateful heart,

ABOUT THE AUTHOR

Dr. Rebecca G. Harper is a professor of language and literacy in the College of Education and Human Development at Augusta University where she teaches courses in literacy, qualitative research, and curriculum, and serves as the EdD program director. Her research focuses on writing and critical literacy and the ways in which authentic literacy can foster engagement, agency, and empathy in students. She is the director of the Augusta University Writing Project and the author of *Content Area Writing That Rocks (and Works)!*; *Write Now and Write On: 37 Strategies for Authentic Daily Writing in Every Content Area*; *Writing Workouts: Strategies to Build Students' Writing Skills, Stamina, and Success*; and *Literacy Practices in Sports and Coaching: Developing Literacy Competencies in Interdisciplinary Environments*.

Chapter 1

IN THE BEGINNING, WE WRITE

My kindergarten students can't read yet; they aren't ready to write.

My students struggle with spelling.

They have a hard time coming up with their own ideas.

If they tell you their story it's great, but if you ask them to write that all down? Forget it.

Trying to stay on topic is a struggle.

Whenever I model writing, everybody in class copies my example. If I write my story about my dog, Frisky, then everybody in the class writes about **their** *dog named Frisky.*

So many of my students don't know how to organize their ideas. They just put everything in one big paragraph.

I have trouble getting my students to write a sentence, much less a paragraph.

Does any of this sound familiar to you? These are some of the comments and concerns I hear from teachers across the country when they talk about their students and writing. In fact, I bet some of you wondered if I have been lurking outside your classroom because these remarks describe the students sitting in your classroom right now. The fact is these are not unusual concerns. They are rather common and even transcend grade levels and content areas.

At this point you may be asking yourself, so why does this happen? Most often this is because students simply lack confidence and do not have a significant amount of experience with independent writing. Getting better at any skill requires practice to gain experience, but many of our students just don't have the needed background. It's almost like applying for a job to gain experience for a specific career, but the job that would give you the needed experience requires experience in order to get hired. Kind of silly, right? Yet how many of us as teachers have standard sets that assume students walk in the door with base line understandings despite the fact that they are all coming from different backgrounds with different literacy experiences. This is especially true for young learners with writing, but it is also evident with middle and secondary students.

The reality is that while many of our students may come to us with limited academic writing experiences, they often have alternative literacy experiences from their home and family lives that can be leveraged in the classroom. Upon examination, you may find that students in your class are proficient in storytelling, singing songs and rhymes, artistic representations, and more. Finding ways to celebrate literacies like these can help bridge the gaps between home and academic literacies. In fact, remember that our youngest students who may not actively be reading words yet, are reading the world. Like Freire and Macedo (1987) say, "before we read the word, we read the world" (p. 35). That's why, despite the fact that many of our students might not be able to identify letter sound relationships and subsequently decode words, they are already reading their worlds, acquiring home literacies, and learning how we use words to communicate our thoughts and ideas in multiple settings. Plus, research indicates that home literacy practices have a direct effect on students' development of reading, language, and writing skills (e.g., Burgess et al., 2002; Puranik et al., 2018; Sénéchal & LeFevre, 2002; Sénéchal et al., 1998) and there is emerging evidence that a child's home literacy practices have a direct impact on their emerging writing skills (Aram & Levin, 2001; Puranik et al., 2018; Skibbe et al., 2013).

Let's reflect back on those initial concerns that began this chapter. Of course, each of those items are valid and are certainly not unusual in the classroom setting, especially the elementary setting.

> **My kindergarten students can't read yet; they aren't ready to write:** While some of our students are not reading alphanumeric texts yet or may be striving readers, they can still take part in writings that focus on pictorial images by orally telling stories that can be transcribed by an adult.
>
> **My students struggle with spelling:** Students who may not be the best spellers can still be excellent writers. In fact, I know plenty of brilliant teachers who aren't the best spellers!

Being a good speller does not make you a good writer and correspondingly, being a poor speller does not make you a bad one. Instead, we look for ways to address this through a variety of instructional strategies. One way might include active utilization of the print that is posted in the classroom. Many times, students don't pay attention to all the words that are posted in their classrooms and if they simply looked around, they could find some of the words they need help with. Another simple strategy is to use a substitute you know how to spell. If you can't spell melancholy but you can spell gloomy, use gloomy! One of my favorite stories about finding a substitute word goes back a couple of decades to my mother's third-grade classroom. She had a parent who had written a medical excuse and after crossing out multiple incorrect spellings of the word *diarrhea*, the parent had written: "Please excuse Sam. He had the runs." ☺

My students have a hard time coming up with their own ideas: While some students may profess that they don't know what to write or can't think of a good topic, using quality mentor texts, video clips, images, props, and digital tools to help students think of possibilities that they might consider writing about. In particular, children's literature offers numerous opportunities for story ideas that can emerge not only from the story itself, but from the discussions after. Plus, when we use books that focus on everyday activities, like a trip to grandma's (*Saturdays and Teacakes*), the barbershop (*Crown: An Ode to the Fresh Cut*), and family traditions (*We Had a Picnic This Sunday Past*), students can begin to see that their everyday activities are worth writing about too! With this in mind, this book offers a myriad of writing strategies that build on a variety of mentor texts. When we use these types of texts as models, we are able to get more bang for our buck. Not only do we provide students with a possible topic idea, but we also can expose them to a variety of genres, which can lead to big payouts in the classroom and on assessment days.

If they tell you their story it's great, but if you ask them to write that all down? Forget it: Emerging writers often meet with more challenges when writing than those who are proficient and have had a lot of practice. Think about what many of our writers have to navigate as they think about writing their ideas down in print. They are not simply considering what they might include in their story, but rather they are considering what words they should use, where punctuation might go, when they need to capitalize letters, and how should they spell a particular word. That's a lot of deliberation that deals mainly with the structure and format of writing and not necessarily the overarching idea or gist of the story they are telling. Plus, the reality for many of us is that talking about our ideas is a little easier than writing them down. For me personally, I can say a lot more in less time and with greater ease. Have any of you readers ever taken an online class with a discussion board? Then you probably know what I am talking about! Or, have you ever gotten a text or email and decided that it would be easier to call or swing down to someone's classroom instead of writing your response? Then you kind of have an idea of why some of your students might want to choose to tell you about their story rather than write it down.

Trying to stay on topic is a struggle: Once beginning writers connect with an idea, staying on topic and writing their thoughts down in an organized fashion can sometimes be a challenge. In fact, these are skills that come along with additional experience. For some writers, if there is a somewhat related detail connected to their story, they think it relates and is on topic. For example, if a student is writing about an important figure in their life—grandma—who often takes them to Walmart, then Walmart seems like a relevant detail. Now all of a sudden you find yourself reading about the time grandma took them to Walmart and bought them a hot wheels set and how she hit the buggy corral with her Buick. Try explaining to a second grader why Walmart isn't really important to the story! In my experience, it can sometimes be difficult for students to identify in their own writings what might be off topic or may need to be reorganized, which gives us all the more reason to find strategies and tactics that can help build this crucial skill. Later we will discuss ways to address this through the use of sticky notes, paint strips, and index card sorts which can make organization and on topic writing much more attainable for your students.

Whenever I model writing everybody in class copies my example. If I write my story about my dog, Frisky, then everybody in the class writes about *their* dog named Frisky: Building strong students writers means lots of teacher writing as well. We know how important instructional modeling is for our students to see the process and product of writing, but when they copy our exemplar or even our "Don't do this" sample it can be incredibly frustrating. Part of the copying can sometimes occur simply because our students don't feel confident enough to write their own compositions. The more often students are given opportunities to write, the more their proficiency and confidence can improve. What if we made certain that students had opportunities to practice their writing skills on a daily basis? Then it's possible that they wouldn't need to copy the teacher's example because they have their own ideas. Plus, if they are writing about items that are unique to their own lives, there's less of a need to copy.

So many of my students don't know how to organize their ideas. They just put everything in one big paragraph: Frequent opportunities for writing can aid writers in developing well-organized, comprehensive, and thorough compositions. Expounding upon and idea or explaining thoughts and ideas can make the difference between an effective piece of writing and one that falls flat. To do this, writers need practice and specific strategies that they can use. This might include adding descriptive details, incorporating evidence for support, or answering questions that might be posed about a topic. Rest assured that we will talk about some instructional strategies that can help get your students writing more and expanding on their thoughts and ideas.

I have trouble getting my students to write a sentence, much less a paragraph: While some of our students might struggle with writing extended pieces, every extended piece of writing begins with a sentence, and each sentence begins with one word. When I work with students of all ages, I always tell them that we can work with whatever they put on the paper. We can revise, we can re-write, and we can change, but if there is not anything written on the paper, we can't work with nothing. Many of the writing strategies listed in this book focus on simple starts that can be extended into more thorough writings, but they all start with words that become sentences and move into extended compositions.

As you can see, there are ways in which to address writing concerns so that our students meet the instructional standards their grade level requires, but also help them become more confident and experienced writers. There's no quick fix or remedy that is one size fits all, but with strategic instructional planning, we can work on managing these concerns. Providing students with the space and place to practice their writing skills, along with feedback and reflection within a community of writers can propel students to success. This book aims to do just that.

Universal Lessons From a Kindergarten Classroom

One of the best parts, I think, of working with young students when it comes to writing, is the fact that many haven't developed strong feelings of disdain toward writing. In fact, several years ago when I conducted a study in my middle daughter's kindergarten class, almost all of the students indicated that they loved to write *and* they held a strong understanding of the interconnectedness of reading and writing. Hearing the words, "We write to read," was almost like a class mantra in that kindergarten class. In working with these young children, it became apparent that they held at least a rudimentary understanding of writing and its overall purpose and process as a vehicle for communication and expression.

For example, during my time in that classroom, my daughter Macy Belle produced this writing:

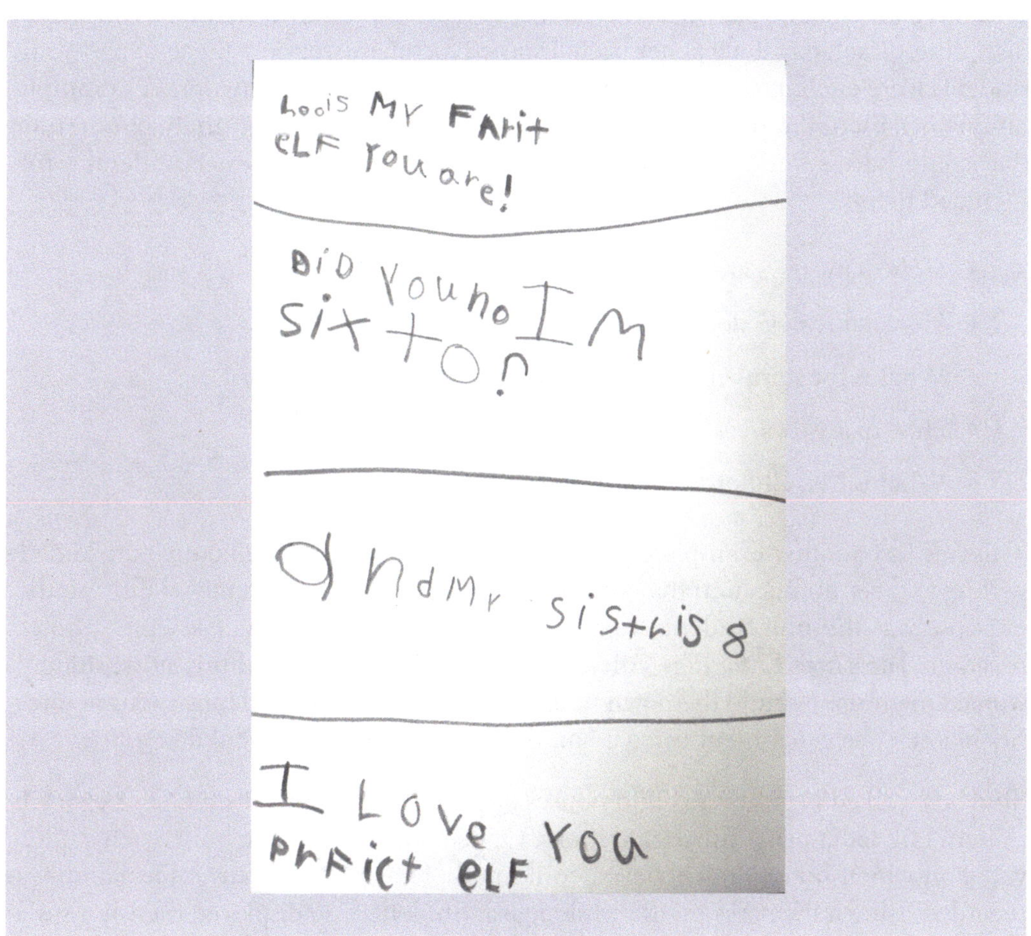

If you notice, she only uses exciting punctuation (exclamation points and question marks), and she draws a line after each sentence. Now as a mother, I am proud of her emerging literacy skills, but as a literacy educator? Holy smokes! This writing sample is beyond intriguing. Why does she only use certain punctuation, and why are there lines dividing her paper? Upon asking her the impetus for the dividing lines, she responded, "So you'll know I'm done talkin' about what I'm talkin' about." Mic drop, Macy Belle. In all seriousness, that writing sample and her explanation showed me that she has a basic and rudimentary understanding of organization AND that sentences should be complete thoughts, hence the lines after each one. Thus, this writing sample represents an emergent understanding of the function of writing. Now, she thinks I kept that writing sample because of the fact that she wrote it, and that is partially true. However, to be honest, no matter what kindergartener authored that sample, I would be just as intrigued simply because it provides me with some needed insight into how young writers think and process information. It also offers some insight into how the student is beginning to conceptualize literacy concepts, which can aid educators in their future planning and instruction.

Yet this was not the only interesting tidbit that came from my visits in that classroom. I also observed students who were articulating their own questions based on the content presented in class, developing inquiry projects that required significant communication and research, and were responding to their classmates' writings on a regular basis. Plus, they were taking part in literacy engagements that utilized multiple skills across disciplines. Each day the teacher posted some type of answer on a piece of paper and students were encouraged to write a question that matched that answer. For example, on one occasion, the posted answer was seven. Students wrote a variety of questions that could have seven as the answer. Some of the questions/queries students wrote included these:

- How many days are in a week?
- How many dogs do I have?
- What is the number between six and eight?
- How many dwarves were there in Snow White?
- What is Ms. Clifford's room number?

This was just another example of how students in that class were taking part in daily writing and communication that was helping them build their literacy skills. Another example was the unit students completed on fairy tales and their research project based on *The Three Little Pigs*. After reading multiple versions of this story, students worked in groups to build their own houses which they later tested for structural integrity in a science experiment using a hair dryer. Here's how that went down.

Students worked in groups to build houses out of different materials such as Lego, aluminum foil, toilet paper tubes, and more. Once their houses were built, each student voted on which house they believed couldn't be blown down. This information was recorded using tally marks on the whiteboard. Students also displayed their houses in the hallways with paper ballots and other students, teachers, and family members cast their votes as well. On the experiment day, the teacher brought in her hair dryer and they tested their hypotheses by attempting to "blow the houses down." They increased the "wind speed" by turning the hair dryer on different speeds and recorded their observations on the board. Once they completed their experiment, they compared their results to their hypotheses.

Photo by Alysha Krier Mooney

Talk about engagement! These five- and six-year-olds were invested in this project! After completing the experience, each one wrote about their thoughts and then shared how they might adjust their builds if they were to do this again. Mind you, this started with a fairy tale that many of the students had already heard before, but they took it to the next level with these reading and writing extension activities that also crossed multiple content areas. In this one project, the teacher was able to assess reading and writing skills, math concepts, and science content. Plus, the students were actively involved in the entire learning process and were guiding the learning. One student even asked if the temperature could affect the outcome as well. (Remember, some hair dryers have high heat and a cold blast button.) We (the adults) had not even considered that as a variable!

This kindergarten class is a perfect example of how writing can be used for engagement, understanding, and communication. One item to note about this classroom in particular is the wide range of readiness levels in that class. Many of the students qualified for special education services and had extensive IEPs while others were reading and writing well above grade level. Because of the collaborative nature of this project, it allowed for all learners to participate no matter their readiness level.

The Nature of Writing Development

The fact remains that even young writers, though they may not have a strong command of formal writing conventions, are still able to effectively communicate their emergent understandings of writing as communication. Plus, many are making observations about the world in which they live where they see examples of literacy. In all grades, when teachers make connections between these personal experiences and the literacy experiences in the academic classroom they can see improvement in motivation and performance. In addition to making these connections, giving students frequent opportunities to write can yield multiple benefits. When going through a box of papers my mother kept from my time in school, I noticed that there were multiple examples of my writing from early preschool on. Granted, much of what my early writings looked like were scribbles and stick figures, but they represented an important stage in early literacy. While some of the samples might be hard to decipher, they served as a method of communication and an initial piece of literacy evidence. In some instances, my contribution was that of a scribble line, with some teacher or other adult deciphering my marks and translating what those scribbles meant.

At other times, I attached letters and words to my drawings as I began to piece together letters and sounds to write messages to my parents or stories in my classes.

Even my son, Vin, who will profess, much to my heartbreak, that he doesn't like to read or write, is actually reading and writing on a regular basis both in and outside of school. I often find notes he has scribbled next to his computer that are not in any way connected to school, including:

- Minecraft maps with locations labeled
- To-do lists
- Fortnite sites and passwords
- A list of passwords he has tried when he got locked out of an account
- Notebook paper-size posters with him depicted as a 6'2" point guard
- Stories he has started (all Minecraft of Fornite based, of course)
- Birthday and Christmas lists
- Lists of his friends and their nicknames

What does this tell me? First of all it is a reminder that even at a young age, he is utilizing his writing skills to achieve his personal goals—goals that may not be directly connected to his academic ones. Second, it is another reminder of how children are making sense of the use of writing to live and function. In my time in schools across the country, I often observe children doing a significant amount of writing that has nothing to do with their academic endeavors. Frequently I watch students creating their own comics or versions of graphic stories, drawing pictures of their favorite characters, making lists of their favorite friends, and writing stories or songs that are connected to their personal interests. Finding ways to capitalize on these writing engagements that students are already completing can have numerous benefits in the classroom.

Even at a young age, many children understand that we use words and pictures to communicate. If you have ever sat with a toddler holding a book and listened to them create a story simply based on what they see from the illustrations, you know what I am talking about. Later, we'll talk about how to use wordless picture books to build strong descriptive writing lessons that can be used from the primary grades to the secondary setting.

As a young child, one of my favorite books was, and still is for that matter, *There's a Monster at the End of This Book*. My mother read that book to me so many times that I eventually memorized the words and proclaimed to my father that I could read—just listen. My dad reminded me that I was not actually reading, but rather I had just memorized the words in the book. Now, granted, there was some truth to that statement, but also some falsehoods. That memorization of the familiar story and my recall and recitation served as an important stage in learning to read. Around that same time, my sister and I had a set of cassette tape audio books that we listened to on repeat. Listening to those audio books—the ones that "dinged" when it was time to turn the page—were pivotal in both my sister and me learning to read. We used those literacy experiences at home, along with what we were learning in school, as a way of solidifying an understanding of reading and writing. Similarly, my "copying" of a familiar story in my own writing served as an important stage in learning to write. Do you remember the part in *Charlotte's Web* (1952) where E. B. White describes the barn? He explains, "The barn was very large. It was very old. It smelled of hay and it smelled of manure. It smelled of the perspiration of tired horses and the wonderful sweet breath of patient cows . . . It was the kind of barn that children like to play in.

And the whole thing was owned by Fern's Uncle, Mr. Homer L. Zuckerman" (p. 13). As a young writer, borrowing those sentence starters and craft from White helped me craft a narrative about my childhood home. As a middle grades teacher, one of my favorite quick write activities asked students to borrow a line from a poem, excerpt of literature, or song lyric and use that line as inspiration for a new writing. Many of my seventh- and eighth-grade students wrote beautiful responses that were inspired by lines in other works of literature.

Working With Developing Writers

In *Writing Workouts* (Harper, 2023), I discussed how many students have not been trained for writing instruction, which can result in several hurdles when approaching writing tasks. I compared this type of training to athletic training and workout regimens, as there are several parallels that can be drawn. If someone wants to get better at running, they run—simple as that. Correspondingly, specific training principles are employed to run a marathon, which are different from the training required to run a 5K. Different types of physical activities require different training plans and teaching writers is no different. While I argued for more specific and strategic training in *Writing Workouts*, I have to wonder, what if we started our students' school experiences with writing from the onset? What if instead of proclaiming that our youngest students aren't ready to write, what if we walked in with the assumption that they are in fact ready? Now I know that many of our youngest students come into our classrooms and may not know the alphabet or any letter–sound relationships, but there are numerous ways in which students *can* write that don't require them to initially know this material. Instead, they can use pictorial descriptions and orally develop and create stories that can be transcribed. Starting students early on with daily writing and drawing opportunities can build a strong foundation for the upper grades where reading and writing demands are more significant. If we begin early by showing students how to claim their identities as writers and show them how to have success in writing, as they progress to more difficult and complex literacy tasks this can aid them in building their self-confidence and writing proficiency. Plus, when we show students that writing takes on a variety of formats (infographics, graphic novels, pictorial representations, multi-paragraph compositions, etc.) it is much more likely for students to see that they are, in fact, writers. When we define writing as having a specific structure, with a format that appears a certain way, many students, if they are not proficient in that particular structure, assume that they are not writers. By exposing students to a variety of reading and writing engagements, we can begin to cast the net wider, thus helping more students call themselves writers. And this notion is not simply beneficial for students, but teachers as well. When teachers embrace the idea that writing is fluid, takes multiple forms and structures, and is utilized for a variety of purposes, teaching writing can also become more accessible.

Another important item to note is our young children's' proficiency in digital literacies. Remember, most of the students in your classroom have grown up with access to a digital device or other piece of technology. They have only known smartphones and probably are unaware that just two short decades ago, phones were simply used for calling people. Not surfing the web. Not updating your socials. Just phone calls. Today's students are frequently using the internet for more than just school research. They are using digital entities for socialization, gaming, communication, and more. Yet, how often do we lean into those literacies especially in the elementary setting? My son Vin is frequently using the internet to locate the best videos that offer tutorials for any one of the multiple video games he plays, and he is frequently utilizing the chat feature to communicate with his friends. When someone's microphone was broken last week, his friends Face Timed so they could communicate and they shared directives in the chat room. In addition, when he joined in on a game after his friends, he was able to get up to speed on their communications by reading the chat transcript and summarized the entire conversation he missed. Plus, I watched him scroll through the transcript and re-read some of the conversations when his friends started talking about something that he had missed. While this is something I observed at home, I would be willing to bet that this is not exclusive to my home. In fact, research indicates that many students are utilizing digital platforms for multiple means of communication (Kumpulainen et al., 2020; Marsh et al., 2017). Thus, utilizing these platforms that students may already have a strong proficiency can also help students build their confidence in writing.

While this book is meant to address writing in the elementary setting, you will notice that many of the lessons can be modified and adjusted based on the skill level and developmental stage of your students. Many of the strategies can also be used to support content-area lessons not just English language arts, and the modifications, extension ideas, and suggestions for ways to abbreviate the strategy or lesson are presented in an easy-to-follow format. Student samples are included so you can see what a finished product might look like once complete.

Below are highlights from each chapter that may help you determine just where you want to start reading first. You'll notice that this book is not laid out by genre, but instead is organized based on end goals and themes. Because many strategies transcend genre, the purpose is to be able to locate lessons and strategies based on your instructional goals and plans, which might not be strictly bound by genre. Looking at the brief synopsis of the chapters below provides information on what types of engagements are included in each section. Doing this first can help ensure that the time spent is not wasted on strategies or engagements that don't fit your purpose or time availability. You may find that you dip in and out of this book as you locate strategies that best fit the goals of your instruction. Each chapter addresses big ideas in the writing world and can help you plan and guide instruction that best suit the needs of your students. With this in mind, it isn't necessary to start at the beginning and read straight through to the end. Instead, think about what your students might need or consider lessons or standards where you feel you need some additional tools for teaching and start there. Regardless of where you begin, each chapter offers unique and novel approaches for developing and nurturing your writers in multiple settings.

Chapter 2: Breaking Into Story

We all have stories and live what scholars call "storied lives" (Rosenwald & Ochberg, 1992). While much of those stories have been saved for adults, children have a variety of experiences from which they can pull to build and tell their own stories. This section focuses on writing engagements that provide inspiration for an array of writings that celebrate the gift and expression of story. Using a variety of children's literature and authentic literacy experiences as inspiration, this section explores the importance of crafting our stories.

Chapter 3: Tell Me More

Adding rich descriptive details to writing can lift words off the page and provide readers with a picture that is vivid and true. This section focuses on the art of detail and description. Mastering the art of showing rather than telling can be one of the most enjoyable types of writing when coupled with quality mentor texts and authentic experiences. Plus, the art of description is genre fluid, meaning it can merge and easily integrate with a variety of writing types, audiences, and purposes. Yet elaboration and description are not only for descriptive and narrative writing—learning this craft can aid in the construction of argument, research writing, and constructed response writing, as well.

Chapter 4: Learning Through Writing

Whether we realize it or not, many of us conduct research on a daily basis. This is no different for children. They read books about their favorite activities, watch shows around a specific topic, and often look online to locate interesting facts about animals, sports figures, video games, and more. With this in mind, this section focuses on writings that are research based. But don't worry; these fun writing engagements are anything but your typical research report. Instead, they focus on many of the research skills our students are already employing and demonstrate how to incorporate these practices in the classroom on a regular basis.

Chapter 5: Finding Your Voice

Making your writing sing involves a symphony of individual components of craft that can help students develop well-developed and powerful pieces of writing. Often, these items are more challenging for students to take up and implement in their writing due to their somewhat nebulous and ambiguous nature. However, when these components of author's craft are coupled with quality mentor texts and examples, they can become more manageable and accessible for students. This section focuses on the subtle nuances of writing that can propel pieces to the next level. It includes ideas for teaching voice, dialogue, character development, and more.

Chapter 6: The Art of Persuasion

In the persuasive genre, writers are tasked with mastering specific writing skills in order to effectively convey their message and convince their readers. These skills often are employed in the genre of argument as well. Therefore, engaging in lessons that focus on these skills is a must. Plus, these craft ideas can aid students in crafting writings in other genres or in general responses to literature. This section focuses on lessons and strategies that can be used when teaching the persuasive genre, but also can be modified for use in other genres.

Chapter 7: The Measure of Success

While teaching developing writers is at the forefront of this book, the need to monitor and assess their learning as they progress is also important. This section focuses on different forms of assessment, suggestions for feedback, and ways in which teachers might monitor student progress, but also engage students in this process as well.

Appendix: The Rest of the Story

This appendix includes book lists, templates, materials lists, supplemental resources, tips, and other resources mentioned throughout the book. Downloadable PDFs of the appendices are available on the book's companion website: **https://companion.corwin.com/courses/writefromthebeginning**

Chapter 2

BREAKING INTO STORY

Story is a natural part of our lives. In fact, stories are woven into almost every part of our lives, as it is fundamentally an essential part of our human existence. They allow us opportunities to share, connect, and reflect upon the world in which we live. In many instances, we begin our explanations and communications with story by default, due to its natural connection to our lives and worlds. Think about the conversations that we have on a daily basis that are based on a story:

- Tell me about your day.
- Remember when we . . .
- Why do you think _____ happened today?
- Remind me of that movie we saw.
- Tell me about that time you got in trouble in school.
- Have you ever been to _____? Tell me about it.

While those short prompts above might seem inconsequential, they are tangible examples of how we use story in our daily lives to communicate our thoughts and feelings in a variety of settings. The *Oxford Dictionary* defines *story* as "an account of imaginary or real people and events told for entertainment," and "an account of past events in someone's life or in the evolution of something." When you consider those definitions, it is easy to see the natural fit of story in our daily lives. Aside from the fact that we use story as a vehicle for communication, we also use it as a way to account and share events from the past.

As a young child, one of my favorite parts of going to my grandmother's house were the stories she would tell about my mother and her sisters. It was an opportunity to experience and learn about events that occurred long before I was born about people

I knew and loved. If you look at storytelling from a cultural perspective, many cultures pass down history and accounts of events and traditions that are of significant importance to their people. In fact, in some cultures, there are designated storytellers who are responsible for sharing their people's stories, ensuring that these important histories and traditions will transcend generations. Several years ago my family decided to surprise my grandmother with a written account of stories we recalled of my grandfather who had passed away some 30 plus years ago. What started out as a small family project for us to create a written record of our stories of my grandfather, expanded to encompass not only immediate family, but extended family and friends as well. We collected stories from pastors, work colleagues, siblings, friends, children, and grandchildren. While collecting those stories took a lot of legwork, the culminating project was priceless.

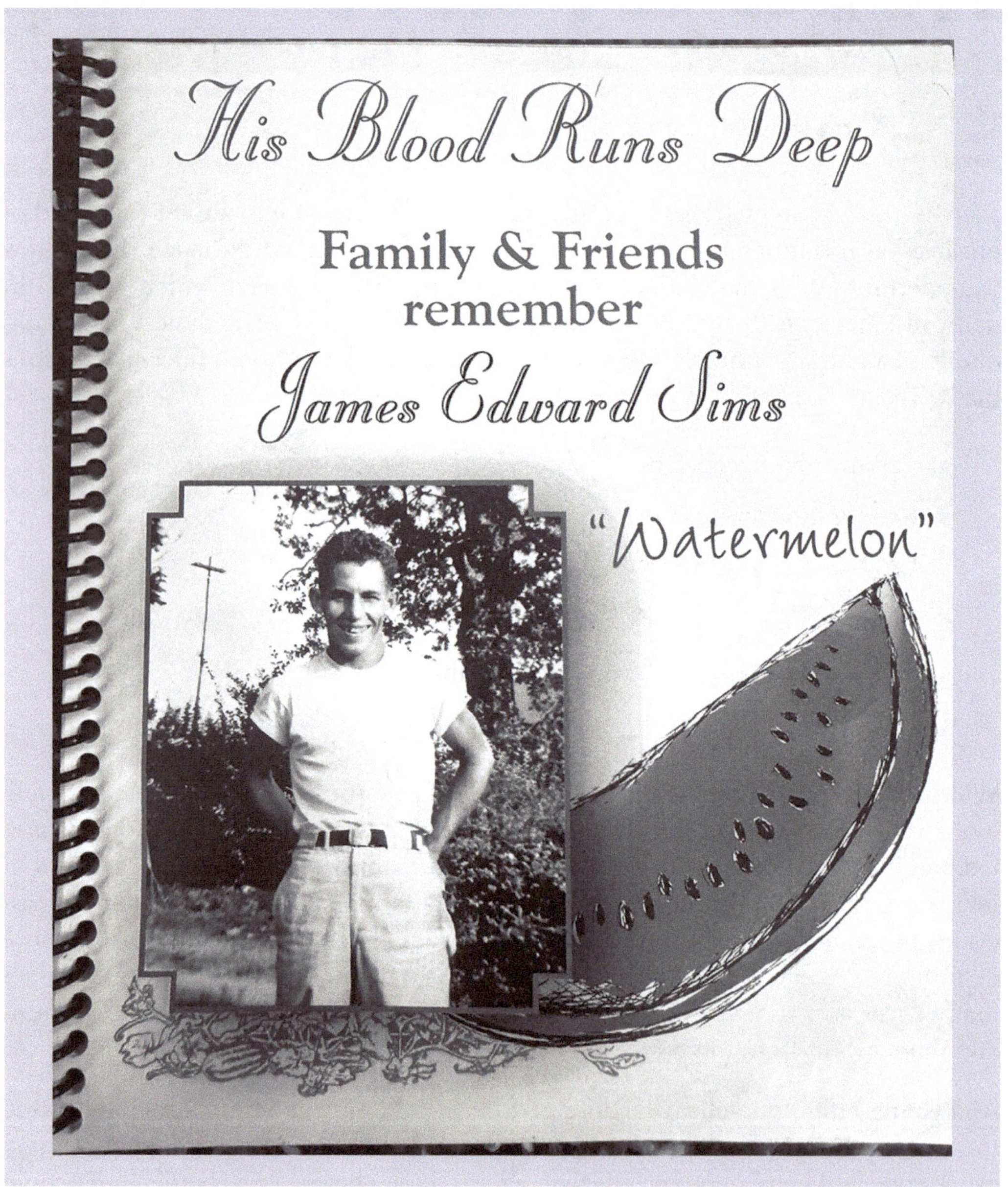

After completing that project, I began to think more about the importance of recording our stories so that others could share and reflect on our experiences and memories. Plus, I was reminded of the fact that even our youngest children can share their stories about their families and lives. As young children, sharing lived experiences can help lay the foundation for a number of literacy skills and engagements. Not to mention the fact that it is often easier for writers to write about what they already know and have experienced than something that is brand new and potentially foreign to them.

While story certainly is natural, have you considered how they also are additional opportunities to reinforce story elements and components? When I tell my own children about a story from my childhood, each one includes the same basic components: characters, a setting, a problem, and a resolution. All of these are standards-based academic skills and competencies that even our youngest children are charged with learning and constructing and represent one more example of how reading and writing are intertwined in all areas of our lives and have a natural fit with how we communicate and function in the real world.

At the elementary level, we spend a significant amount of time on the genre of personal narrative, as many of the standards focus on the construction of narratives. Yet there is so much more to the story than just the personal narrative. Don't get me wrong, stories can start there, but they can also be used to transcend multiple genres and purposes. Utilizing stories for multiple purposes, audiences, and content can help strengthen students' writing skills and overall understanding of writing and its purpose. Think about what stories can do.

Stories can

- Build characters
- Frame a backstory
- Describe an event through a story lens
- Teach and explain information
- Share a moral or bit of wisdom
- Offer explanations for events
- Provide a vignette or snapshot with descriptive detail
- Offer an elaborative example

Casting the net a bit wider with story can help students embrace its versatility and become more proficient at utilizing it for a number of purposes. By helping students recognize how often they share their stories both in and outside of the academic classroom, we can help improve their success when completing academic assessments or related tasks in the narrative genre. An as students begin to recognize their success it can help improve their overall confidence when writing narratives in the academic setting. Because reading and writing can be intimating for learners at all ages and stages of their development, it may help improve performance and increase their confidence when students see that they are already doing what is required in their own lives.

Story also offers opportunities to explore different perspectives, moods, and topics. Think about Judy Blume's *The Pain and the Great One*, for example, which explains events told from the perspective of siblings—an older sister (The Great One) and a younger brother (The Pain)—or Wendelin Van Draanen's *Flipped*, which shares the alternating perspectives of two young neighbors who see the world and their relationship from completely different lenses.

Stories can make you laugh, reflect, cry, scream, feel scared, and more. They connect you to characters, take you to new places, and help you experience characters and events that might be new or unknown. Plus, stories, when written from personal accounts, can have healing components, allowing writers to share their feelings and thoughts about specific events. Not to mention their capacity for empathy and understanding. As a former middle grades teacher, I found that many of my students found their own unique and individual voices through their construction and reconstruction of stories. Plus, in many instances, their collective retellings and explanations helped them make sense of events they had experienced. I often noted that my students would tell me so much more about their lives through their writings instead of through our conversations. That quality is often reflected with writers across generations.

One of my favorite people in the world is an accomplished and award-winning writer, who like all of us, has had a number of challenging experiences occur in his life. When I read his novels, all of which are fictional accounts of made-up characters, I see fragments of his life and story reflected in his narration and characters. As such, his fictional stories have become, I think, one more vehicle for his healing as an adult. Through the stories he constructs in a fictional town with fictional characters, he is funneling some of his childhood and life events through the vessel of characters and their experiences. Our students are no different. For many, their fictional stories become another avenue for sharing and processing their experiences—their hurts and their hopes, all through the vein of story, and all under the guise of an academic task or expectation.

Stories can heal, they can help, and they can offer hope. Not to mention that the construction of story addresses a number of academic standards on their own. Perhaps the most important component of story is the capacity to give a writer their own voice and platform for sharing and showcasing their thoughts, dreams, and fears—the good, the bad, and the ugly. By starting our writers off with opportunities for sharing their own stories, we can offer spaces for collaboration, reflection, and growth, all while celebrating the uniqueness of our own storied lives.

With these characteristics in mind, this book begins with lessons and strategies that celebrate and focus on the construction of story. Each can be modified and adjusted to fit the needs of a variety of learners and multiple mentor texts can be dropped in for accompaniment. All focus on the ways in which we can celebrate and teach the art of story in classrooms across grade levels.

WHEN I WAS YOUNG IN . . .

Using a common or shared experience can serve as a catalyst for strong writing. In this lesson, students focus on a shared experience or time period in their lives (e.g., When I Was Young in First Grade) to write about their personal experiences. Because of the shared nature of the experience, many students can find encouragement and confidence by writing about experiences that are shared and valued by their peers.

Focus Genre: Personal Narrative

Target Grade Level: K–5

Standards

Write narratives to develop real or imagined experiences or events using effective techniques, well-chosen details, and well-structured event sequences.

Anchor Texts

When I Was Young in the Mountains by Cynthia Rylant

We Had a Picnic This Sunday Past by Jacqueline Woodson

Momma, Where Are You From? by Marie Bradby

The Memory String by Eve Bunting

Our Class Is a Family by Shannon Olsen

Materials

- Anchor chart paper
- Sticky notes
- Paint strips

Teach It

1. Begin by reading *When I Was Young in the Mountains* by Cynthia Rylant.
2. Ask students to share how the character described her experiences with life in the mountains. Make note of how Rylant never clarifies if the events occurred over multiple visits to her grandparents' house or if everything occurred during one particular visit.

You don't absolutely have to start with this book, but I believe it is the best fit for this writing lesson.

3. Have students brainstorm as a class places or things that they experience in their current grade level. (e.g., "When I was young in kindergarten, I . . .")
4. Make a list of the things students share (e.g., "When I was young in kindergarten, I played on the playground.").
5. From that list, determine which ones should be the focus of the writing. Condense them down to 5 to 7 examples.
6. Record each of those examples on a sheet of large anchor chart paper, one idea per sheet of chart paper.
7. Post the chart paper in different places in the classroom.

Quick Tip!

Words or pictures can work here. If students draw pictures, when you share them with the class, write the words on the sticky notes next to the pictures that were drawn.

8. Give students sticky notes to record their own thoughts and ideas as they read the anchor charts.
9. Have students circulate around the room with their sticky notes and pencils. Instruct students to record their ideas for each of the anchor chart topics on sticky notes and then place them on the appropriate anchor chart.

10. Go around the room and give a debriefing of each of the anchor chart lists with the sticky note information.

11. As a class, begin writing sentences connected to each of the anchor chart topics listed. Make sure to model how to do this for the class. Demonstrate how to take the notes students have written and use them to construct complete sentences.

12. From this point on, you can continue the lesson in a variety of ways. You can construct a collaborative writing composition including material from all anchor charts that you compile into a classwide writing or you can have students choose an event that they want to write about and construct an independent sentence about their own experiences.

Try It

- Use this when you want students to write about experiences that they have in common with their classmates.
- Because this writing has a predictable starter, "When I was young in . . .," it connects well with other works that follow a predictable series of sentences, which can be beneficial for emerging readers.
- Try this if you want to experiment with a collaborative writing engagement. Working with a partner or in groups can help students increase their confidence in writing.
- Use one of the other mentor texts and complete another writing engagement using that text as a frame. For example, when reading *We Had a Picnic This Sunday Past*, have students use that title as a frame: "We went to music this Monday past and we . . ."

Extensions

- Incorporate a family literacy component by including a take home writing assignment for parents and caregivers to write about their own experiences in that grade level.
- Have each student complete their own "When I was young in . . ." page into a class collection and whole class book sharing all of their experiences.
- Use this writing as a frame for writing about historical figures or characters from novels. Instead of using the "When I was young in . . ." frame, change it to a sentence stem that is connected to a historical character or literary character (e.g., "When I was young during the American Revolution . . .").

Quick Tip!

This connects well with the *You Wouldn't Want to Be a . . .* books that focus on periods in history and what life was like then.

Photo by Alysha Krier Mooney

Modifications

Emerging Writers

- Create pictorial examples of their experiences. Have a classmate or the teacher dictate and label the picture.
- Collect pictorial examples from the class and create a class storyboard of the experiences.
- Use magazine images to locate pictures that show what students might do in each of the settings or places they described. Have them attach the appropriate pictures to the different anchor charts.

Proficient Writers

- Have students interview classmates, other teachers, or family members about when they were young during that time period. Have them record their findings and discuss with their classmates.
- Complete a comparison analysis of how different generations explain their experiences of the same event or occurrence.
- Conduct a collaborative project between upper elementary students and primary students. Have them write together about what they did or do in a specific grade or a particular place.

See It Sample

By Macy Belle

When I was young at the Beche
I got Drtey.
In the Drt I
like Bilding a Hool. We
got on
BugeBoofDse. DaDy got
stug By a
jeLefishe OW!

WE ALL SAW A . . .

Providing written accounts of everyday events is an important skill for students to master. In this lesson, students recall events and explain and describe their observations in their daily lives. Because of the collaborative nature of this writing engagement, it is a great classroom community builder as well.

Focus Genre: Personal Narrative

Target Grade Level: K–2

Standards

Write narratives to develop real or imagined experiences or events using effective techniques, well-chosen details, and well-structured event sequences.

Record observations and ideas and use them to create real or imagined stories.

Anchor Texts

They All Saw a Cat by Brendan Wetzel

See the Ocean by Estelle Condra

Night in the Country by Cynthia Rylant

The Bear Ate Your Sandwich by Julia Sarcone-Roach

Materials

- Crayons, colored pencils, markers
- Lined paper
- Anchor chart paper
- We All Saw a . . . template (p. 233)

Teach It

1. Read students the main anchor text *They All Saw a Cat* by Brendan Wetzel.
2. Have students share all the different animals that saw the cat and how the images and pictures in the story changed based on who saw the cat.

Quick Tip!

There are some great science connections with this book since different animals see images differently. This lesson in general has strong science connections, since so much of what is required in science is connected to observations.

3. Have the class brainstorm all the places they might go during the school day while they are at school. Make sure these are places that all students will experience and not ones that might only be available to some students.
4. Record these places on an anchor chart or digital whiteboard.
5. Create an anchor chart with each place listed (e.g., the playground, library, cafeteria, or hallway).

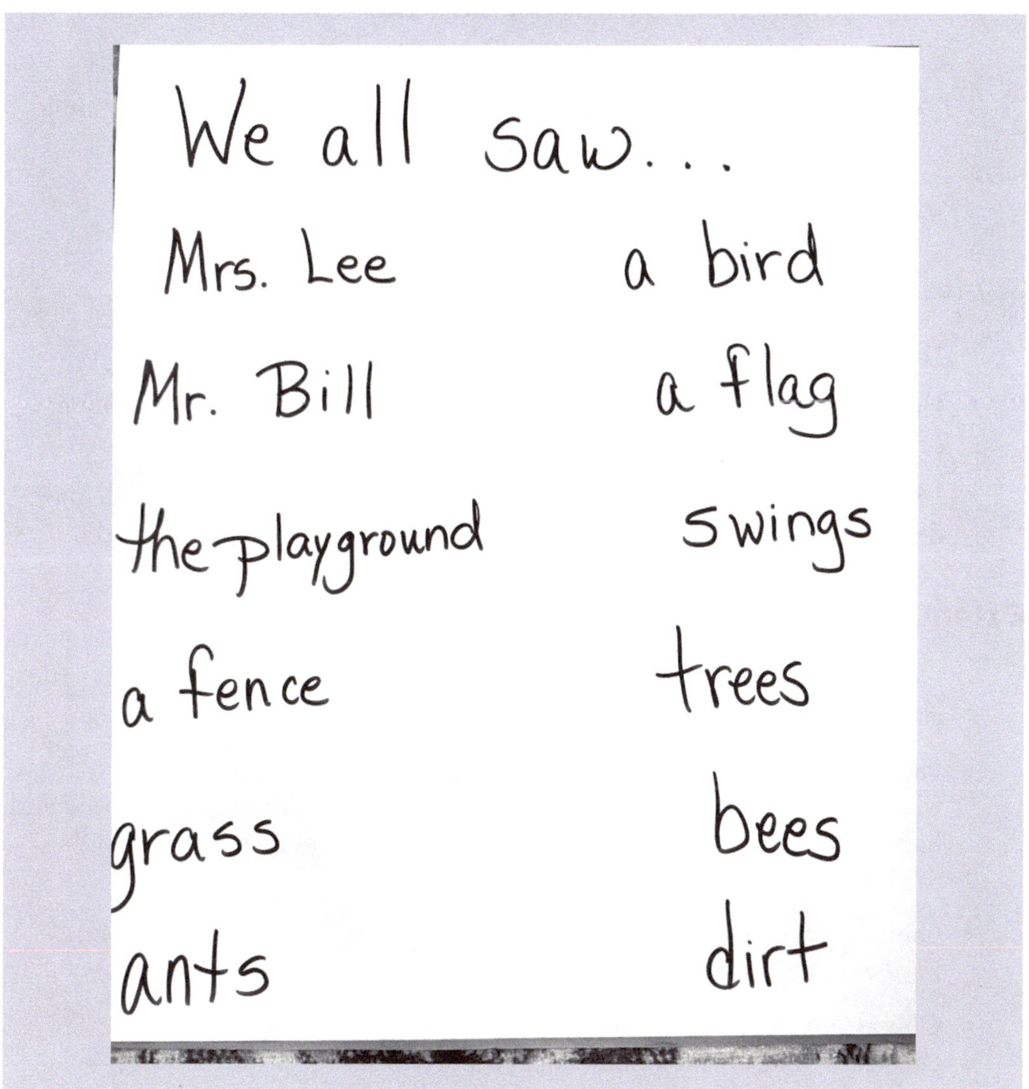

6. Explain to students that they are going to start observing what they see when they go to each of the places listed on the anchor chart.
7. For the next week, after visiting each of the listed places on the chart paper, have students share what they saw and collect details about each place on the chart paper.

Quick Tip!

You can also have students record this information in their writing journals if you want to incorporate an independent writing component.

8. After about a week of collecting their observations, model with students how they might take the observations and write them in a sentence, for example, "We saw ________ when we went to the playground."
9. After modeling this for the students, have students complete a gallery walk of the anchor charts so they can determine what details they want to include in their own writing.
10. Using the We All Saw a . . . template (page 233), have students write their own "We saw a ________" or a "I saw a ________."
11. Share these with the class.

Try It

- Use this as a lesson that incorporates a collaborative writing component.
- Have students use this lesson as a way to collect their observations about a setting or an event.
- Use this as practice for descriptive writing since students have to recall and describe what they saw and experienced.

Extensions

- Connect this to the *When I Was Young in . . .* lesson and have students write about items they saw when they were in a specific place.
- Have students use these writings to create riddles so that the reader can guess what item it was they saw based on their descriptions. Or, flip this around and have students create riddles for readers to guess where they were when they made their observations.
- Complete a Sketch to Stretch (Harper, 2023) activity with this lesson and have students include images and pictures to accompany their writings.
- Connect this to character writings and have students write from the perspective of a character in a book or novel.
- Connect this lesson to the Memory Map Memoirs activity (p. 36) when considering what students might include on a memory map.
- Compile each student's writing into a class book of things they saw around the school.
- Connect this to a wordless picture book by assigning a specific page to students and have them describe what they see. Then have other students see if they can determine who had which picture.

Modifications

Emerging Writers

- Complete this lesson as a collaborative writing engagement where students write with partners or groups about different items they saw.
- Have students create a pictorial writing and use teacher dictation for the sentence construction.
- Write one main composition as a class using oral feedback from the students. Record this class story on chart paper.

Proficient Writers

- Have students use address labels to label the pictures in their story; connect this to text features in different text types.
- Divide students into collaborative teams and assign each team a specific anchor chart. Assign them the responsibility for composing the story about all the items their classmates saw in that specific place.
- Have students take this concept and apply to a historical figure or write about what that person or character might have seen.

See It Sample

We saw a

Fulton: bee, butterfly, black eyed susan, ball, pine tree, pumpkin

Damien: eagle, pinecone, wasp, dog, children

JD: Dove, bee, watermelon, zinnia, grass

Photo by Shirley Groves

STORY BAGS

Writing creatively, in some instances, gets overlooked in lieu of writing that focuses on technical or informational aspects. With Story Bags, students are required to use objects to construct a story that is entirely made up and centered around the items included in the bag.

Focus Genre: Narrative

Target Grade Level: 3–5

Standards

Write narratives to develop real or imagined experiences or events using effective techniques, well-chosen details, and well-structured event sequences.

Anchor Texts

The Patchwork Quilt by Valerie Flournoy

The Story Blanket by Ferida Wolff

One Little Bag: An Amazing Journey by Henry Cole

Those Shoes by Maribeth Boelts

The Keeping Quilt by Patricia Polacco

Aunt Flossie's Hats and Crabcakes Later by Elizabeth Fitzgerald Howard

Materials

- Random items
- Bags or boxes for item collection (e.g., plastic or paper bags or small boxes)

Teach It

1. Begin by collecting a variety of objects. These might include things like ticket stubs, game pieces, figurines, coins, small toys, etc. The more random the better.

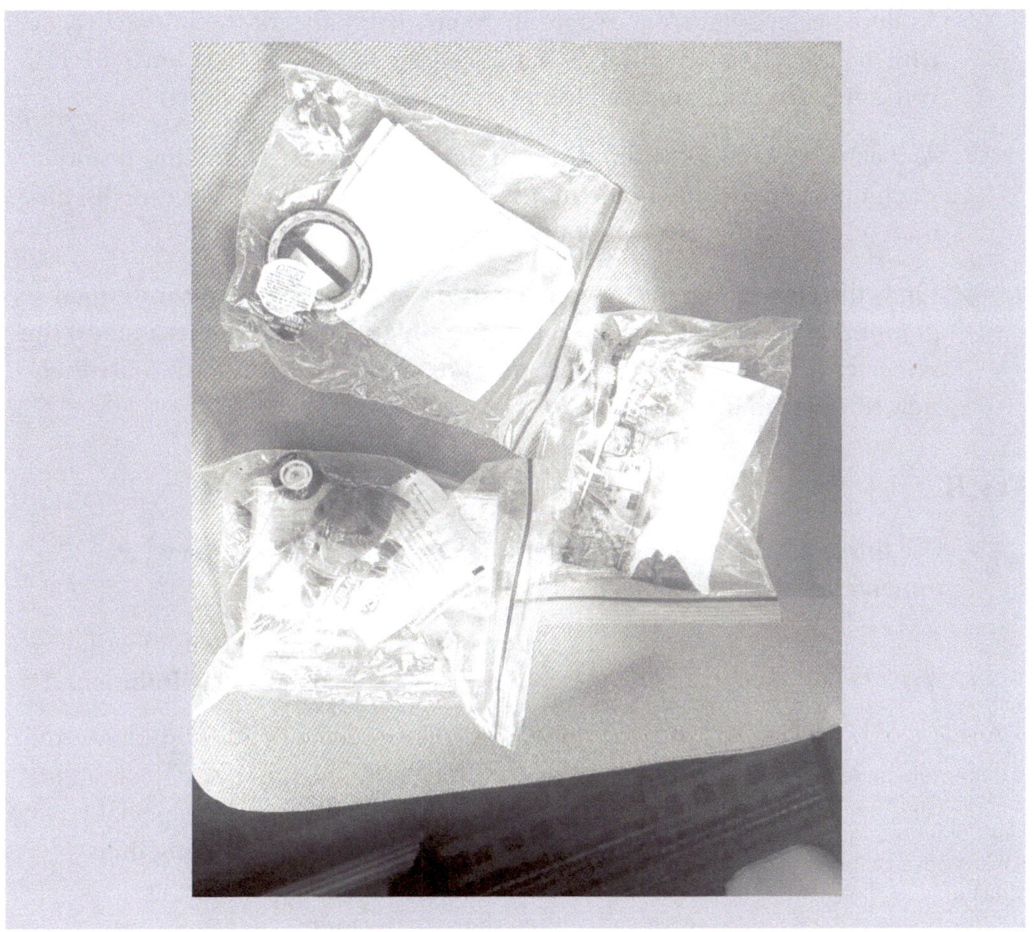

2. Place about five random items in a bag or box.
3. Explain that as a class, you are going to create a story using all of the items in the bag.
4. Show students each of the items. Ask them to tell you what each item is and where you might use it or see it.
5. Hold up one item and begin brainstorming a story that includes the object. Have students share ideas that are connected to the object and begin drafting a quick story using the object somehow in its construction. (This is important practice for students!)

Quick Tip!

By random, I mean just that. One time we used the following:

- a receipt
- tube of lipstick
- penny
- paperclip
- lottery ticket

These were all items I had in my purse, and we created a quick story using those items just for fun.

6. As students give you ideas, record them on chart paper or the interactive whiteboard. (Initially, start with brainstorming ideas; once you have this list, you can begin using material from the list to construct the story.)

7. As a class, use material from the brainstorming list to start building a story. Each time you use one of the items, mark it off of the brainstorming list and then underline the item when you include it in your story.

8. Once the class has created a collaborative story, divide students into small groups or partners and give them their own story bags. Have them repeat the same activity working with their partner or group. Have students share their new stories with the class.

Try It

- Use this as a springboard or opener into character prop writings when responding to extended pieces of literature (p. 245).
- Try this when you want students to write creatively in a collaborative environment.
- Try this when you want to offer students the opportunity to utilize physical objects and props for writing—this can be especially helpful when students are sharing their writings since they can hold the items as they share their stories.

This lesson is extremely beneficial for students who might get nervous speaking in front of the class or who might need visual reminders. Having physical objects can aid with both of these.

Extensions

- Have students bring in their own objects for story creation. Have them explain why they chose to bring the objects they included. As a class, use the items the students brought in to write a new story.
- Connect specific objects or items to characters in a novel or to specific events in a story or event. Have students explain how each item is directly connected to the text.
- Connect this writing activity to the construction of a Six-Room Image Poem using the template (p. 235).
- Use this as an extension or spin-off to the Pearls on a String strategy.
- Use this as an opener or practice for the Book in a Box strategy (p. 263).

Modifications

Emerging Writers

- Construct a whole-class writing so that students can get used to using physical objects to draft stories.
- Share a ready-made story with students based on a set of objects or props so they can see how the story is connected to the objects. Have student volunteers display the objects when the item is referenced in the story.
- After reading a picture book or novel, ask students what items might be connected to the story or character. Use those items to build a retelling.
- Show students a couple of objects. Have them brainstorm what kind of character the objects might belong to or what kind of story might include them.

Proficient Writers

- Have students create oral stories on the spot. Give students objects just like before but have one student start crafting the story and then hand the story off by giving an object to a classmate for them to continue the story.
- When developing or creating a character, have students start with a series of objects and build a character around the items.

See It Sample

PEARLS ON A STRING

Retelling stories is crucial for reading comprehension. Plus, this lesson can aid students as they construct their own stories. By offering students opportunities for collaborative retellings that focus on reading comprehension aspects, students can practice the skill or retelling, which is closely connected to the construction of a summary. This also allows them an authentic opportunity to practice the important skill of story construction.

Focus Genre: Narrative/Story Retelling

Target Grade Level: K–5

Standards

Retell familiar stories using main story elements in a literary text.

Retell familiar texts by identifying the topic and supporting details in an informational text.

Anchor Texts

For this lesson, most any text can be used as an anchor text. Below are some familiar examples (and some of my favorites) that students may already know and have experience with, which can help students as they practice this important skill.

The True Story of the Three Little Pigs by Jon Scieszka

Memoirs of a Goldfish by Devin Scillian

Memoirs of a Hamster by Devin Scillian

Martina the Beautiful Cockroach by Carmen Agra Deedy

Spoon by Amy Krouse Rosenthal

The Day the Crayons Quit by Drew Daywalt

Materials

None

Teach It

1. Begin by reading one of the stories suggested from the anchor text list. (Remember, most any story will do. You may find that your class has a

favorite story they have enjoyed being read to them over and over again. That would be a good one to start with.)

2. After reading, ask students to tell you a detail they remember.
3. Select a student volunteer to share their detail. Once they have shared, have them come to the front of the room.
4. Ask the rest of the class, "Who remembers a detail that came before or after ________'s detail they shared?"
5. Select another student volunteer. Have them share their detail. Based on the content of the detail, place them either before or after the student who is already standing in front of the room.
6. Repeat this process until you have the story retold in front of the class.

Photo by Alysha Krier Mooney

7. Ask any students who are not in the front of the room to add any new details that should be added for the retelling to be complete.
8. Perform the entire retelling by having each student share their detail until the entire story is complete.

Try It

- Use this as a springboard into written retellings by starting with an oral retelling first.
- Instead of a traditional paper pencil comprehension assessment, use this as a substitute.

- Use this with language learners and have them share their details in their home language or English.
- Try this as a way to check comprehension when reading an extended work like a novel that might take several weeks to complete.

Extensions

- Use an anchor text that has an ambiguous ending or one that ends in a cliffhanger. Have students extend the story by completing the ending.
- When sharing their oral sentences, give students a notecard and have them write their sentence down. Use the notecards to create a written account or retelling.
- Have students add images or drawings to accompany their oral or written retellings.

You could also do this if you want students to consider what came *before* the story began, as this can help them develop backstories and cut scenes that can tell an additional aspect of the story or the character.

Modifications

Emerging Writers

- Divide students into pairs and have them collaborate to remember and share a detail.
- Have a few details already written on notecards or sentence strips. Use those as starting points for the retelling.
- Start retellings like this by focusing on the beginning, middle, and end. Have students share a detail from each of those major parts first.

Proficient Writers

- Have students begin by writing their detail on a notecard before sharing. Proceed as normal with the lesson.
- Have ready-made details recorded on notecards or sentence strips. Have students put them in the correct order for the story retelling. If you want, omit key details and have students determine what these key details are.

See It Sample

Grandma was sick.

LRRH took a basket to Grandma's

The wolf ate Grandma.

The wolf tried to trick LRRH.

LRRH was saved.

MEMORY MAP MEMOIRS

Writing about moments in our lives is one of the most important and natural types of writing our students can do. In this lesson, students focus on a specific memory or moment to draw and write about. Using, images, words, and the oral component of story can help students construct vivid stories centered on a specific moment.

Focus Genre: Memoirs and Personal Narrative

Target Grade Level: 3–5

Standards

Write narratives to develop real or imagined experiences or events using effective technique, well-chosen details, and well-structured event sequences.

Anchor Texts

How Angel Peterson Got His Name by Gary Paulson

Memoirs of a Parrot by Devin Scillian

Memoirs of a Hamster by Devin Scillian

After the Fall by Dan Santat

The Bad Seed by Jory John

Going Down Home with Daddy by Kelly Starling Lyons

Saturdays and Teacakes by Lester Laminack

The Name Jar by Yangsook Choi

Your Name is a Song by Jamilah Thompkins-Bigelow

Materials

- Chart paper

Teach It

1. Begin by reading aloud one of the texts from the anchor text list.

2. Discuss the anchor text. Make sure to focus on the expanse of time. Memoirs are examples of exploding moments in a character or narrator's life. In many instances, you will find that moments that make up memoirs are often short and include small events that have been exploded and expanded so that the reader is able to fully experience all that occurred during that brief moment.

I almost always start with Paulson's book because it is one of my favorites. It is a fantastic example of memoir, as Paulson shares individual memories from his life in short story format. However with primary students, I would not start with this book simply because it is likely too long for young children to listen to in one setting.

3. Have students brainstorm and make a list of the components that were included in this description. Pay special attention to the amount of time that passes. It is important for students to see that in many cases, these expanded stories are actually short expanses of time where the author uses descriptive tactics that make the event seem longer than it actually is.

4. Make a list of moments or events in your life that you could write about and explode into a bigger story. Model this for the class.

5. Explain to students that instead of creating the written story first, you are going to start by drawing a picture called a *memory map* that can help you remember the events during that moment.

6. To model this for your students, begin by drawing a picture of the place, people, and event you want to write about. As you are drawing, share with the class why you chose to include specific items in your picture.

Photo by Alysha Krier Mooney

7. Have students think about a few events that they could write about. Record their ideas on chart paper or the interactive whiteboard.
8. Ask students to select a moment in their life that they would like to share.
9. Have them draw their own memory map and share it with a partner or the class.

Try It

- Use this when you want students to focus on a specific moment or event for writing.
- Try this as a warmup for extended memoir writing.
- Try this as a low-stakes brainstorming session.
- Early in the school year, this can work as a classroom community building activity where students get to learn about their peers.

Extensions

- Have students connect this strategy to novels and extended works. Instead of having them write about moments in their own lives, have them choose moments from a character's life to explore.
- Use this as a way for students to create extended memoirs since they begin with a low stakes writing engagement.
- Connect this strategy to the research genre of biography and have students craft a version of the memory map connected to their biography subject.

Modifications

Emerging Writers

- Start by creating class memory maps. With this modification, the class chooses several events or memories that they share together. Post each memory idea on a sheet of chart paper. Have students rotate through the room and add their drawings to each of the sheets of chart paper. Once this is completed, the teacher can add any words or phrases that go along with the images.
- Give students a specific event or idea to draw or write about. This can help them focus and complete the task.
- When connecting this to a novel or other reading, have students work together to create a collaborative memory map of details from the story.

Proficient Writers

- Have students create multiple memory maps for their memoirs in storyboard format. This can be extended into a graphic composition that utilizes multiple drawings and pictures to tell their story.
- Have students use their memoir maps as a prewriting or brainstorming component of a formal memoir composition.

See It Sample

Photo by Alysha Krier Mooney

WHO IS IN MY HEART?

Empathy, understanding, and compassion cannot be undersold in today's classrooms, and students need opportunities to write about those they love and care about. Sharing their feelings and thoughts about whom they love and care for can help students share their gratitude and care for others but can also allow students to connect with their classmates.

Focus Genre: Personal narrative/story telling

Target Grade Level: K–5

Standards

Write narratives to develop real or imagined experiences or events using effective techniques, well-chosen details, and well-structured event sequences.

Anchor Texts

A Chair for My Mother by Vera B. Williams

I Am Enough by Grace Byers

All the Places to Love by Patricia MacLachlan

Yo! Yes? by Chris Raschka

The Secret Life of Squirrels: A Love Story by Nancy Rose

The Kissing Hand by Audrey Penn

The Invisible String by Patrice Karst

If you have never completed a heart map, I think you will find that they are fantastic writing engagements that can allow students to consider those in their life who mean the most to them and who are closest to their hearts. Check out Georgia Heard's *Awakening the Heart: Teaching Poetry K–8* and read how Heart Maps got started.

Materials

- Chart paper
- Heart Map template (p. 236)

Teach It

1. Begin by reading one of the books from the anchor text list or use one that is connected to the same theme.
2. Talk with students about some of the people or things that they love.

3. Make a brainstorming list of the ideas that students share.

4. Using the Heart Map template (p. 236), model what you might include in your own Who Is in My Heart? writing. Include words, drawings, phrases, etc.

5. Give each student their own heart template and have them include their own thoughts about who or what they love.

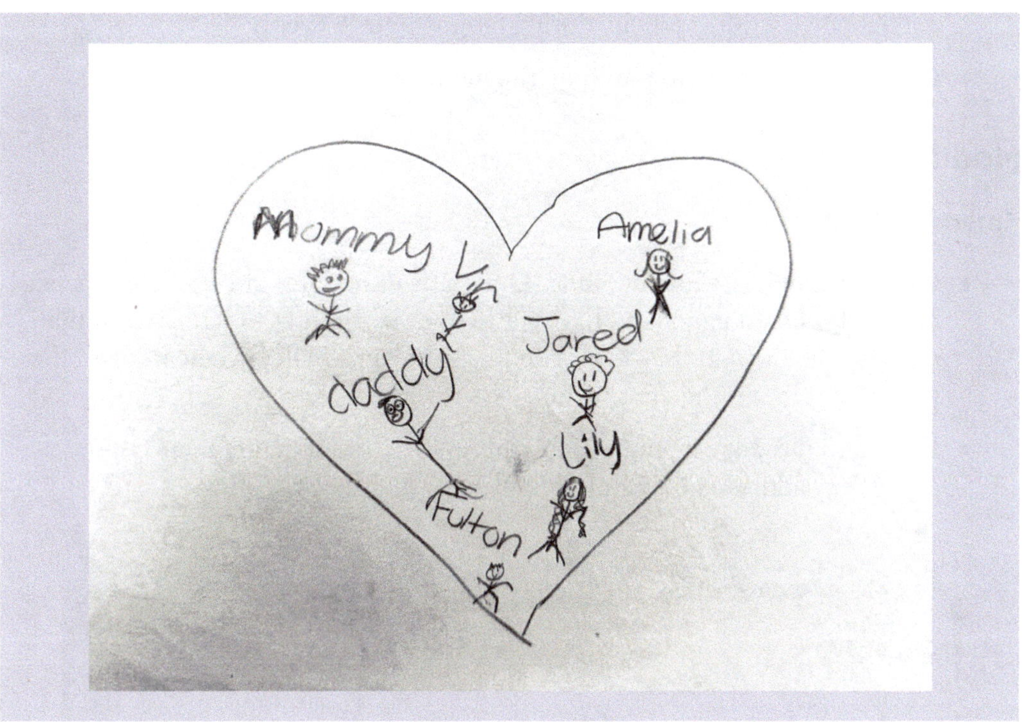

6. Have students share their finished work with the class.

Try It

- Try this as a writing engagement that reminds students of all those people in their lives who they love and who love them back.
- Use this as a way to get to know the students in your class and help build classroom community.
- This works well as a low-stakes writing assignment that focuses on personal interests and experience.

Extensions

- Extend this into a heart map poem and encourage students to use material from their heart writings to compose a short poem.

For instructions and other related materials on heart maps, check out Georgia Heard's website: https://www.georgiaheard.com/heart-maps

To scan a QR code, you must have a smartphone or tablet with a camera. We recommend that you download a QR code reader app that is made specifically for your phone or tablet brand.

- Connect this to a particular character in a novel or picture book and have students write about what that particular character loves.
- Use this as a springboard or brainstorm that can help students think about events and moments for their memoirs.
- Extend this to include contributions from students' family members. Send home a blank heart template for family members to complete or use this as a collaborative writing activity during family literacy events.
- Connect this writing to the Body Biography writing (p. 124).

Modifications

Emerging Writers

- Create a giant class heart writing. Draw a heart on large sheet of chart paper or bulletin board paper and have students draw pictures or write words that explain who or what they love. Use this to create a collective heart of all the people and things the class loves.
- Have students draw pictures of the things they love. Dictate their responses onto sticky address labels and stick them to their heart writings.

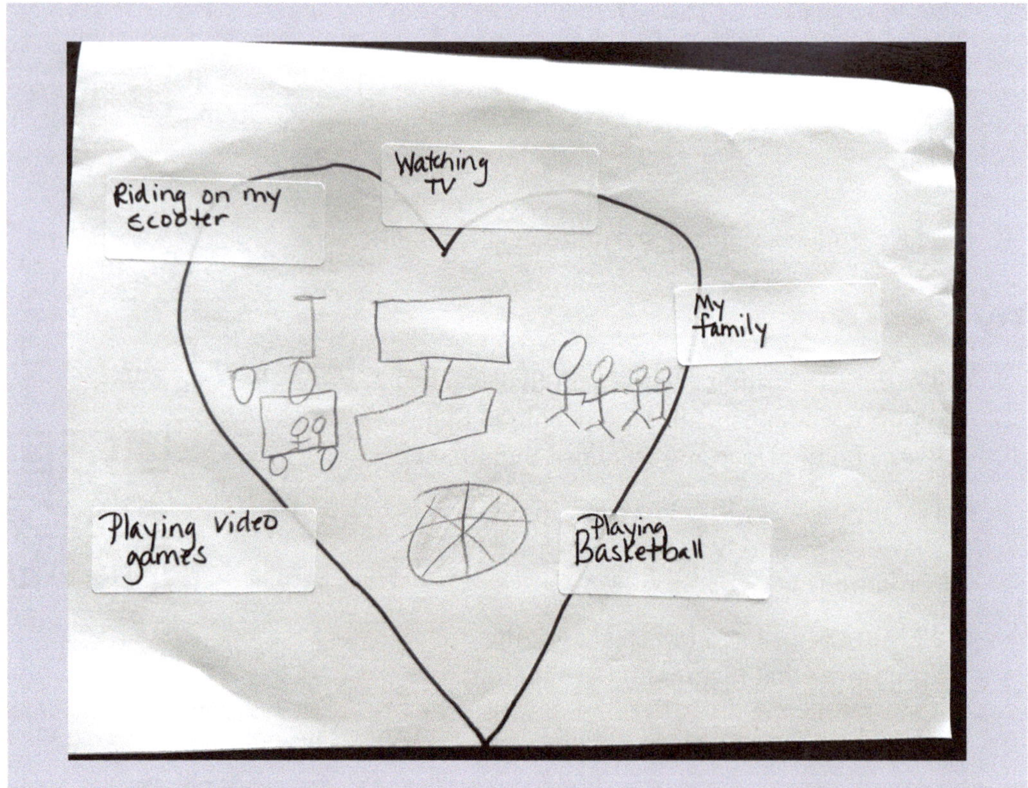

- Send home communication about the writing assignment to families and request family pictures that can be included on the heart writing.

Proficient Writers

- Have students use these heart writings as brainstorming or prewriting sessions for extended compositions on the same topic.
- Divide the heart template into sections or topics and have students include a detail for each topic. For example, you might include a section for the people you love, a section for your favorite things to do, another section for favorite animals.

See It Sample

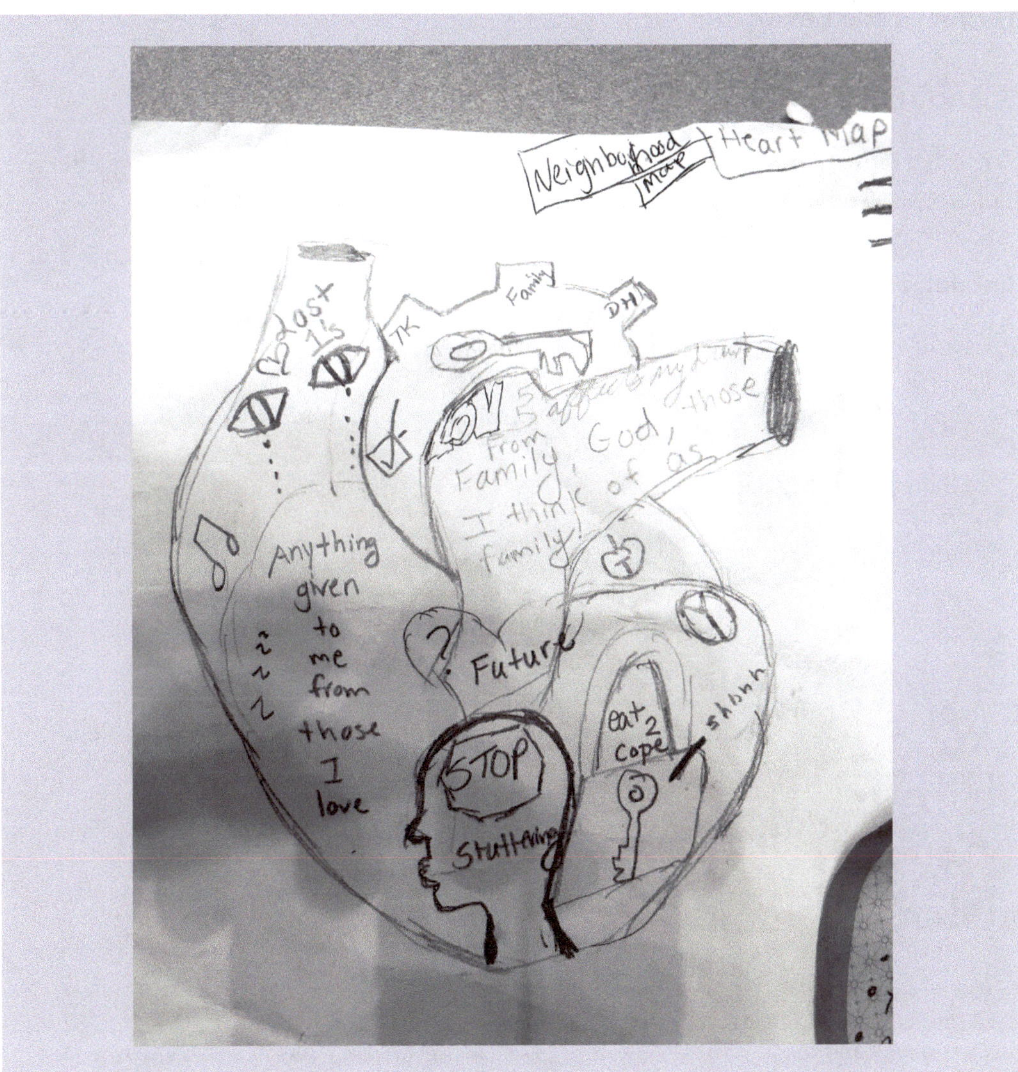

Photo by Alysha Krier Mooney

EVERYDAY WRITING

Understanding and recognizing the potential for story in the world around us is important for all learners. In fact, some of the best stories and ideas come from our experiences in everyday occurrences and day-to-day activities. In this lesson, students focus on the power of story that emerges from our daily experiences in a variety of settings.

Focus Genre: Narrative

Target Grade Level: K–5

Standards

Write narratives to develop real or imagined experiences or events using effective techniques, well-chosen details, and well-structured event sequences.

Anchor Texts:

Crown: An Ode to the Freshcut by Derrick Barnes

Bippity Bop Barbershop by Natasha Tarpley

Jabari Jumps by Gaia Cornwall

Saturday by Oge Mora

My Papi Has a Motorcycle by Isabel Quintero

Last Stop on Market Street by Matt de la Pena

We Had a Picnic This Sunday Past by Jacqueline Woodson

The Honest to Goodness Truth by Patricia McKissack

The Secret Olivia Told Me by N. Joy

Goin' Someplace Special by Patricia McKissack

Another great text to use is *The Wishgranter*, which is a short film that tells the story of a wishing well and those who drop their wishes in it. Scan the QR code or visit the link below to learn more: https://www.imdb.com/title/tt6192248/

Materials

- Everyday Writing template (p. 237)

Teach It

1. Begin by reading one of the books from the anchor text list or a related title.
2. Talk with the class about the subject of the reading and discuss how the story involved something that was an everyday activity or part of a regular routine.
3. Make a list of the ways in which the author described the everyday event. Pay special attention to the language, words, and phrases used, how the author uses sensory details to tell the story, if dialogue is used, etc.
4. Make a brainstorming list of places or routine events that people take part in. Ideas might include going to the grocery store, the barber shop, playing a game, going to the park, etc.
5. Have students choose an event that they might write about for their everyday writing.
6. Begin by creating a brainstorming map about the event, or use the Everyday Writing template (p. 237).

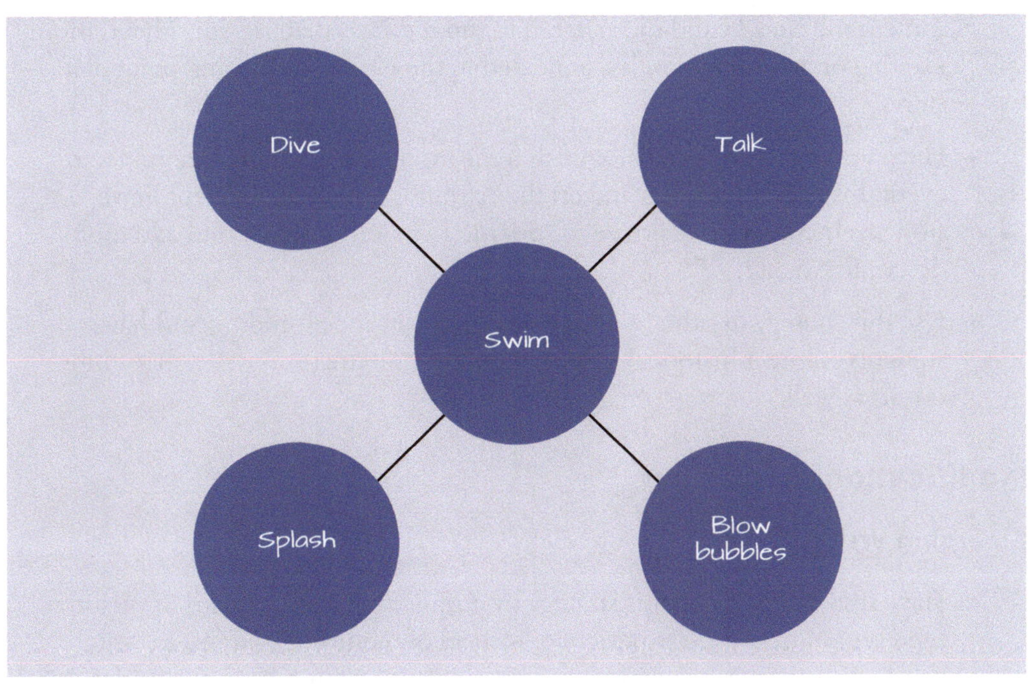

7. Once students have completed their brainstorming map, begin drafting the composition. To do this, model an example from someone's brainstorm map. This is especially important, as students need to see how shorthand note-taking shifts into complete sentences.

8. Have students construct their writings and share with the class.

Try It

- Use this when students might run out of topics for writing or might feel like they are short on writing ideas.
- Try this to practice writing about everyday occurrences that students might overlook or undervalue.
- When students struggle with ideas for composition, shift to everyday experiences as a springboard for writing engagements.
- Use this to practice writing about common day-to-day life and share how even routine daily experiences can emerge into beautiful stories.

Extensions

- Have students use this type of writing to help add details to other writing compositions that might have a more detailed focus on a specific conflict or problem. When students understand that they can add additional detail to events that might be considered as routine and daily occurrences, they may understand how to add more detail to those events that are considered more exciting or are more closely connected to the climax or turning point of a story.
- Have students focus on dialogue as a means to add additional detail to an event. Instead of just focusing on the narrative aspect of an event, have students incorporate dialogue in order to help tell the story and add more descriptive detail.
- Use this strategy in other content areas, such as social studies, and have students connect historical events to different figures and write about those events as well.

Modifications

Emerging Writers

- Have students practice this strategy by completing a story board or pictorial representation of their experience. Instead of requiring students to write words and sentences, begin by drawing pictures of an everyday experience.
- Have students orally tell about their experiences and then have the teacher dictate the sentences to accompany the images.

- Have students make a list of the daily experiences they might write about. Complete a shared writing about an experience that the entire class might have.

Proficient Writers

- Have students practice integrating different types of descriptive detail into their everyday writing. Challenge them to incorporate specific examples of imagery, figurative language, or dialogue in order to better describe their event.
- Connect this strategy to a novel study or literature connection and encourage students to write about a daily event that a character might experience.
- Connect this to the Memory Map Memoirs activity (p. 36) in order to get students thinking about moments or events they might write about.

See It Sample

Photo by Skylar Clay

I AM FROM . . . WRITING

Getting to know students is one of the most important parts of building a positive classroom climate and establishing classroom culture. Students come from diverse backgrounds with varying beliefs, traditions, hobbies, familial structure, and more. When thinking about writing topics, what do we know more about than ourselves? That's why starting off extended writings with topics that address *who* students are and where they see themselves in the world can serve as a gateway into writing for those who might be inexperienced or unmotivated. I Am From . . . Writing can serve as a fantastic opportunity for students to get their feet wet with extended writings and for their classmates and instructors to learn about each other.

Focus Genre: Personal Narrative

Target Grade Level: K–5

Standards

Write narratives to develop real or imagined experiences or events using effective techniques, well-chosen details, and well-structured event sequences.

Anchor Texts

Momma, Where Are You From? by Marie Bradby

When I Was Young in the Mountains by Cynthia Rylant

The Relatives Came by Cynthia Rylant

We Had a Picnic This Sunday Past by Jacqueline Woodson

Materials

- Chart paper
- I Am From . . . template (p. 238)

Teach It

1. Begin by reading *Momma, Where Are You From?* by Marie Bradby.
2. After reading, brainstorm details that the author used to tell us where the main character was from. (These items include family, neighbors, traditions, food, and everyday life activities.)
3. Model your own I Am From . . . brainstorming template for the class to observe.

4. Have students complete their own I Am From . . . brainstorming using the template (p. 238). For example, a student's map might look like the following:

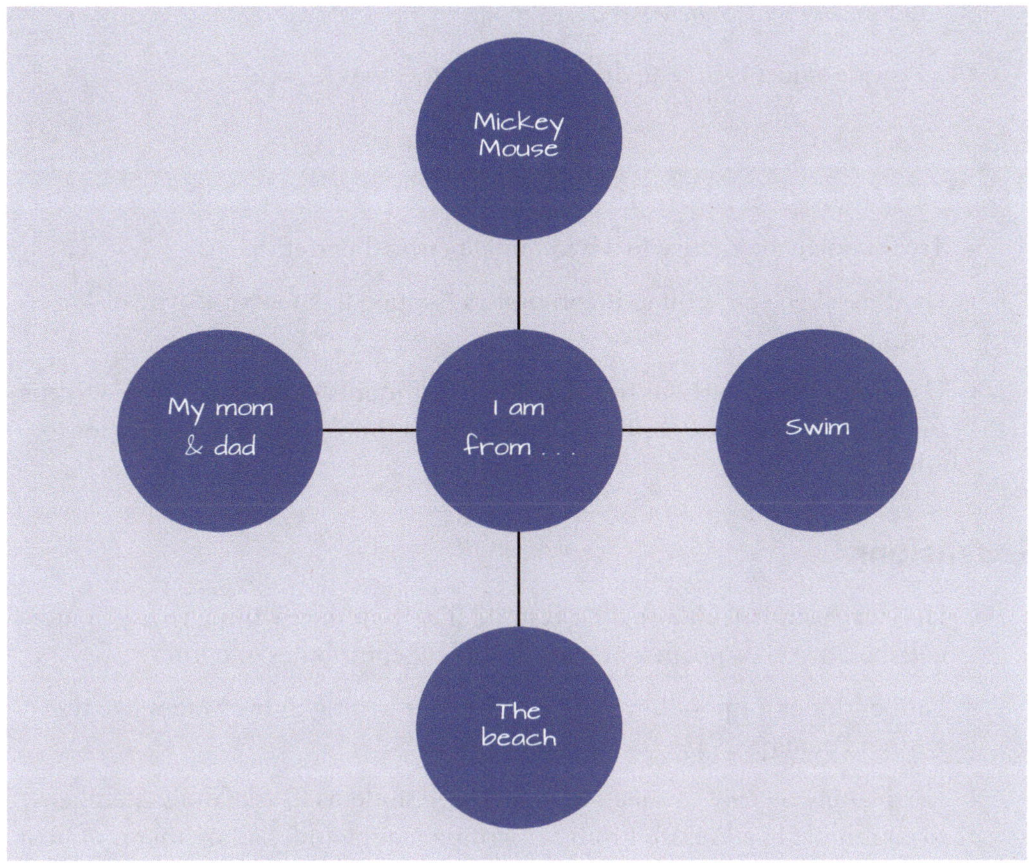

5. Encourage students to share items from their maps or as you are reading or checking their maps, share a few with the class. (e.g., "Hey guys! I was just reading Vanessa's I am From . . . map, and did you know that they raise chickens and goats? Do any of you have something similar you could add to your map?") It is important to share this aloud with the class because it can help students think of additional items to include on their templates as well.
6. Open the next day's class by reading the book *When I Was Young in the Mountains* by Cynthia Rylant.
7. Ask the students to consider what today's read aloud and yesterday's have in common.
8. In both texts, many of the sentences start with the same sentence frames. (I am from . . . ; When I was young in the mountains . . .)
9. Have students refer back to the original text and discuss how the author described where she was from by listing parts of her daily life in sentences.
10. Model how students might take the material from their brainstorming template and write it using the frame "I am from . . . " For this, students

need to start off every sentence with, "I am from . . .," using items from their brainstorming template. This is important to do so students can see how they might take the material they wrote about and mimic what the author did in *Momma, Where Are You From?*

11. Provide students time to draft and share their work.

Try It

- Try this as an alternative to a traditional personal narrative.
- Use this when you want to incorporate a "getting to know you" type of writing.
- Use this writing early in the year to give students experience with writing for an extended time, but on a topic that is more personal and easier to address.

Extensions

- Have each student choose their favorite line from their writing to use in a collaborative class poem where each student contributes one line.
- Partner students up so they can perform their writing in two voices like the Partner Poem (p. 171).
- For a family literacy connection, encourage students to ask family members to contribute to a We Are From . . . writing that includes all members of their household.

Modifications

Emerging Writers

- Provide students with the I Am From . . . Part 2 template (p. 239) and have them complete their writings on it. This template also includes room for an illustration.
- Create a class, We Are From . . . shared writing on a large sheet of chart paper. Have each student contribute a sentence to the chart paper so that everyone has input on the class writing.
- Have students work with a partner to create a sentence that describes them both.

Proficient Writers

- Have students write their I Am From . . . writing following the format of a Pinterest Paragraph (Harper, 2021). Using Pic Collage, Canva, or other online image collage app, students can collect images of each part of their poem and add text boxes for their sentences.
- Have students record their writing online and respond in a classroom chat like a BackChannel.

See It Sample

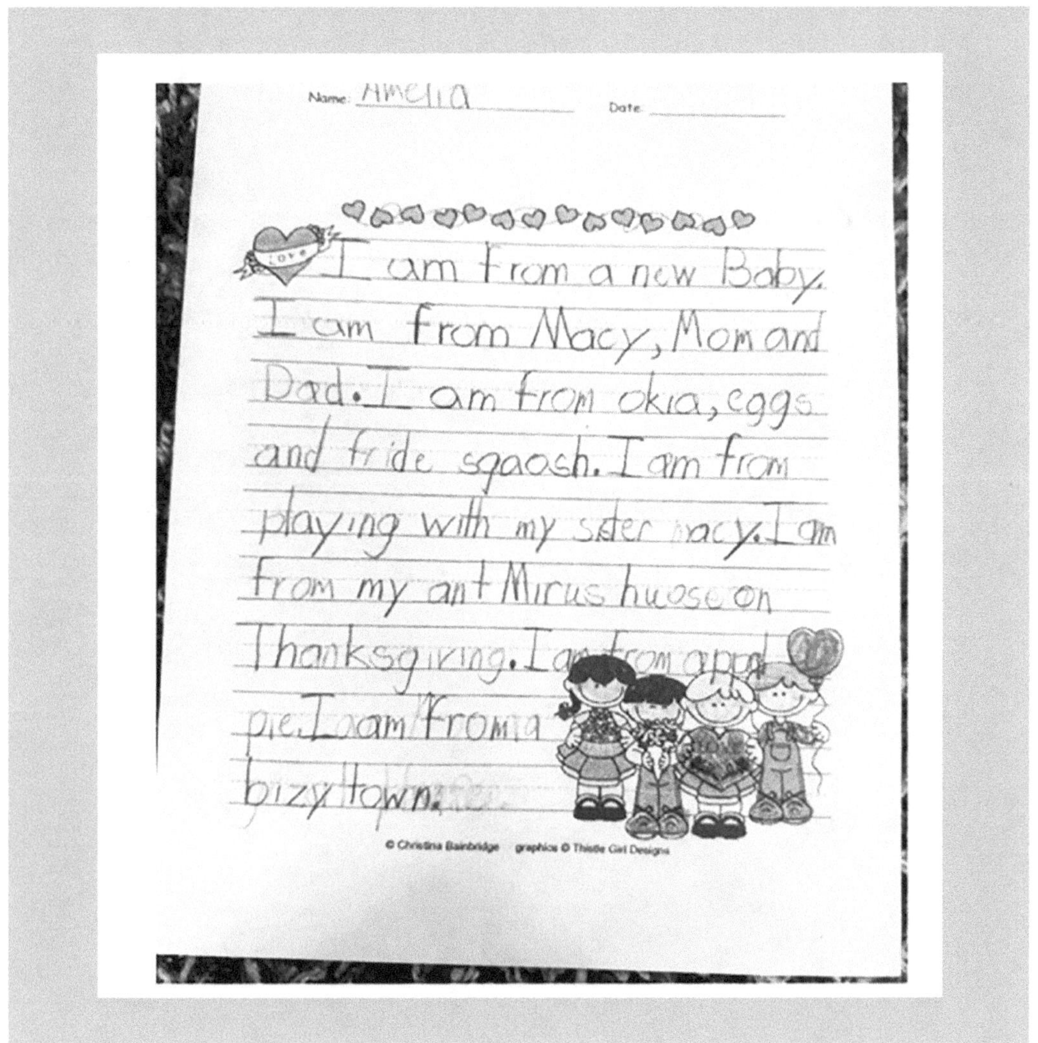

Name: Amelia Date:

I am from a new Baby. I am from Macy, Mom and Dad. I am from okra, eggs and fride sqaosh. I am from playing with my sister macy. I am from my ant Mirus huose on Thanksgiving. I am from appl pie. I am from a bizy town.

© Christina Bainbridge graphics © Thistle Girl Designs

(Continued)

(Continued)

Name: Amelia Date:

I am from keeping My mom and dad Happy when they are sad. I am from a great place.

© Christina Bainbridge graphics © Thistle Girl Designs

Chapter 3

TELL ME MORE

While there are certainly times when getting to the point is helpful and conservation of words is needed, in many instances, rich descriptions can help readers build important visuals in their minds as they are reading. Plus, the craft and skill of elaboration is not exclusive to a specific genre. Instead, it is important to employ across genres. In fact, some of the most well-crafted pieces writing utilize a variety of descriptive techniques, which can help clarify the content presented. In the narrative genre, we often focus on the notion of showing and not telling, which is important, but there are other ways to elaborate as well. In some cases, offering the reader an illustrative example along with a fact or including specific information can go a long way. This is especially true with nonfiction texts where an illustrative example, figure, or image can offer another layer of information, thus helping students fully understand a concept. In many instances, figures and diagrams can provide readers with as much, if not more information about a concept or idea. Plus, as students move on in the upper grades, constructed response writings increase, which often require students to position textual evidence in support of claims and reasoning in order to fully flesh out a strong response. As such, the task demands that students elaborate and explain their reasoning with extended responses.

Now, for some students, this notion of saying more is sometimes confused with simply writing more of the same. I bet many of you have read papers that go something like this:

> *My dog Billy is my best friend. He is very, very, very sweet and cute. He is really cute when he wears his dog sweater. He is really really cute with that sweater. He is very, very, sweet when he sits in my lap. I like it when he is sweet and sits with me for a long, long, time.*

Now, while the sample above is a great example of primary writing, it also is indicative of what some students think writing more entails: simply saying the same item over and over or the repeated use of the same word. (Think very, very, very or really, really, really.)

Of course, there is certainly a place for repetition and emphasis in certain types of writing. Repeating a line in a composition can emphasize a point or overarching theme—think how the chorus functions in a song—but that is different than adding more details to build a thorough and well-thought-out explanation. Helping students identify areas in which they might apply additional descriptive details or information can aid them in creating solid written compositions.

Getting students to write more doesn't have to be a daunting task when teed up with the right literature and strategies. Utilizing a variety of tactics to promote elaboration can help students understand when and where more detail might be needed. Now, here's the kicker—some writings need to stay short and sweet. There is a careful balance between writing effectively with solid descriptions and using all the words in the room. Showing students a mixture of types of writings that call for those different characteristics can help grow and build proficient writers. One way to do this is to implement read alouds into your instructional routine on a daily basis, as this gives students the ability to hear examples from multiple genres and writings that are crafted for numerous audiences and purposes.

Here's something else to consider: There is a difference between a written composition that is in need of elaboration and more detail and one that simply is too short because it did not address the components of the prompt or assignment. Those are two different revision goals with a different overall purpose. While both are centered on the notion of elaboration, their purpose and reasoning are different. In one instance, elaboration is needed to give a more thorough explanation or overarching picture of a phenomenon, whereas the other instance requires elaboration that fully answers or addresses a query. Offering students the opportunity to practice both of those elaboration types and tasks can help them determine in later writings what might be needed to develop a thorough understanding of a concept in a written composition. Now for those of you who might be wondering about our youngest writers who might be drawing pictures as a precursor to alphanumeric text, elaboration can still be addressed through prompts that ask students to consider adding more details to their drawings and artistic renditions. In fact, after asking students to add more details to their drawings, teachers could then go back and use address labels or sticky notes to label items in their drawings. This idea could be used with primary students to focus on critically analyzing an illustration. Students would practice labeling components of an illustration from a wordless picture book, photograph, or piece of artwork.

Sometimes elaboration can be examined through a specific type of author's craft using a mentor text as a frame for writing. For example, in *Writing Workouts* (2023), we talked about how authors sometimes employ specific tactics to add details to their writing. Think about how some authors arrange the words on the page to simulate the meaning of a word, thus elaborating on the meaning simply through the placement of the words on the page. In Julie Danneburg's *First Day Jitters*, the author mimics the action of the word *stumbled* by writing it like this:

s

t

u

m

b

l

e

d.

Do you see how with that particular example, the author actually showed the reader visually what the word means? Another example is in Jeron Ashford Frame's book *Yesterday I Had the Blues*, the author writes this phrase:

The kind of blues

make you just wanna just

turn

down

the

volume.

Without really adding more words, the author has given the reader more details simply by arranging the letters on the page so that they become a visual example of the definition of the word. Instead of providing another example of what that word means, showing the reader that action on the white page has elaborated in some fashion. Now, while this is certainly an example of adding more details, most of what students will utilize when it comes to the addition of details will be centered on the addition of words or phrases to solidify their descriptions. Another example of this type of word elaboration comes from the book *Watercress* by Andrea Wang:

> Finally we load everything, the soggy bag, my sopping shirt, our sodden selves, into the car and headed home. Our original destination is long forgotten, a memory of something unfinished. (p. 14)

In this example, the author uses three separate words to describe the fact that the characters in this story are wet: *soggy*, *sopping*, and *sodden*. Instead of saying they were really wet over and over again, she describes three different items and uses a synonym to further explain how truly soaked and drenched they were. One way to practice this particular piece of writer's craft might be to have students look at *Watercress* as an example and then try to employ something similar in their own compositions. For example, in my own writing I might say this:

> When we left the beach, we threw our damp towels into the beach wagon, our sopping wet suits into the bag, and our salt-sprayed shirts over our shoulders, careful not to rub them across our blistered, red backs, sunburnt from our afternoon fun.

The example I created above is one way that students might try to utilize that same tactic in their own writing simply by using a quality mentor text as inspiration. Providing students with a frame or example of how elaboration might look in their own writing can help them be more successful at writing their own examples. Plus, by creating one of my own for students to see, it can help build a strong community of writers, especially when I share writing that I draft live in front of the class. If we want our students to feel comfortable sharing their own writings, which require students to embrace the vulnerability they might feel when they share, we as teachers have to be willing to be vulnerable alongside of them.

Strategies in this chapter focus specifically on the nature of elaboration and rich descriptions. One of the best parts about these strategies is their versatility. Many can be utilized in multiple settings and across genres for a number of purposes. For example, Stretch a Sentence, Sensory Writing, and NVA^2 can all be used across genres and subjects. Getting students to not only write more but also write more with a purpose and goal in mind is the focus for the strategies that follow.

YESTERDAY I HAD THE . . .

Developing stories and ideas that *show* instead of *tell* can sometimes be daunting for students. In this lesson, mentor texts with vivid imagery and description are employed so that students have a tangible example of this writer's craft. By describing moods through words, actions, and imagery, students can create written compositions that go beyond simplistic explanations and instead capture the complexity of the overall emotion.

Focus Genre: Personal Narrative

Target Grade Level: 3–5

Standards

Write narratives to develop real or imagined experiences or events using effective techniques, well-chosen details, and well-structured event sequences.

Make sure to start with *Yesterday I Had the Blues* anchor text since the subsequent writing task is directly connected to this text. Feel free to drop in any of the others as you see fit.

Anchor Texts

Yesterday I Had the Blues by Jeron Ashford Frame

Red Sings from Treetops: A Year in Colors by Joyce Sidman

The Day the Crayons Quit by Drew Daywalt

Green by Laura Vaccaro Seeger

How Are You Peeling? Foods With Moods by Saxton Freymann and Joost Elffers

When Sophie Gets Angry—Really, Really Angry by Molly Bang

My Many-Colored Days by Dr. Seuss

The Way I Feel by Janan Cain

The Color Monster: A Story About Emotions by Anna Llenas

Materials

- Paint strips in a variety of colors. (These can be different length configurations based on the needs of the students.)

> **Quick Tip!**
>
> I get paint strips at various hardware stores. Check with the paint department to see if they have discontinued any paint colors as they will often have those laying around.

- Different color sticky notes. (These can be used instead of paint strips.)
- Yesterday I Had the . . . template (p. 240).

Teach It

1. Read aloud the book *Yesterday I Had the Blues*.
2. Discuss how the author used different examples of actions to describe each character's mood. If needed, refer back to the text for specific examples to recall.

> **Quick Tip!**
>
> For the best results, make sure that students have heard this book at least once prior to this task. That way, students are already familiar with the story (characters, plot, setting, etc.) so they can focus on the specific details needed for the writing in the subsequent readings.

3. Ask students to brainstorm different moods they might have and what colors that might be associated with those moods. Record these on the board or on chart paper for students to see. Students can also record this information on their Yesterday I Had the . . . template (p. 240).
4. Together as a class, assign a specific mood to each color. (These will vary based on the brainstorming session, but some examples might be Red: Anger; Yellow: Joyful, Happy; Blue: Sad, Melancholy, etc.)
5. Together as a class, select one color to use as a model. Have the class collaboratively develop examples that could be connected to that color and its designated mood. Record each example on one block of the paint strip until the entire paint strip is filled. This gives students an example of the culminating writing product. **Note:** If using sticky notes, use one colored sticky note per example and then connect them together.
6. Once the class has completed their example, have each student choose a new color. Using that color and the mood that has been assigned to it, have students create their own Yesterday I Had the . . . writing. If using a paint strip, students should include one example per block on the paint strip. If using colored sticky notes, tell students how many sticky notes to include.

Try It

- Use this as a new way to approach mood in writing.
- Try this when you want students to complete a personal narrative that allows them to describe moods through colors and actions.
- Use this to practice developing characters by exploring different moods and what might occur with each one.
- Use this to help flesh out characters in personal narratives.

Extensions

- Have students trace the many moods of a character in a novel by utilizing different colored paint strips to chronicle the moods of a character.
- Use the material gathered on the Yesterday I Had the . . . template (p. 240) as a starting point for describing characters in other works and their moods.

Integrating art and music adds another layer of understanding to moods by giving them a visual and auditory example of specific moods.

- Connect this to artwork by using the colors and associated moods to collect examples of artwork that fall on the continuum.
- Integrate music into the lesson by having students locate songs that correspond with the chosen mood. Record them on the paint strips.

Modifications

Emerging Writers

- Have students collaboratively complete this activity by rotating moods and colors. For example, if using paint strips, place them in a pile on the floor or on a table. Have students pick up a paint strip and add an example based on the color or mood. Throw the paint strip back in the pile and pick up another. Repeat until all blocks are complete. In this modification, students are creating a collaborative writing example since multiple students contribute to the final product. (See examples below.)
- Use one extended paint strip to create one sentence describing the color and mood. Instead of having an example on each block of the paint strip, reduce this to one word so that the students have one paint strip sentence.

Proficient Writers

- Challenge students to create a paired writing by utilizing two opposing moods (e.g., anger and joy). Have students use two paint strips to create their opposing compositions.
- Have students brainstorm leveled-up color words. For example, instead of green, try words like jade, lime, olive, or emerald.
- Have students complete this activity based on characters in a story or novel. For example, you might say, “Miss Lana from *Three Times Lucky* had the reds when . . . ” In this modification, students look for examples from a literary work that serve as evidence for a particular character’s mood.

See It Sample

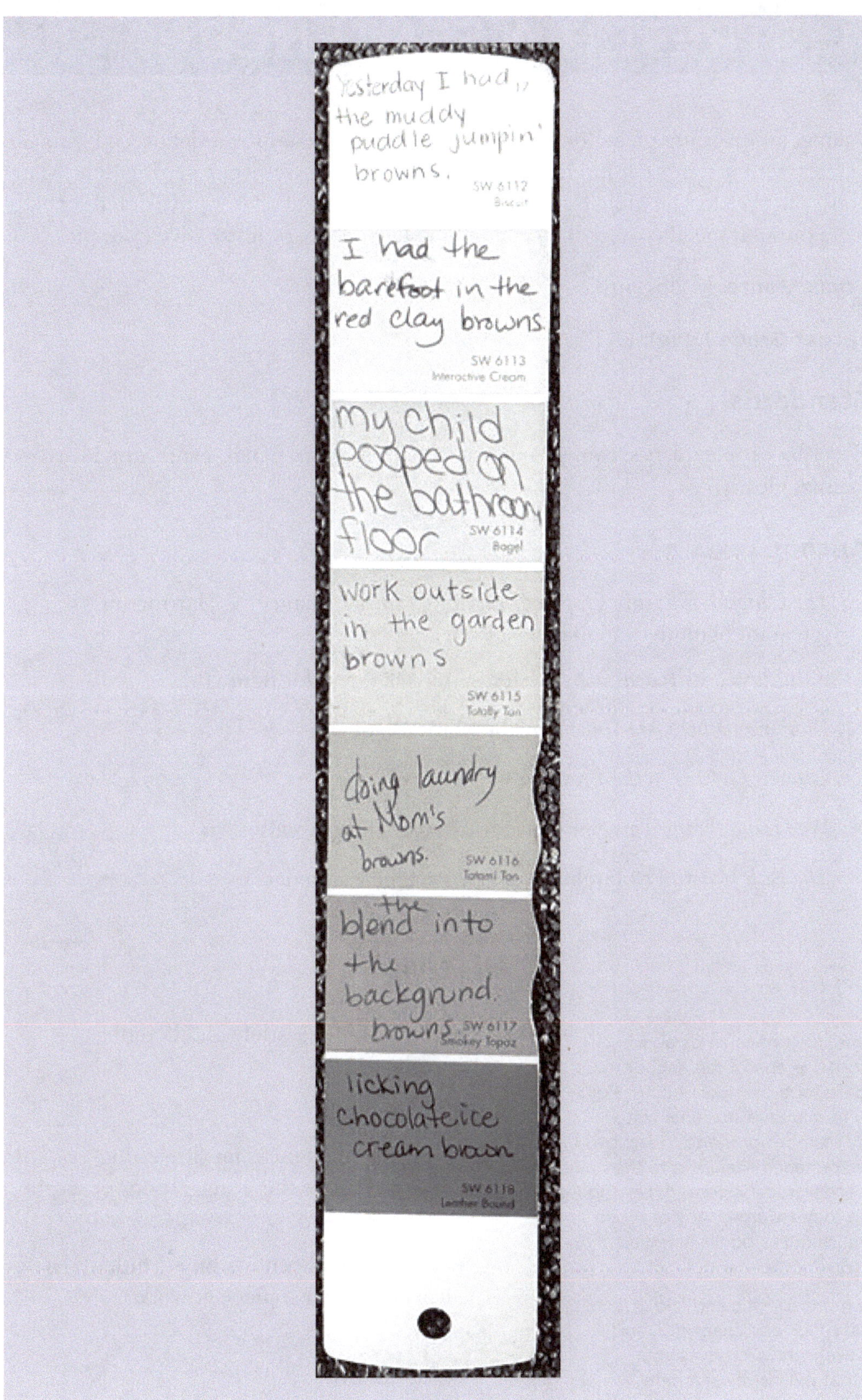

STRETCH A STORY/ STRETCH A SENTENCE

Taking an existing piece of writing and adding descriptive detail can provide readers with a more comprehensive understanding of an event or situation. Many books offer readers tangible examples of how to incorporate descriptive details or elaborate through specific word choice, additional evidence, or illustrative examples.

Focus Genre: Multigenre

Target Grade Level: K–5

Standards

Describe people, places, things, and events with relevant detail, expressing ideas and feelings clearly.

Anchor Texts

The Chicken Chasing Queen of Lamar County by Janice N. Harrington (great for figurative language)

Saturdays and Teacakes by Lester Laminack (great for nouns)

Momma, Where Are You From? by Marie Bradby

Crown: An Ode to the Freshcut by Derrick Barnes

We Had a Picnic This Sunday Past by Jacqueline Woodson

The Raft by Jim LaMarche (great for stretched sentences)

Quick Tip!

If your students don't have an established piece of writing, use one of the anchor texts as a springboard for a piece of writing. For example, you might have students write about a family member or friend, describe an everyday experience like a trip to the barbershop or the grocery store, or tell the story of where they are from. Any of those ideas work well with the books listed as anchor texts.

If you need a more specific and laid out lesson for this, check out Chapter 2, and use one of those writing ideas as your composition that will be revised here.

Materials

- Sticky notes (variety of different colors)
- Sentence strips
- Sample Sentences for Stretching (p. 241) (Use these suggestions or create your own.)
- Existing pieces of writing (Students each need their own piece of work.)

Teach It

1. Read aloud one of the books from the anchor text list.
2. Discuss how the author used descriptive details in the writing in order to show and not tell. (For example, in Laminack's *Saturdays and Teacakes*, he describes his Mammaw's kitchen this way: "In Mammaw's big kitchen, sunlight poured through the windows like a waterfall and spilled over the countertops, pooling up on the checkerboard floor.")
3. Ask students to share specific examples from the story where the author used descriptive details.
4. Pick a sample sentence from the story and have students discuss what types of details were included. (Prompts for this might include the following: Who are they talking about? What is happening in the sentence? Where is this happening? How do they describe the characters, setting, etc.?)
5. After discussing the sentences from the story, have students practice stretching a sample sentence by doing things like adding more detail, using additional adjectives, or including information that tells the reader who is involved, where the action occurred, and why. (Use one of the sample sentences in the appendices for students to stretch or create your own.) Have them work independently or with a partner to stretch a sample sentence.
6. Once they have practiced, have them take a sentence from one of their prior writing compositions and practice stretching it. Share with the class.

Try It

- Use this as a collaborative engagement for adding detail to sentences.
- Try this when you want students to complete a personal narrative about an everyday experience and then stretch their sentences by adding more detail.
- Use this in tandem with one of the lessons from Chapter 2 and have this serve as the revision aspect of that lesson.

Extensions

- Use this as a partner revision strategy during peer conferencing time.
- Have students take existing sentences from mentor texts and rewrite and revise using this strategy.
- Use this in tandem with the NVA² strategy (p. 82).
- Have students do the opposite of this strategy—Shrink a Sentence—for revising overly wordy sentences or run-ons.
- Connect this strategy to the Slinky Sentences in *Writing Workouts* (Harper, 2023).

Modifications

Emerging Writers

- Have students work in pairs to stretch sentences.
- Use this idea in a station format by putting individual words on notecards. Instruct students to create a short sentence with the words on the notecards. After they create a short sentence, have them use other words to stretch the sentence out.
- Write parts of sentences on sentence strips and distribute them to students. Have students take their sentence part and find classmates who have details or other sentence parts to stretch their sentences.

Proficient Writers

- Have students stretch their sentences by adding companion illustrations or figures. This works well if students are working on storyboards or for a graphic novel or comic strip format.
- When using this strategy in the research genre, have students elaborate by finding evidence from other sources in order to stretch their writing. This works well as an introduction for citation and research utilizing additional sources.

See It Sample

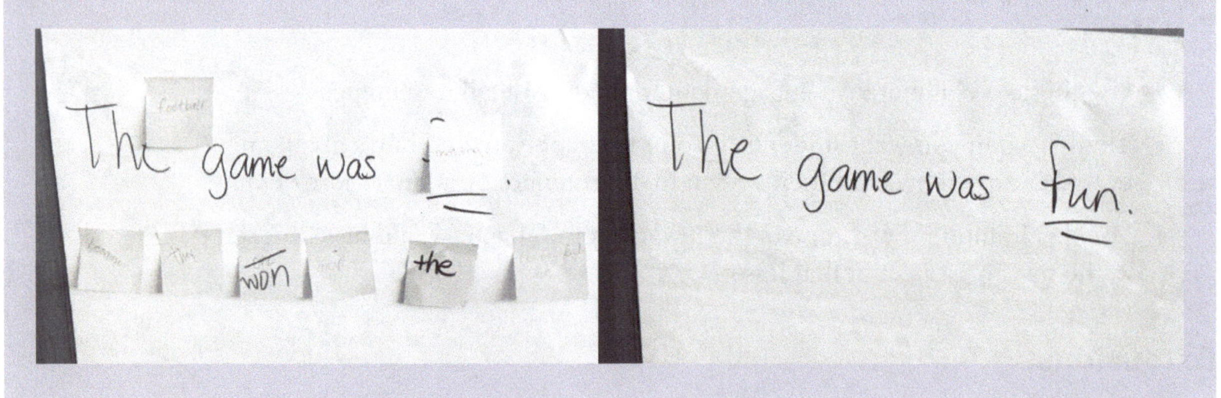

PICTURE POINT OF VIEW

One language arts focus that is constant across grade levels is point of view (POV). While early literacy classes tend to focus on who is telling the story, as students progress in their schooling, POV becomes more specific and detailed, with students reading and writing stories told from multiple points of view. In the upper elementary grades, students must recognize, identify, and navigate multiple options for POV including first person, second person, third person limited, and third person omniscient. For some students, the lines between the different types of third person points of view becomes a little blurry, and yet for others, they see the pronoun, "I" they automatically assume the text they are reading must be written in first person.

Most tasks that address this skill tend to approach it from an identifiable stance, meaning students are asked questions like, "Identify the point of view in passage A." "From what point of view is passage B told?" Those types of questions or tasks require students to read and label: Passage A is first person; passage B is third person limited. The problem with these types of tasks is that they do not allow for the *experience* of point of view. One way that teachers can attempt to create a more thorough understanding of POV is through a strategy called Picture Point of View. **NOTE:** This lesson should be used as a review. If your students do not know different points of view yet, save this lesson for when they have seen them all and use it as a review.

A lot of students confuse perspective with POV. Perspective addresses the attitudes and stance, if you will, that the narrator assumes when telling a story. POV focuses on the *type* of narrator telling the story.

Focus Genre: Narrative

Target Grade Level: 3–5

Standards

Compare and contrast point of view; understand the difference between first and third person.

Anchor Texts

Zoom by Istvan Banyai

Because of Mr. Terupt series by Ralph Buyea

The Pain and the Great One by Judy Blume

Flipped by Wendelin Van Draanen

Zoom is a wordless book, so I mainly use it as a way to see how point of view and perspective might look visually. *After the Fall* is one of my favorites to use because you can compare the original Humpty Dumpty nursery rhyme to this new account told in first person by Humpty himself.

The True Story of the Three Little Pigs by Jon Scieszka

The Bear Ate Your Sandwich by Julia Sarcone-Roach

After the Fall by Dan Santat

The Bad Seed by Jory John

They All Saw a Cat by Brendan Wenzel

Windows by Julia Denos

The One and Only Ivan by Katherine Applegate

Another great book to use for this activity is *Counting by 7s* by Holly Goldberg Sloan. It is one of the few books I have seen that alternates point of view based on the chapter.

Quick Tip!

You might find it beneficial to give students a word or phrase bank to use related to each specific point of view to help them with their writing.

Materials

- Sticky notes (variety of colors)
- Images from magazines or online
- Chart paper

Teach It

1. Begin by discussing each form of narrative point of view as a reminder and review. This is especially important when you are utilizing first person, second person, and third person limited and omniscient.
2. Read one of the anchor texts from the list and then discuss the point of view used in that example. Discuss how this affected the story and how it was presented.
3. Divide the class into four groups of students. Distribute a different colored sticky note to each group of students. You should use four different colors, one for each point of view.
4. Explain what color represents which point of view. Explain to students that the color sticky note they receive indicates which point of view they will focus on for this activity.
5. Display an image on the interactive whiteboard or document camera.

6. Have students work with their group to brainstorm narration that would fit the picture in the point of view they were assigned. Give students about 5 to 7 minutes to complete this task.

7. Have each group share their ideas.

Photo by Shelly Tanner

8. Divide students into four new groups and assign each group a new color sticky note, similar to Step 3. Direct students to areas in the room where new pictures are posted.

9. Explain to students that they will be completing a gallery walk around the room and will be writing about each image from the new point of view they have been assigned.

10. Give students about 5 minutes at each station before moving onto the next station.

Quick Tip!

Consider posting images on large sheets of chart paper as shown in the student sample. This allows students to post their ideas all around the picture as they complete their gallery walk around the room.

11. Once the class has rotated to all stations, have the last group at each station share all the collected information from each point of view with the class.

12. Have students comment on how the point of view affected the details that were provided in the writings.

Try It

- Use this when you want students to practice writing with images as a starter. Because this strategy uses images as the central method for developing a story, students aren't spending significant amounts of time unpacking the text.
- Try this as a warm-up for writing in different points of view.
- Use this as a collaborative writing engagement.

Extensions

- Encourage students to take an existing piece of their writing and switch the POV. Compare how those POVs affect the story.
- Use a mentor text from the list (or another that you enjoy) and have students compare the POV in that account with that of the original nursery rhyme, tall tale, etc.
- Use this as a lead-in for writing in different POVs and in a variety of genres.
- Connect this lesson to ones on voice, mood, and perspective, as each adds a unique layer to a text's overall meaning.
- Use this as a lead-in for discussions of audience and purpose and how POV might be modified based on those.

Modifications

Emerging Writers

- Have students practice sorting sentences that are written in different POVs into correct categories based on their POV as an opener for this skill.
- In a station format, have students match up different narration sentences to different sample images and use those to begin drafting their own writings in different points of view.

Proficient Writers

- Have students complete the task using different colored markers to designate the point of view that is the focus. Instead of requiring students to always write in a designated point of view, students can choose to add to the chart in the POV of their choice. Make sure students know what colors are for which POV so the information and ideas don't get mixed up.
- Have sample narration examples already created for students to use. Based on the POV assigned, students have to locate which ready-made details fit that POV.
- Have students practice modifying the perspective from which they write but keep the POV constant. Discuss how perspective alters the story.
- Use this as a way to teach the different points of view initially. Instead of reviewing the different points of view, have students record information on each piece of chart paper as a summary to the day's lesson on a specific point of view. By the time your unit on point of view is complete, your students will have written about each point of view on every chart paper example.

See It Sample

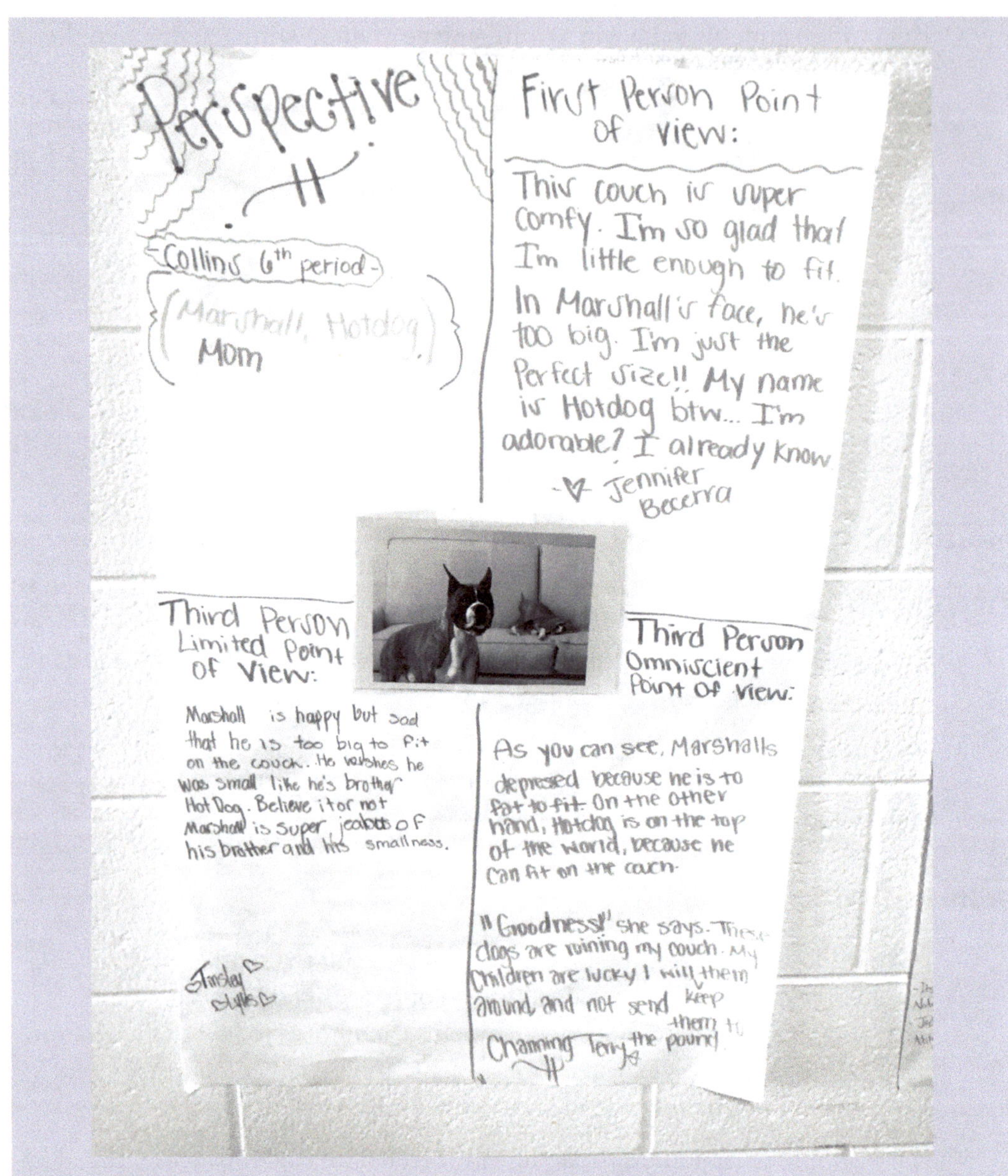

Photo by Shelly Tanner

STRETCH TO SEE

One of the best resources for writing ideas and topics can come from images, photos, artwork, and models. Because the number of images available is infinite, the possibilities for a writing class are endless. Plus, images offer another awesome added benefit: You can drop in any number of photos into a lesson with very little planning (Forgot your bell ringer for the day? Search for a unique image and start writing about it.), or they can be strategically placed and purposely connected to a bigger idea or lesson. In addition, for many of our youngest writers who may be learning to read letters and words, or for English learners, using pictures to start a story or other type of writing can help them craft ideas and begin the drafting process. In this lesson, by asking students to describe an image or a portion of the image, this can help build observation and descriptive detail skills in a fun, low-stakes way, both of which aid them when writing. Images can also be helpful in setting up a reading, either fiction or nonfiction, by activating or building prior knowledge through visual means. In fact, check out this email I received from my mom (Dr. Gayle S. Lee, 1956–2016) when she used this activity in her fourth-grade classroom.

> Hey Sweetie, you will have to tell MB that she (and this picture) are a star in my classroom. I used the picture for a lesson on using analytical thinking skills to determine who, what, when, where, and why. The students gave answers for *who* of: Macy Belle, Rebecca Harper's daughter, Amelia's little sister, and Dr. Lee's granddaughter. For *where* they said: bathroom or kitchen, her house, my house, a house. For *when* they said: morning, afternoon, during the day, before dance class. For *what* they said: getting ready for dance, posing for a picture. For *why* they said: she was getting ready for dance, she enjoys dressing up.
>
> I had some answers like 2:00 in the afternoon and in Aiken, etc., but they were able to determine what was the difference between saying daytime (because of the light from the windows) and a specific time (because there was not a clock on the wall) and saying in a house (because they haven't ever visited our houses to know for sure where she was), but they knew it was not a business or a school bathroom.
>
> Oh, they do like your bathroom. They also concluded that the towel hanging on the wall was just for decoration BECAUSE the towel on the floor and the towel on the side of the tub both match the towels in the corner cabinet. They also included that someone had recently taken a bath because the towel on the side of the tub looks "used" or "wrinkled". Isn't teaching fun!!! Nothing that I receive it safe from being shared with my students.
>
> Love you bunches,
>
> Mom
>
> **Gayle S. Lee, Ed.D., NBCT**
>
> Fourth Grade Teacher
>
> Indian Land Elementary

Focus Genre: Narrative, descriptive writing

Target Grade Level: K–5

Standards

Apply a wide range of strategies to comprehend, interpret, evaluate and appreciate texts.

Employ a wide range of strategies to write and use different writing process elements appropriately to communicate with different audiences for a variety of purposes.

Anchor Texts

See the Ocean by Estelle Condra

Night in the Country by Cynthia Rylant

Seven Blind Mice by Ed Young

Sierra, *Mojave*, *Mississippi*, or *Heartland* by Diane Sibert

Sleep Tight Farm: A Farm Prepares for Winter by Eugenie Doyle

Materials

- Random images (these can be digital or physical copies)
- Paper for jotting down ideas

Teach It

1. Display an image for the class to see. Discuss the image and what the students notice.
2. Give students a specific item or concept to find in the photo. For example, you might ask students to find the math in the picture. Have them record their noticings on their papers. (By the way, you'd be amazed at how many math concepts are hidden in photos: angles, lines, shapes, volume, reflections, and more.)

Notice that this lesson does not begin specifically with the reading of an anchor text. Of course, feel free to include a read aloud that is visually appealing, In fact, you might consider using multiple wordless picture books so that students can practice looking for specific details in images.

3. Have students share their observations.

4. Choose another item or concept for students to find. For example, you might ask them to describe the image using figurative language. Other sample nudge questions might include: Who is in the photo? Where do you think it is taken? What is happening in this image?

5. Have students share their noticings and inferences with the class.

Try It

- Use this as a way to discuss illustrations and images that accompany alphanumeric text. This can be helpful when students want to add illustrations to their writings.
- Try this when you need an impromptu quick write for a lesson.
- Try this as a way to facilitate class discussion and conversation.

Extensions

- Use this as an opener for the NVA^2 activity (p. 82).
- Connect this to wordless picture book writings (p. 76).
- Extend this to a fully executed descriptive writing lesson like the one on page 86.
- Use this as a starter for Sticky Note Poems (p. 94).

Modifications

Emerging Writers

- Provide students with a series of specific prompts to use when analyzing or observing a specific photo or image. This can help them stay on track and pay attention to specific details.
- Glue photos or images on chart paper and have students rotate around the room recording their observations and noticings on the chart paper.
- Use illustrations from familiar picture books and have students write down their observations about the images.

Proficient Writers

- Have students bring in an image to class and create their own writing prompts or nudge questions to use with the photo.
- Use historical photos, math problems, science figures, or primary sources instead of random photographs for content-area connections.
- Crop images so that there is a significant part of the image missing. Have students make inferences about the cropped image. Show them the original image and have them make adjustments to their inferences as needed.

See It Sample

Penguin Photo → find all math items
- # of penguins
- depth of water
- temperature of air
- height/weight of penguins
- elevation
- time of day

↳ find science items
- habitat
- animal
- coral
- water
- motion

↳ find SS items
- population
- emigration
- leadership
- nat. resources
- environment

Photo by Alysha Krier Mooney

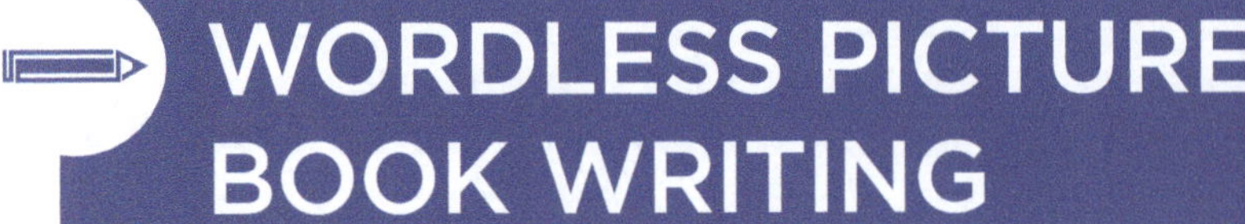

WORDLESS PICTURE BOOK WRITING

Wordless picture books are not just for primary classrooms. Instead, they are valuable resources that can be used in middle and secondary classrooms as well. Plus, some wordless books often have very sophisticated illustrations that warrant careful examination, and many times have complex story lines that require students to reread sections in order to fully understand the message.

> **Stop & Think**
>
> While some may argue reading a wordless picture book isn't really reading, it actually is! Since reading is about meaning making and understanding, when students read images and develop a story or create meaning based on what they have seen, they are actually reading and building their visual literacy skills. And remember, texts are not restricted to books that have words. Instead, texts can be images, pictures, dramatic interpretations, and more.

In primary grades, standards almost always address a student's ability to match words to illustrations. While this might be a primary focus, students in upper grade levels can benefit from using picture books to craft solid sentences and extended paragraphs that correspond to the images presented in the work. Using wordless picture books for the creation of extended written responses allows students to take a low stakes text (wordless picture books) and expound upon them as they develop solid, extended written compositions. Plus, they are able to move beyond simply making sure that the words and images match, but that each sentence matches the one that comes before and the one that comes after.

Focus Genre: Narrative

Target Grade Level: 3–5

Standards

Apply a wide range of strategies to comprehend, interpret, evaluate and appreciate texts.

Employ a wide range of strategies to write and use different writing process elements appropriately to communicate with different audiences for a variety of purposes.

Anchor Texts

Flotsam by David Wiesner

Mr. Wuffles by David Wiesner

Journey by Aaron Becker

Unspoken by Henry Cole

Flora the Flamingo by Molly Idle

Small Things by Mel Tregonning

Fly by Mark Teague

One Little Bag: An Amazing Journey by Henry Cole

Materials

- Sticky notes
- NVA² template (p. 242)
- Notecards or sentence strips
- Pages from a wordless book of your choice

> **Quick Tip!**
>
> Because of copyright law, don't make copies of the pictures in a wordless book. Typically, what I do is purchase a second copy of my favorites and then cut the pictures out of the book. Note: To do this activity, you would need two extra copies of the book since pages are printed double-sided. Put the originals in plastic sleeves or laminate them so you can reuse as needed.

Teach It

1. Display an image from one of the wordless picture books.
2. Distribute an NVA² template to each student and provide them with a notecard or a sentence strip.
3. Instruct students to look at the image and draft a sentence that describes what is occurring in the sample image using the NVA² template or format. (See instructions for that format written on page 82.)

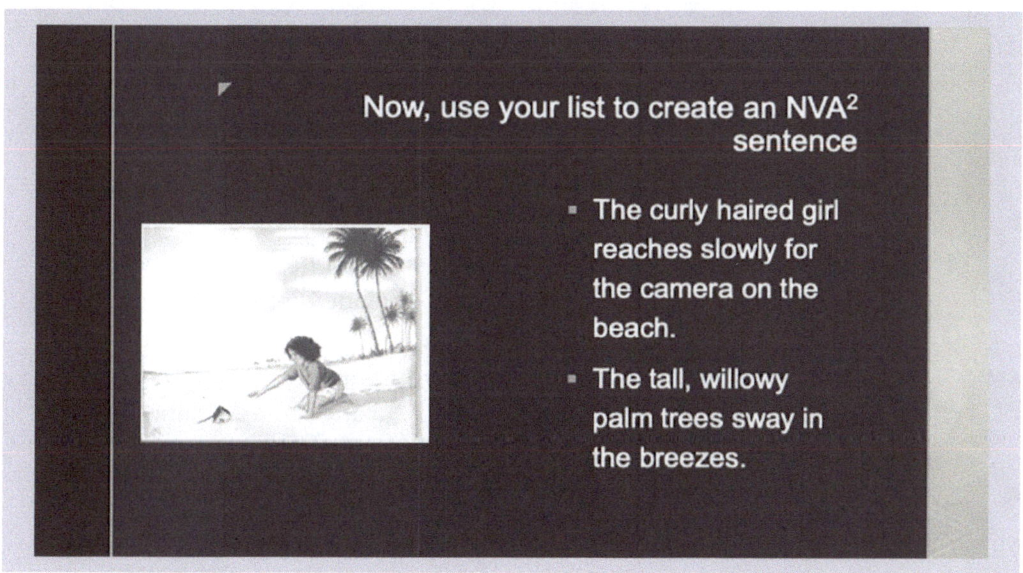

4. Have students share their work with the class. Note how some of the sentences might vary despite the fact that everyone used the same image.

5. Distribute the remaining pages of the book, one page per student.

6. Have students repeat Steps 2 and 3. They should draft a sentence that describes the new image they have been given using a second NVA^2 template and an additional sheet of paper.

7. Once students have written their sentences, start putting the story back together.

8. Call out the page numbers starting from page one. Have students lay their images on the floor in the hallway or classroom and put their sentence right below it.

> **Quick Tip!**
>
> For a large class, you might choose a longer book with more pages. Similarly, when completing this activity in small groups or with a smaller class, a shorter book will suffice. Make sure you have these pages numbered so they can be put back in the correct order.

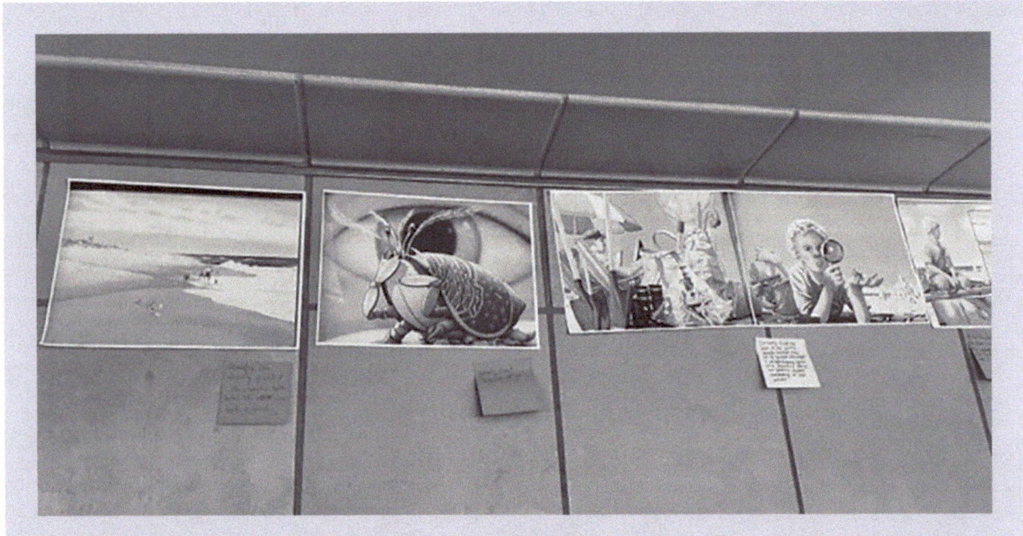

9. Repeat this for the entire book.

10. Once the entire story has been rebuilt, divide students into groups.

11. Have each group read the story. When doing this, they should look at the images and the accompanying sentences. Provide them with a notecard or sticky notes to make notations of sentences that need revisions, those that may not work where they are, or any other observations. You could also have students use sticky note flags to attach to any sentences and pictures that should be revised.

12. Once everyone has viewed the entire story, have students discuss their observations as a class.

13. Remind students of the whole class activity they completed before they started the activity. In that example, students were only responsible for looking at their specific image and drafting one sentence that supported that image. However, once they re-built the story, not only do the sentences have to match the individual images, but they also must match the sentences that came before and after. Help students understand that building a coherent story relies on much more than simply matching words to images.

14. Ask students if there are certain pages or sections that should be revised. (These should have been recorded on their notecards or sticky notes.)

15. In pairs or small groups, have students choose which image's sentence they plan to revise. Give them a blank notecard and have them revise their chosen section.

16. Once the revisions are complete, have the class reread the story with the revisions and discuss it as a group.

Try It

- Use this as a way to incorporate literature in the classroom.
- Use this if you have emerging readers or English learners in your class who might be reading below grade level.

- Try this when you want to get students up and moving with a hands-on activity.
- Use this when you want students to conduct a close read with a different type of text (illustrations).

Extensions

- Have students create their own wordless picture book using photos or images.
- Use scenes from silent movies for students to create accompanying scripts.

Modifications

Emerging Writers

- Use a book that has words and black out the words. Have students write their sentences and then compare them to the original ones from the text.
- Instead of using an entire wordless book, use scenes from a book or divide the book into parts so it is completed in sections.
- Have students draft words for each picture first and then progress to sentences.
- Create sample sentences that students might use and have them match the sentences to the appropriate illustration.

Proficient Writers

- Make some placeholder blank pages instead of using all the pages from the book. Have students draw pictures and write sentences for the place holder pages using material from the existing pages to help them determine possibilities for inclusion.
- Have students create their own wordless picture book. Then have them swap books with a partner and have their partner write the words for the book.

See It Sample

CHAPTER 1 In the Beginning, We Write
CHAPTER 2 Breaking Into Story
CHAPTER 3 Tell Me More
CHAPTER 4 Learning Through Writing
CHAPTER 5 Finding Your Voice
CHAPTER 6 The Art of Persuasion
CHAPTER 7 The Measure of Success

CHAPTER 1 In the Beginning, We Write
CHAPTER 2 Breaking Into Story
CHAPTER 3 Tell Me More
CHAPTER 4 Learning Through Writing
CHAPTER 5 Finding Your Voice
CHAPTER 6 The Art of Persuasion
CHAPTER 7 The Measure of Success

NVA² DESCRIPTIVE WRITING

Teaching grammar effectively can often be challenging, as traditional methods tend to focus on the utilization of skills-based worksheets or grammar exercises in isolation. As a former writing teacher, finding ways to make grammar instruction effective and engaging was often a struggle. However, what worked best were lessons that incorporated grammar into the writing the students were already doing. Experiencing it in context helps students do more than simply identify grammatical elements in writing, but rather experience it as they are writing, thus offering them more authentic opportunities to engage with the ways in which language and words work and function. NVA² is a great strategy that incorporates grammar into writing composition.

Focus Genre: Descriptive Writing/Grammar Lesson

Target Grade Level: 3–5

Standards

Apply knowledge of language structure, language conventions (e.g., spelling and punctuation), media techniques, figurative language, and genre to create, critique, and discuss print and nonprint texts.

Employ a wide range of strategies as they write and use different writing process elements appropriately to communicate with different audiences for a variety of purposes.

Anchor Texts

For this lesson, you don't really need a specific anchor text since you are mainly focusing on images. However, any wordless book you enjoy would work well here. See page 76–77 for examples.

Quick Tip!

A great image repository is https://www.pics4learning.com/

Materials

NVA² template (p. 242)

Teach It

Display an image for the entire class to see. You can also use a page from a wordless picture book.

1. Have students use the NVA² template (p. 242) or create their own NVA² chart on a sheet of paper.

2. Instruct students to first record a list of nouns that go with the image in the N column.

3. Have students move on to the V column and make a list of verbs that go with the image.

4. Have students move to the A column and make a list of adjectives that go with the image.

5. Once students have filled up their template, write NVA^2 for the students to see. Instruct them to take one noun, one verb, and two adjectives and write an NVA^2 sentence that describes the image posted for the class to see. For example, here's what one class produced:

Noun	Verb	Adjective
Tree Water Wood Umbrella Leaves Sky Rocks Shells	Moving water Wind blowing the leaves Moving clouds	Green Brown Blue Red White Powder white
The beach has a shell moving clouds and powder white sand.		

Noun	Verb	Adjective
Palm Tree Sand Beach Shells Ocean Pine straw Clouds Leaves Poles	People walking	Blue sky Blue ocean Green leaves Brown wood Brown pinestraw White clouds Tan sand Orange poles White poles Clean beach
The beach is where a lot of people walk when the sky is blue with no clouds because they think it is gonna rain and ruin their walk and they are gonna be soaked wet so that is why I pick that sentence.		

6. Have students share their sentences with the class.

Try It

- Use this as a way to incorporate grammar into writing engagements.
- Try this when you want students to practice crafting descriptive sentences that include specific parts of speech.
- Use this as a low stakes way to have students practice descriptive writing.

Extensions

- Add a fourth A category for adverbs. Have students write a new NVA[2] sentence that incorporates a noun, verb, adjective, and adverb.
- Have students repeat the sentence construction process and construct a descriptive paragraph.
- Extend this strategy into a fully involved descriptive writing composition using one of the descriptive writing strategies from this book on pages 86 and 94.
- Have students collect their own images and complete their lists and sample sentences. Display the images in the class for everyone to see. Then distribute the sentences and have students see if they can match the sentence to the correct image.
- When students orally share their sentences, have their classmates identify the different parts of speech in their sentences.

Modifications

Emerging Writers

- Start with one or two parts of speech first and have students practice with those before you move on to the next.
- Provide students with a ready-made word bank that they use to select the words they think compliment the image.
- Divide students into groups and assign a specific letter from the NVA[2] chart for each group. Have one group focus on the nouns, another on verbs, and another on adjectives. Then divide students into new groups and have them collaboratively write their NVA[2] sentences.

Proficient Writers

- Have students create multiple sentences and build a descriptive paragraph.
- Use multiple images and paste each one on a sheet of chart paper. Have students complete a gallery walk and add applicable words to each chart paper and image.
- Have students locate or bring in their own images for use during this lesson.

See It Sample

Nouns	Verbs	Adjectives
girl	smiling	sunny
cat	purring	green
Mom	holding	furry
animal	hugging	blonde
pet	standing	blue (shirt)
leaf(ves)		yellow (eyes)
fence		
garden		
porch		

or even for KG/1 = person, place, thing

Now create a NVA² → The furry yellow eyed cat purrs.

The photo displayed for the class was of a blonde woman holding a cat, while standing on a deck outside.

SENSORY WRITING

In many instances, when students write, they rely heavily on one type of sensory detail: sight. However, in order to create compositions that are rich, vivid, and full of description, appealing to all five senses is important. Revising compositions to include different sensory details can sometimes be daunting for students because they may not know exactly where to put the new details. By annotating and color-coding their paragraphs, determining which details should be added becomes more manageable.

Focus Genre: Descriptive Writing

Target Grade Level: 3–5

Students employ a wide range of strategies as they write and use different writing process elements appropriately to communicate with different audiences for a variety of purposes.

Anchor Texts

Night in the Country by Cynthia Rylant

Watercress by Andrea Wang

Fireflies by Julie Brinckloe

Roller Coaster by Marla Frazee

A Moment in Time by Jennifer Butenas

I typically use crayons, which I put in small plastic bags for easy distribution. I include five colors (green, red, blue, yellow, and purple) so everyone has the same colors and can annotate their papers accordingly.

Materials

- Colored pencils or crayons
- Existing writing students have drafted
- Sensory Writing template (p. 244) *(optional)*

Teach It

1. Begin by reading one of the descriptive anchor texts.
2. Discuss with the students the different types of details that were included in the story. (If you want them to take notes on the different sensory details included in the read aloud for sharing, distribute the Sensory Writing template [p. 244] for them to record their details.)

3. Discuss how using sensory details can be helpful in creating rich descriptions in a story.
4. Have students take out one of their latest writings.
5. Assign a specific color to each sense and display a key for students to reference throughout the lesson.

The NVA[2] activity (p. 82) would be a good composition to start with. However, you can use any draft students are currently working on.

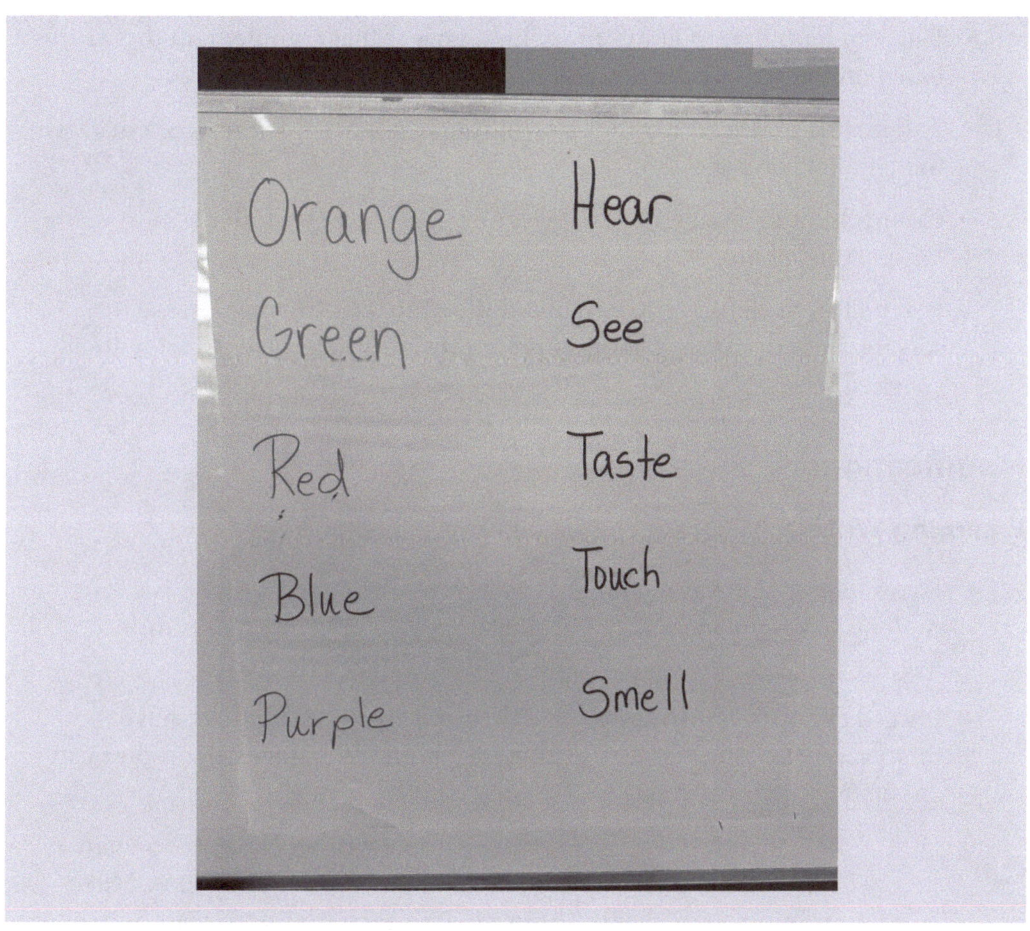

6. Instruct students to take their own writing and annotate it based on the colors listed on the board. For example, they might underline all details related to the sense of sight with the color blue, while those that appeal to the sense of smell are coded with a green crayon.
7. Once they have marked up their entire composition, ask them to consider what sense is missing by looking at the colors they have used in their annotations.
8. Based on what color is missing, have students revise for that specific sense. Make sure you model how you might incorporate a new sensory detail in the writing.
9. Have students share their revisions with the class.

Try It

- Use this when you want students to revise with a specific purpose.
- Try this as a way to get students to reread their compositions and revise accordingly.
- Use this when you want students to revisit an existing composition but look at it through a different lens.

Extensions

- Have students draw pictures or include images that complement the writing based on the sensory details.
- Extend this strategy into other writings such as a Six-Room Image poem. Use the template on page 235.
- Connect this to Candy Revision (Harper, 2023) where students must revise for specific reasons.
- Extend this to class discussions about literature by assigning a sense to a specific student so they can respond or provide a statement utilizing their assigned sense.

Modifications

Emerging Writers

- Focus on one sense at the time. In fact, you might decide that it is enough for students to simply include details that appeal to only two senses instead of all five.
- Instead of having students evaluate their own personal writings, have them apply the same strategy to an excerpt from literature, which they can annotate.
- Place sample writing excerpts on chart paper and post around the room. Make sure that in each sample at least one sense is completely missing or is very weak compared to the other senses. Divide students into groups and assign them a color and a sense. Instruct them to go around the room and annotate each writing sample. Once every group has visited each sample, assign one sample each to a group and have them identify the sensory detail missing and draft what they could include to improve the writing.

Quick Tip!

Don't have enough copies of a particular book you want them to annotate? Try highlighter tape instead. Highlighter tape comes in multiple colors and can be applied to paper and then removed with no damage to the book. This would be a great tool if you want students to annotate excerpts from their textbooks.

Proficient Writers

- Have students shift their sensory detail revisions to include dialogue and figurative language. Make sure that when they revise focusing on a particular sense, they also include figurative language or dialogue.
- Add another color that represents some other type of descriptive detail like figurative language, dialogue, imagery, etc. Have students annotate their writings to include these additional options as well.
- Use this as a partner revision strategy and have students work with partners to determine what is needed in their writings.

See It Sample

Nickos.
When I go to bed, I like my room dark. In order to stay cool I put the fan on. My pillow is nice and soft. I love the fresh smell of my sheets. When my dad tucks me in, I can taste the toothpaste I used to brush my teeth. I dont like to sleep in silence. I like to hear my parents talk down stairs. Then all of the sudden I see nothing.

- see
- smell
- hear
- touch
- taste

Photo by Nickolas Jokulis

CHARACTER PROPS

Writing about and discussing characters in literature is important for students at all grade levels. When we give students opportunities to discuss fictional characters and their fictional lives in stories, students are able to understand what they have read on a deeper level. Plus, identifying with characters can often assist students in making connections and may improve their comprehension as well.

Focus Genre: Narrative

Target Grade Level: K–5

For this lesson, most any narrative mentor text will do. It works great with a novel or picture book that the class has read or is currently reading. These are a few of my favorite novels that I like to use with this strategy.

Standards

Apply a wide range of strategies to comprehend, interpret, evaluate, and appreciate texts. Draw on prior experience, interactions with other readers and writers, knowledge of word meaning and of other texts, word identification strategies, and understanding of textual features (e.g., sound–letter correspondence, sentence structure, context, graphics).

Anchor Texts

Three Times Lucky by Sheila Turnage

A Snicker of Magic by Natalie Lloyd

Ungifted by Gordon Korman

The Bad Guys series by Aaron Blabey

Materials

- Various props related to the character
- Notecards or sticky notes
- Character Props template (p. 245) *(optional)*

Teach It

1. Determine which characters or figures from reading that will be the focus of the lesson. Select one character to use as a demonstration model for the class.
2. Display four or five objects related to the selected character in the front of the room for students to see.

3. Introduce each object. You might hold up each object so everyone can see and tell the class what it is, but do not tell them which character they belong to.

4. Remind students about the novel or other literary work they have been reading.

5. Distribute a notecard or sticky note to each student and have them record which character they think owns the displayed items. Have them explain and justify their reasoning and then share their thoughts with the rest of the class.

6. Divide students in collaborative groups or partners.

7. Provide students with a list of characters from the novel or book being studied.

8. Have them select a character and then collect five objects that their character would have based on what they know about their character. Remind students to justify and explain their choices. Have students use sticky notes or Character Props template (p. 245) to record their thoughts.

9. Have students share their lists with the class.

> **Quick Tip!**
>
> You could also have students simply make a list of objects or locate images of the chosen objects if collecting physical items is a challenge.

Character Props

Character Chosen: Ms. Lana

Character Traits: caring, dedicated, loyal

Prop	Justification	Textual Evidence (if applicable)
wig	Ms. Lana is always changing her appearance by wearing wigs and different clothes.	"Miss Lana tucked a strand of her glossy Ava Gardner wig behind her ear. . ."
Eiffel Tower	The cafe had a Paris themed menu.	"Glancing around, I pegged today's theme as 1930's Paris—her favorite. A miniature Eiffel Tower graced the counter."
menu	Ms. Lana runs the cafe.	She, "wrote the day's specials on the chalboard."
order pad	Ms. Lana takes orders at the cafe and she wrote a note to the colonel.	"She scrawled across her order pad + handed it to him."

Try It

- Use this when you are reading a novel or other literary work that has multiple characters.
- Try this if you want students to review and collectively discuss characters from multiple works of literature.
- Use this as a way to get students to think beyond using words to convey meaning and include objects and items.
- Try this when you want students to take part in an oral presentation component in addition to writing.

Extensions

- Once students have collected all their objects, instead of having them share aloud, have them set up their objects on display like an exhibit. Then have the entire class rotate through each exhibit and examine the artifacts chosen. Students can then guess which exhibit is for which character.
- Have students use these objects as idea starters when they begin drafting a character analysis.

Modifications

Emerging Writers

- Choose one character from a novel and have the class focus on the same character for the activity. Make a list of objects that character might have and vote on the ones to include as a class. Bring the items in on the next class day and have students discuss and write about them.
- Set the class up initially like an exhibit and have students travel to each teacher created exhibit and record their character choices on the Character Props template (p. 245).
- If you do not have physical artifacts available, use images from magazines to create a Character Collage or use a digital program like Canva to create a virtual option.

Proficient Writers

- Instead of focusing on characters from a specific novel, have students develop a character based on objects you provide. For example, I often use my prom dress as a character starter warm up. I bring the dress into class and show it to students, while I walk around and let them see and feel the sequins and beads on the dress. Then, I ask questions like: Who might wear this dress? Where would you wear this? If this dress could talk, what would it say?
- Bring in a variety of items and have students use the items provided to create props for their assigned characters.
- Use the props to create another story or scene including the character. Make sure to use all the props in the new story. (This would be similar to the Story Bags lesson on p. 28.)

See It Sample

STICKY NOTE POEMS

Poetry, for some, including myself, is a little intimidating. Yes, there are fewer words included on the page, but coming up with the right ones? Sometimes that is easier said than done. Plus, for whatever reason, many students are conditioned to think that all poems must rhyme, which, of course, is not true. There are so many different types and formats of poems and considerable examples that can be used as mentor texts. Since many students have written exclusively in prose, offering opportunities to interact and engage with different genres of expression can be a welcome change of pace.

Utilizing art and peer collaboration, the Sticky Note Poems lesson offers a unique approach to drafting poetry by progressing through a number of experiences: reading aloud, listening, drafting, observing, and drafting. Students are not simply creating a poem, but they are experiencing it as it emerges on the page, framed by a visual image that inspired the word creation and selection. Sticky Note Poems can help nurture the poet in all students.

Focus Genre: Poetry

Target Grade Level: 3–5

Standards

Apply a wide range of strategies to comprehend, interpret, evaluate, and appreciate texts. Draw on prior experience, interactions with other readers and writers, knowledge of word meaning and of other texts, word identification strategies, and understanding of textual features (e.g., sound–letter correspondence, sentence structure, context, graphics).

Anchor Texts

Sierra, Mississippi, Mojave, or Heartland by Diane Siebert

Love That Dog and *Hate That Cat* by Sharon Creech

Joyful Noise: Poems for Two Voices by Paul Fleischman

Moving Words About a Flower by K.C. Hayes

Wonder Walkers by Micha Archer

Dreamers by Yuri Morales

Red Sings From Treetops: A Year in Colors by Joyce Sidman

Green on Green by Dianne White

A *Gift for Amma: Market Day in India* by Meera Sriram

Southwest Sunrise by Nikki Grimes

Saturdays and Teacakes by Lester Laminack

Materials

- Sticky notes
- Chart paper
- Blank paper

Teach It

1. Open the lesson by showing students a photograph. Distribute a sticky note to each student and have them write a word that describes or is related to the displayed image. Post these words on an adjacent piece of chart paper.
2. Distribute a blank sheet of paper to each student. Start by reading students a descriptive text. (This needs to be one with rich detail, lots of adjectives, and highly descriptive sentences.) Don't show the students the pictures if you are reading them a picture book.
3. Instruct students to draw what they hear. You might offer an example, like, "For example, if I hear details about a field with sunflowers, I would draw that on my paper."

> **Quick Tip!**
>
> Make sure that students have heard the story once before but without looking at any pictures. Remember, the first time they hear it they are simply listening to the story. When they hear it a second time, they can pay attention to what they should draw.

Photo by Shelly Tanner

4. After you finish reading the story aloud, have students finish up their drawings and then clear their desks of everything but their drawings.

5. Distribute a stack of sticky notes to each student.

6. Explain to students that they will circulate around the room, looking at each of their classmate's artwork. As they observe, they should write a descriptive word on a sticky note and stick it on their classmate's desk. The word they choose should describe or relate to the image drawn.

> **Quick Tip!**
>
> Make sure you spend remind students that they are not critiquing each other's work, but rather are helping each other develop a word bank they can use as starters for their writing.

7. After students have circulated and seen all the artwork in the classroom, have them return to their desks. Using these words provided by their classmates, have students construct a poem about their image.

Photo by Shelly Tanner

8. Before students begin constructing their own poems, model how this might be done using the sample photo and words that students brainstormed that you opened class with in Step 1.

9. Have students use the words at their desks to construct their own poems. Follow the same procedure with filler words by providing them with additional blank sticky notes in a different color.

You don't have to use all the words that students brainstormed, but try to use as many as possible. If you need to add filler words, record those on a different color sticky note so you can see which were originals and which ones were added.

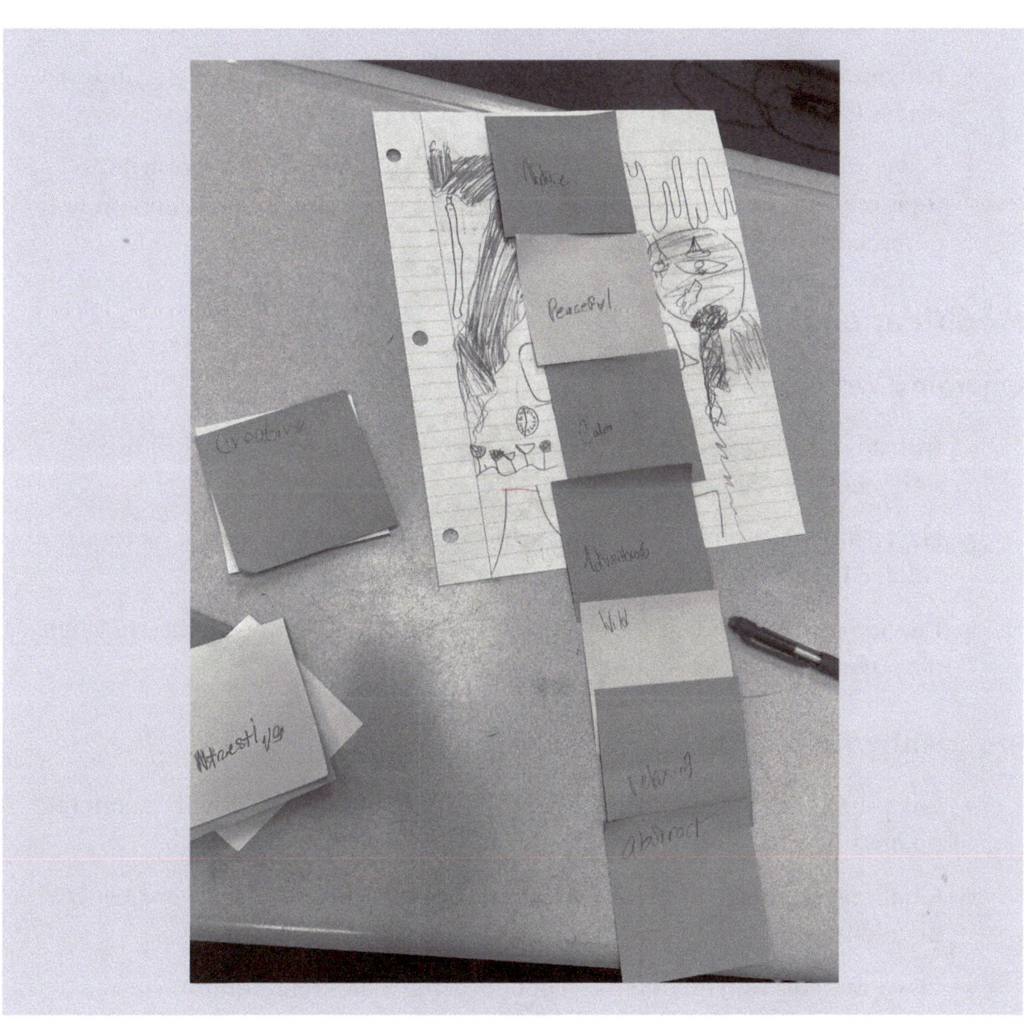

Photo by Shelly Tanner

10. Have students share their poems with the class.

Try It

- Use this as a way to connect art to poetry and capitalize on arts integration.
- Try this when you want students to practice constructing poetry in a low-stakes setting.
- Use this as a way to focus on visualization and description when reading and writing.

Extensions

- Have students group or classify the class-generated word bank by parts of speech (nouns, adjectives, verbs, etc.).
- Encourage students to collaborate with a partner to create a poem in two voices like the Character Partner Poem (p. 171).
- Have students display the artwork in the classroom and then redistribute their created poems. See if the classmates can match the correct poem to the correct drawing.

Modifications

Emerging Writers

- Instead of having students write a poem, have them write a descriptive sentence.
- Have students use old magazines to cut out images and create a pictorial collage that represents the material presented in the reading.
- Provide students with some example descriptor words they might use when observing their peers' writing.

Proficient Writers

- Give students a specific type of poem to construct such as a haiku, concrete poem, free verse poem, cinquain, or acrostic poem.
- Challenge students to use all the words from their sticky note word bank with no additions.
- Have students rewrite their new poems using a different point of view.

See It Sample

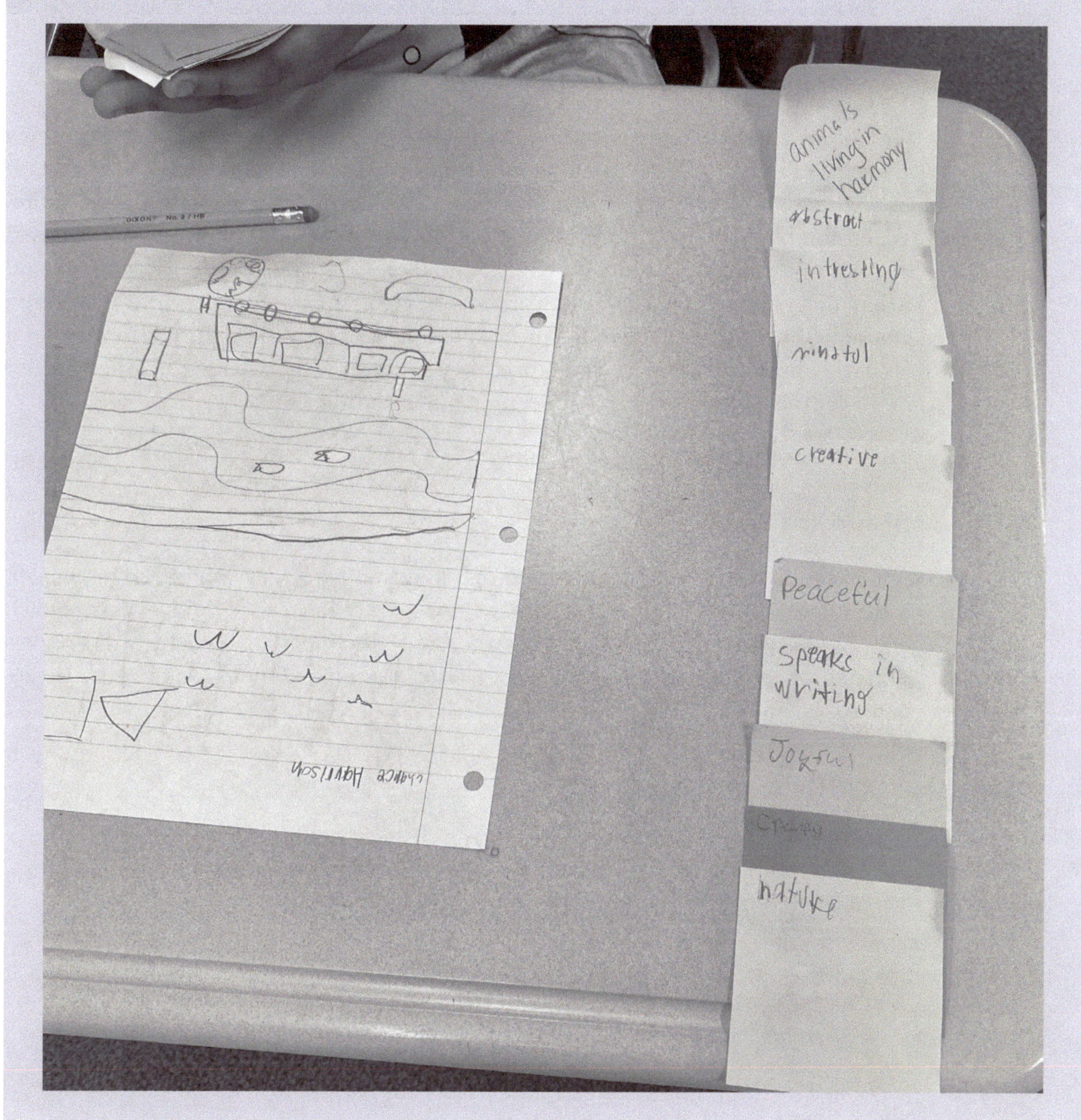

NUMBERS AND ME

Focus Genre: Personal narrative

Getting to know students is one of the most important parts of building a positive classroom climate and establishing classroom culture. Students come from diverse backgrounds with varying beliefs, traditions, hobbies, familial structure, and more. When thinking about writing topics, what do we know more about than ourselves? That's why starting off extended writings with topics that address *who* students are and where they see themselves in the world can serve as a gateway into writing for those who might be inexperienced or unmotivated. I Am From . . . writing can serve as a fantastic opportunity for students to get their feet wet with extended writings and for their classmates and instructors to learn about each other.

Target Grade Level: K–2

Standards

Apply a wide range of strategies to comprehend, interpret, evaluate, and appreciate texts. Draw on prior experience, interactions with other readers and writers, knowledge of word meaning and of other texts, word identification strategies, and understanding of textual features (e.g., sound–letter correspondence, sentence structure, context, graphics).

Anchor Texts

The Boy Who Loved Math: The Improbable Life of Paul Erdos by Deborah Heiligman

All Sorts by Pippa Goodhart

Numbers Everywhere by Linda Leopold Strauss

I'm Trying to Love Math by Bethany Barton

This Plus That: Life's Little Equations by Amy Krouse Rosenthal

Materials

- Chart paper
- Numbers and Me template (p. 246)

Teach It

1. Open the class by reading students one of the books from the list of anchor texts.

2. After reading, brainstorm all the different ways that math was part of the story.
3. Have students share different ways that they use numbers in their daily lives. You might use some of these questions to get the discussions started.
   - How many people are in your family?
   - How old are you?
   - What are the numbers on your street address?
   - How many pieces of candy did you eat yesterday?
   - How many pets do you have?
4. Begin modeling a Numbers and Me writing by putting your name on a large sheet of chart paper. List numbers that are connected to your life on the chart paper.

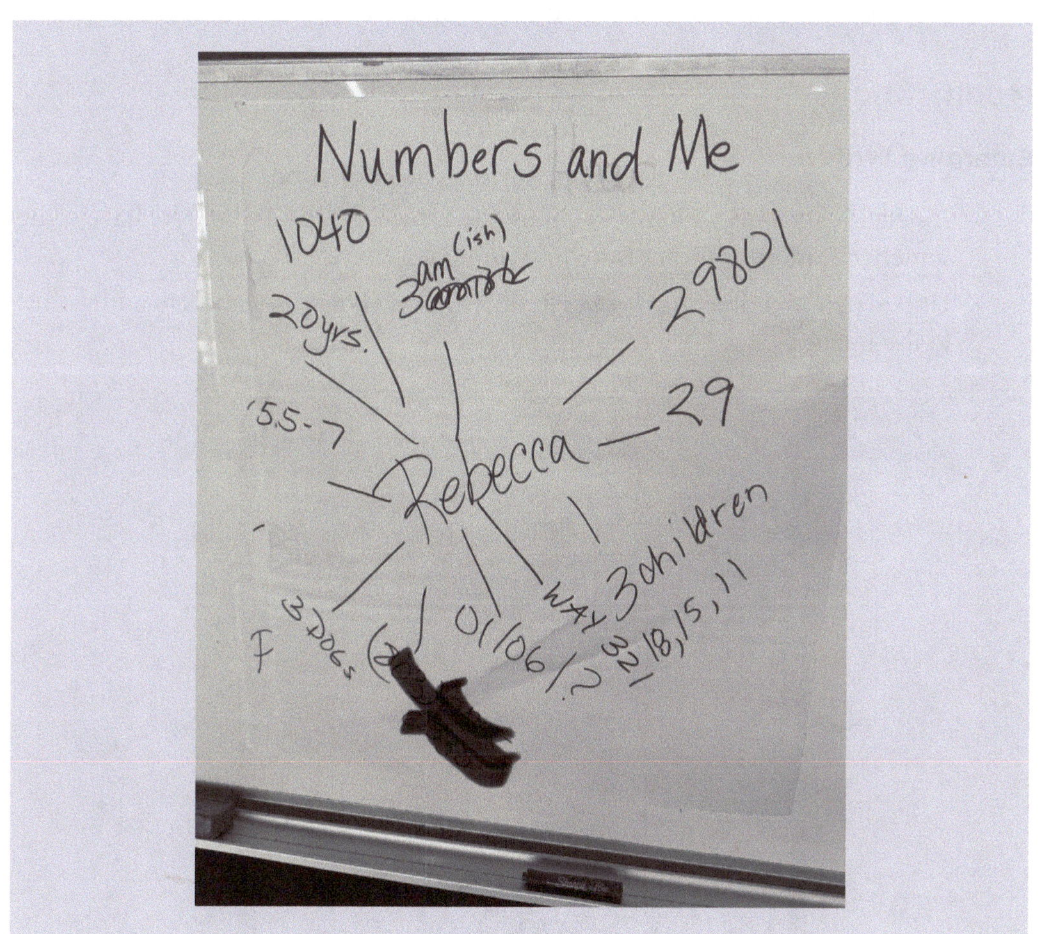

5. Distribute a copy of the Numbers and Me template (p. 246) to each student.
6. Have students begin listing the numbers that are connected to their lives.
7. Give students time to draft and share their work with the rest of the class.

Try It

- Try this as an alternative to a traditional personal narrative.
- Use this when you want to incorporate a getting-to-know-you type of writing.
- Use this writing early in the year since it utilizes a list format which may make it easier for beginning writers.

Extensions

- Have each student choose their favorite detail from the completed template and write that detail in a complete sentence.
- Use the information from the templates to write extended personal narratives.
- For a family literacy connection, encourage students to ask family members to complete their own Numbers and Me template to share.

Modifications

Emerging Writers

- Instead of allowing students to choose their own details to include, have some sentence starters or prompts to help students generate ideas.
- Utilize pictorial drawings for beginning writers. Then use labels to add words to the images.

Photo by Alysha Krier Mooney

- Create a collaborative class Numbers and Me chart with one item included for each student.

Proficient Writers

- Have students create math equations with some of the numbers included (e.g., "I have two dogs and two cats which equals four pets").
- Challenge students to draft questions for which a number would be the answer (e.g., "How many siblings do I have?").
- Have students complete this activity with a partner. Students could interview their partner and create a Numbers and Me interview writing based on what their partner shared.

See It Sample

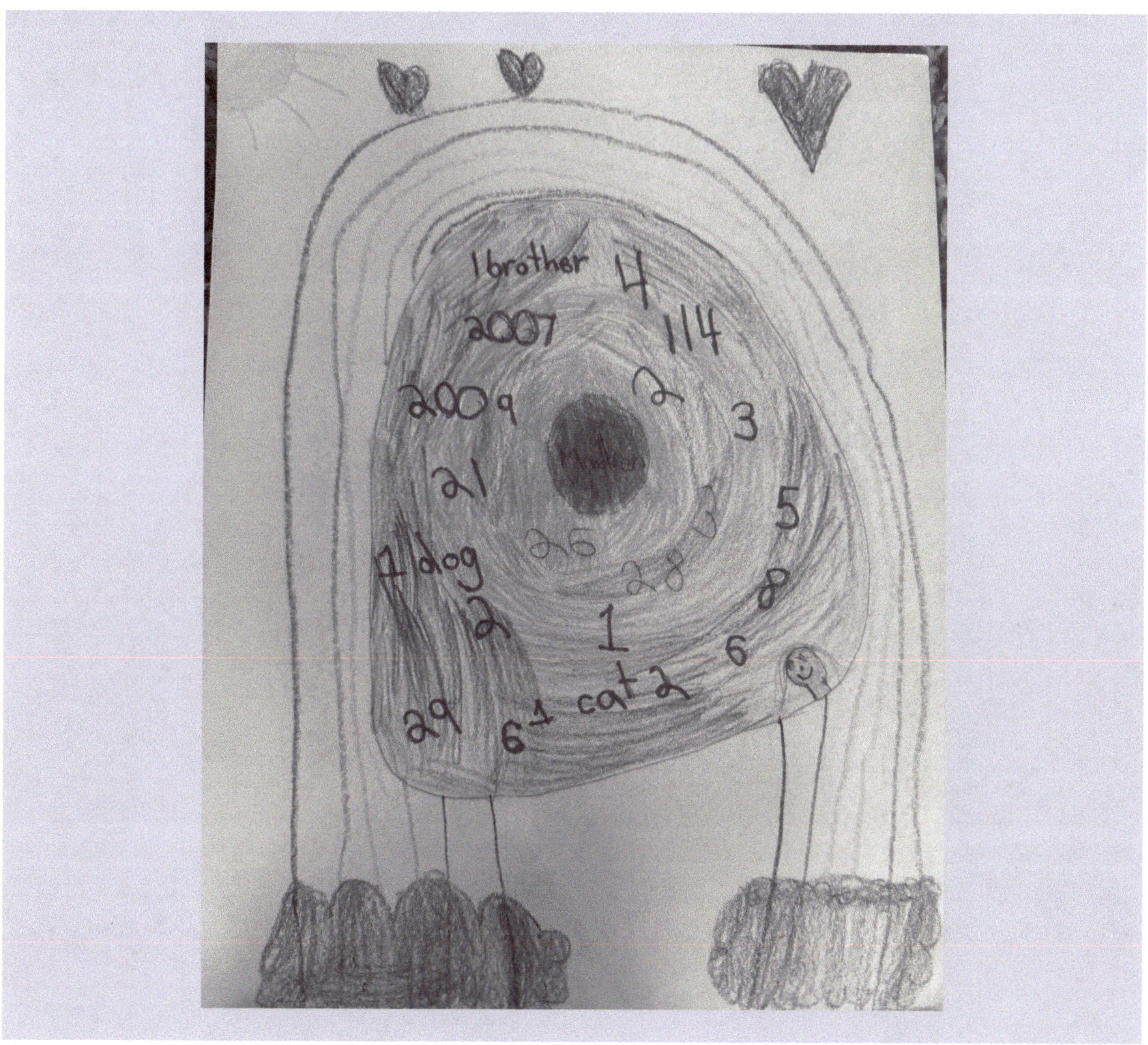

Photo by Alysha Krier Mooney

Chapter 4

LEARNING THROUGH WRITING

Whether we realize it or not, compositions that teach us about a concept or how to do something are more common that we might think. While I have always argued that the majority of the writing we complete is executed as a means to process, learn, and live, when you think about the texts that we consume on a regular basis, a significant amount of them fall in the research, informational, or nonfiction genre. In fact, just today, these are some of the texts I read:

- A passage about the origin of specific clothing items
- An internet posting about the true story of the Deepwater Horizon after watching the blockbuster movie
- A biographic entry about Taylor Swift
- The origin of specific traditions and cultural practices after a hallway office conversation

Plus, I also had to complete mandatory compliance training, accompanied by paragraphs describing cyber threats, peruse explanatory texts about my son's track meet, and check out the nutrition label on a Panera macaroni and cheese container. And those were the texts I could recall when sitting at my dining room table while writing this book.

Want to know how many narratives I read today? Zero. Now, don't get me wrong, I read plenty of narratives and stories on a regular basis, but the largest chunk of my daily reading falls into a completely different type of genre. With this in mind, it is important to consider if the same might be occurring with our students. Now, of course, our youngest readers are often consuming texts that are narrative based, and remember: we live our lives in series of stories. However, if we are preparing our students to be lifelong learners, and we want them to develop skills that are real-world relevant, offering them the space to engage with the types of reading and writing they might find themselves doing outside of the classroom is incredibly important. This is necessary not just because any chance to practice the skill of writing has numerous benefits, but also because writing in this genre has many differences than composing in others.

One of the main differences with this type of writing is how we utilize it or how we plan for the reader to interact and use it. The entire purpose is different. When people sit down to draft a nonfiction composition or an informational writing, they are positioned differently. No longer consumed with plots, setting, or dialogue, these writings focus on facts, information, and explanations. Writings that allow our students to practice this skill can help them not only become better writers, but better readers as well. Plus, for many of our young readers and writers, they enjoy the genre of nonfiction. Think about the *Who Would Win?* series and the biography series *Who Was ________?* In some instances, answering questions about nonfiction texts might seem a little easier for students because those questions are often fact and knowledge based. In addition, when writing compositions under this same genre, some students might find it a bit easier to begin their writings since they know they need to include specific information about a topic. For example, when my oldest daughter was in first grade, we completed a research project using Jerry Pallotta's *Who Would Win?* books as a frame for our writing. We started by reading several from that series and then created anchor charts with information about the types of facts that were always included in those books.

As a result they knew exactly what types of information they should include in their own writings, which made their research much more manageable and focused. The products they were able to create reflected a strong focus and solid execution due to a number of factors including the fact that the students had seen multiple examples of the targeted genre, and they had the opportunity to identify and discuss the components needed for their individual writings. In doing so, the students had essentially created their own sort of checklist or list of requirements when they completed their research. Thus, as they read other books looking for information in include in their writings, they had a strong established purpose because they knew what they should look for. For example, students knew it was important for them to include information about their animal's habitat when they wrote their own *Who Would Win?* book. As they were examining other sources for information, they knew that one item they should look for was the animal's habitat. Doing this aided them in establishing a purpose for reading, which we know improves comprehension (Tovani, 2000). Thus, they were able to locate information that pertained to habitats and include it in their writing. As such, the research writing they were completed became much more manageable because they had a specific focus and direction.

In many cases, students have a significant amount of experience with narratives and stories. The structure is completely different and the way in which we read a text like this is different as well. Think about our students who may have had most of their reading and writing experiences with narratives. What happens when they are tasked with reading or writing an informational or expository composition? Many of them are looking for characters, a setting, plots, and resolution and are disappointed to find only facts, subheadings, and bold print. And let's face it, when kids head on to upper elementary and beyond, the number of informational texts they are utilizing on a regular basis increase exponentially. In fact, in some states, narrative often becomes an afterthought in the upper grades in exchange for the more research-like genre. Showing students how to read and write texts like this can improve their comprehension, vocabulary, and writing skills.

One way that writers make informational texts engaging is by incorporating some of the tactics and styles that are often used in other genres, such as an element of story or a small vignette that is illustrative of the concept. Where literary picture books use images to help tell the story, informational writing often includes images, photos, charts, and figures to help convey meaning and information. In many instances, readers can learn a significant amount of information when reading informational texts simply by examining the diagrams and figures that supplement the text. Incidentally, this is an important feature to introduce as many standardized assessments utilize a variety of source types, including maps, charts, and diagrams for constructed response questions. Giving students opportunities to utilize these types of text features and components can help them improve their reading and writing skills across content areas.

Of course there are multiple ways in which to explore this genre, but starting off in short bursts is best for students. Since research writing can be intimidating, how we begin to introduce it is especially important. Based on experience, I do not recommend that students begin their practice with this genre by writing a fully involved research paper. Instead, I begin by sharing quality literature that can serve as an example for the genre or can offer them ideas for topics they might want to pursue. There are scads of picture books and even novels that can be used as mentor texts. Plus, don't discount the genre of historical fiction as they can often be a starting point for more research on a topic that has been narratively explored in a novel or other fiction text. Think about books such as *The Great Trouble: A Mystery of London, The Blue Death, and A Boy Called Eel* by Deborah Hopkinson, *Fever* by Laurie Halse Anderson, *Potato: A Tale From the Great Depression* by Kate Lied, *A Storm Called Katrina* by Myron Uhlberg, and *The Whispering Town* by Jennifer Elvgren. Each of those books are narratives based on true historical events that can serve as mentor text catalysts for additional research reading and writing. Plus, they can serve as effective and engaging hooks to entice young children to explore different events, concepts, and people. It is also a good idea to give students time to examine the different structure of informational writing simply by reading widely in this genre and annotating texts that are considered research based and informational. One way to do this is through traditional text annotation or with a strategy like text mapping which we will discuss later in this chapter. Regardless, of the strategy, reading and writing widely across this genre can prepare students for the literacy demands of academic classrooms.

Of course, many writing strategies can be utilized across disciplines and are easily modified or repurposed for multiple tasks. However, this chapter focuses specifically on some ways in which students might begin to practice their informational writing skills and capitalize on the ways in which we learn through writing.

ANIMAL PROBLEM WRITINGS

In this lesson, students start with a narrative text that includes animals as main characters and use this as a frame for writing a new story. However, in this lesson, students must use the facts they know or learn about an animal in order to write the narrative sentence, thus blending both genres into an engaging writing activity.

Focus Genre: Informational

Target Grade Level: K–2

Standards

Conduct short research projects that build knowledge about a topic.

Write informative/explanatory texts to examine a topic and convey ideas and information.

Develop a topic with facts, definitions, or details.

Anchor Texts

Cat Problems by Jory John

Giraffe Problems by Jory John

Penguin Problems by Jory John

Odder by Katherine Applegate

Negative Cat by Sophie Blackall

The Littlest Yak by Yu Fraser

I Want My Hat Back by Jon Klassen

Materials

- Chart paper
- Sticky notes
- Animal Problems template (p. 247)

Teach It

1. Begin by reading one of the titles from the anchor text list.

Ideally, the students should have heard the selected book before, as that makes it easier for them to be able to pick out the material needed to write their own composition.

2. Discuss what types of problems the animal in the story had.

3. Ask students to consider why those were the problems for that animal. These might be related to the animal's habitat, food supply, or other basic characteristics.

4. Have students brainstorm other animals that might have problems. Record these on chart paper or the interactive whiteboard.

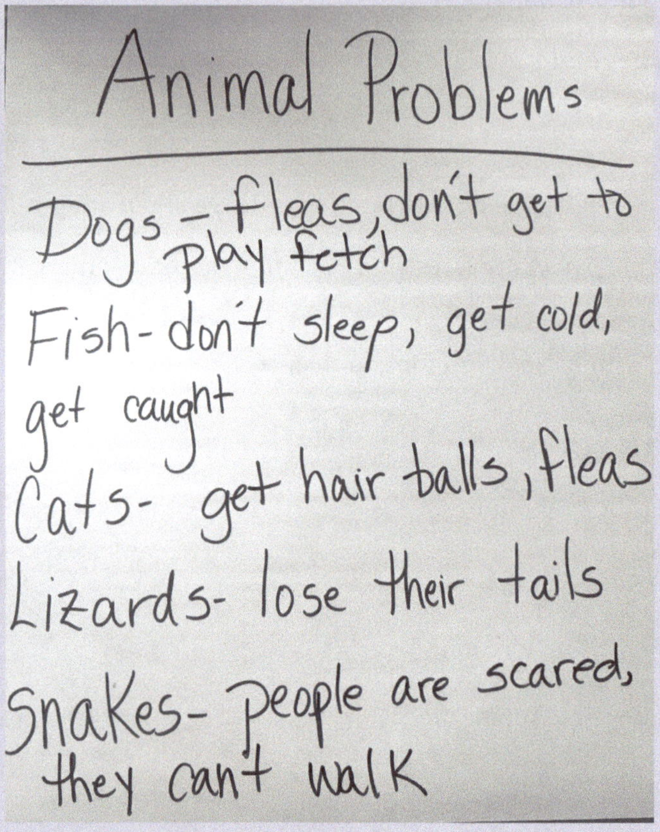

5. As a class, choose one animal and brainstorm some possible problems that animal might have (e.g., Polar bears might get too cold. Cats might get fleas. Snakes can't run. Students may to practice using their research skills for this step, since they may need to go to other sources to locate information about potential animal problems.)

6. Model the writing task for the students using the Animal Problems template and the information brainstormed by the class. Make sure students understand how to use the template to complete their writing.

7. Distribute a copy of the Animal Problems template (p. 247) to each student.

8. Have students choose an animal and write about what their problem might be. Students should also include a picture with their sentence.

Try It

- Use this as a way to merge narrative with informational writing.
- Try this when you want students to practice their research skills.
- Use this as a way to capitalize on student interest and prior knowledge by allowing them to choose their own topics.

Extensions

- Connect this to the Who Would Win? lesson (p. 142).
- Have students annotate their drawings like they did in the Label This! lesson (p. 130).
- Have students write from the point of view of other characters or items. Drew Daywalt's *The Day the Crayons Quit* or *Spoon* or *Chopsticks* by Amy Krouse Rosenthal are great for this!
- Create a new writing activity called Animal Solutions and have students try and solve one of the animals' problems. This could be completed with a partner as each student will have to draft a possible solution for their partner's animal problem.

Modifications

Emerging Writers

- Instead of having students brainstorm new animals, use animal crackers as an activator. Give students some animal crackers and have them pick one to write about.
- Have students complete this activity in stations and allow them to draft their writing as a group on a large piece of chart paper.
- Label sheets of chart paper with different animals. Have students complete a gallery walk and list or draw a problem each animal might have. Have students use the charts to draft sentences on the template.

Plan ahead and teach the Who Would Win? lesson next if you use the animal cracker modification.

Proficient Writers

- Have students conduct research online or with informational text to determine what types of problems each animal might have. Connect these to habitats, food sources, enemies, etc.
- Use the student created templates with problems to develop a guessing game. For example, which of these animals would have a problem because they are always cold?

See It Sample

Photo by Alysha Krier Mooney

TEXTUAL EVIDENCE SCAVENGER HUNT

Many standardized tests include written tasks that require students to locate and position textual evidence to support a claim or answer a question. Even our youngest learners are asked to provide evidence or support when answering questions, and for good reason, as this gives them much needed practice for a type of writing that will only get more complex. One way to ease students into this skill is by making it seem like a game in a Textual Evidence Scavenger Hunt!

Focus Genre: Multigenre/Constructed Response

Target Grade Level: K–5

Standards

Write informative/explanatory texts to examine a topic and convey ideas and information.

Develop a topic with facts, definitions, or details.

Cite textual evidence to support a claim, position, or answer.

Anchor Texts

Any of Jerry Pallotta's *Who Would Win?* series

Actual Size by Steve Jenkins

The Day Glo Brothers: The True Story of Bob and Joe Switzer's Bright Ideas and Brand-New Colors by Chris Barton

Whoosh!: Lonnie Johnson's Super Soaking Stream of Inventions by Chris Barton

I'm Trying to Love Spiders by Bethany Barton

The Mary Celeste by Jane Yolen

The Story of the H. L. Hunley and Queenie's Coin by Fran Hawk

I typically keep items such as pencils, scissors, tape, highlighters, sticky notes, etc. in sets of pencil boxes. That way, each group has their own set of supplies.

Materials

- Magnifying glasses
- Highlighters
- Sticky notes
- Sticky note flags
- Highlighter tape

Stop & Think

In some cases, it might be easier for you to allow students to peruse some of these individually or in small groups. For example, Jerry Pallotta's *Who Would Win?* books can certainly be read aloud, but all the text boxes and extra information can be difficult to share in a read aloud setting. Thus, it is helpful to allow students opportunities to independently read those books as well so they can see these unique text features.

Teach It

1. Start by reading one of the anchor texts to students.
2. Display a sample question based on the text. Distribute the supply kits or individual supplies if you do not have them in separate kits.
3. Using this question, have students work as a class to locate textual evidence that might answer that specific question. For this part, it would be beneficial for you to have photocopies of the page(s) students would need to read to find this information. (Do this if you do not have enough copies of the text for everyone to use. Remember, if you plan to make copies, make certain you use a text or article that has reproducible permissions.)
4. Model how you might highlight or flag evidence, thus showing students how to annotate a text based on the location of evidence.
5. Explain to students that they will be completing their own textual evidence scavenger hunt with a partner or group.
6. Divide students into pairs or small groups. Give each pair or small group a new article or text and a set of questions that they must answer using evidence from the text.
7. Have students use their annotation kits (highlighters, sticky notes, etc.) to locate answers to their questions.
8. Once students have located their evidence, have them share with the class.

Quick Tip!

Depending on your preference or student readiness, you may choose to give all groups the same text or different texts. Even if students all receive the same text, you can further differentiate this lesson by giving them different questions to investigate on their scavenger hunt.

Try It

- Use this as a way to have students practice locating textual evidence for constructed responses.
- Try this when you want students to have an established purpose for reading that is connected to a writing task.
- Use this as a way to have students work collaboratively to locate textual evidence.

Extensions

- Connect this to the Text Mapping lesson on page 138.
- Have students come up with additional text-based items to find in the selected work. Give these new tasks to other groups and have their peers locate the new items.
- Once students locate the evidence from the scavenger hunt, have them use the evidence to draft a written response to a sample constructed response.

Modifications

Emerging Writers

- Start by having students look for simple textual evidence like a character's physical features or dialogue the character said. You could also have students look for a specific number of facts about a topic.
- Start with images and have students provide information from a picture that might answer a question. In this modification, a student's ability to read alphanumeric text is no longer a factor since they are utilizing images or photos instead.

Proficient Writers

- Utilize texts that incorporate multiple figures, charts, diagrams, maps, etc., so that students can get accustomed to using pictorial texts as evidence as well.
- Break a complex constructed response task into parts and have different groups locate evidence for their respective question. Bring them back together to collect all the evidence to answer the complete problem or question.
- Use more than one source for students to complete their scavenger hunts. You could model it as a gallery walk with different texts displayed around the room for students to use in their scavenger hunt. (Think, Resource Roundup, [Harper, 2023], but with props)

See It Sample

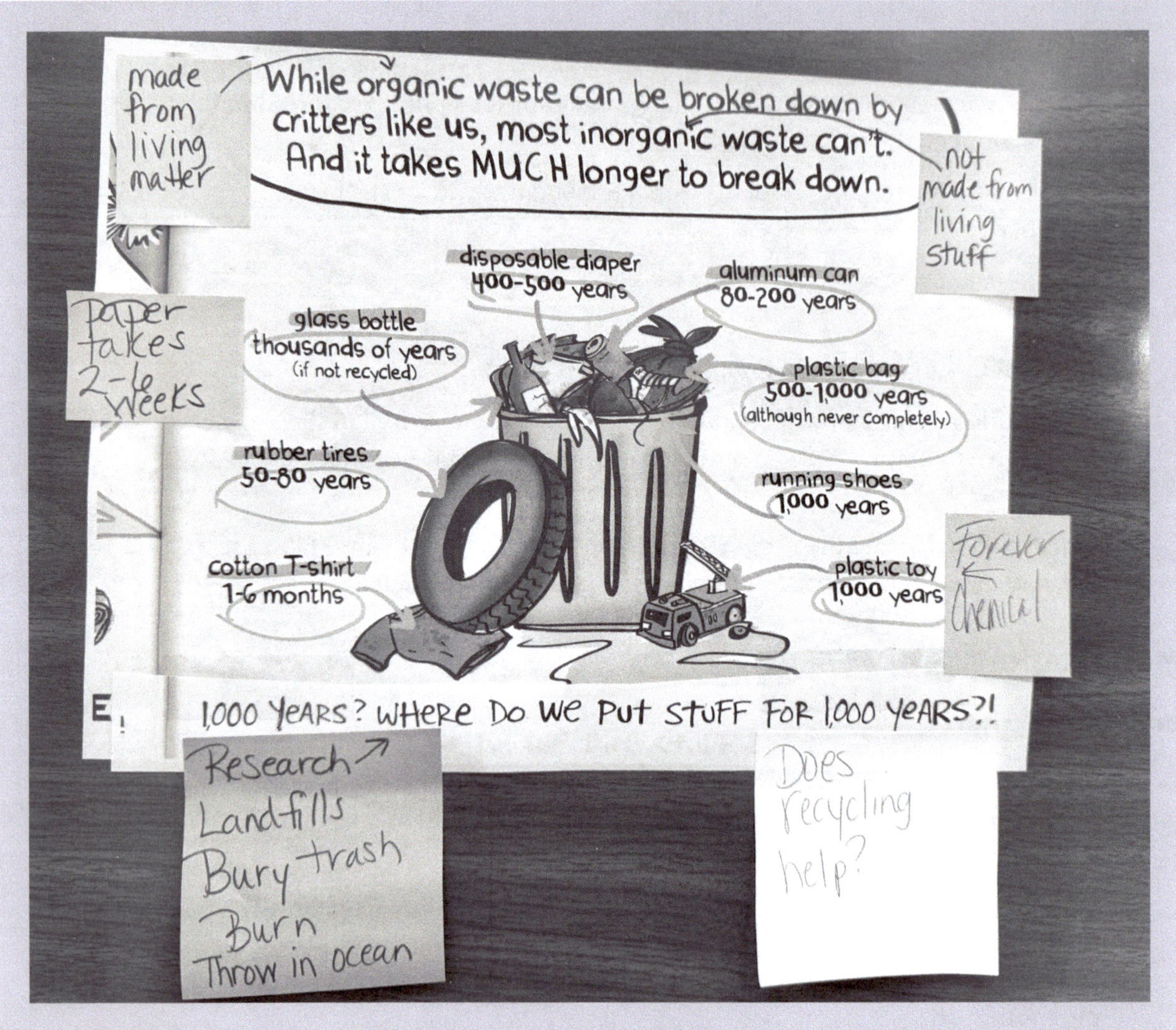

TOP TEN LISTS

While I am not a sports fantastic by any means, I do love watching ESPN's Top Plays. Essentially, this serves as a highlight reel of the day's or weeks' important events or top plays that have occurred. Plus, each individual example on the ranked list has to be discussed quickly and succinctly, thus utilizing many of the same characteristics and qualities needed when writing a summary.

Focus Genre: Informational

Target Grade Level: 3–5

Standards

Summarize key details and ideas in a text.

Develop a topic with facts, definitions, or details.

Anchor Texts

You Wouldn't Want to Be a . . . series

Who Was . . . ? series

Ice Cream Man: How Augustus Jackson Made a Sweet Treat Better by Glenda Armand and Kim Freeman

Overground Railroad by Lesa Cline-Ransome

Papa Put a Man on the Moon by Kristy Dempsey

Baseball Saved Us by Ken Mochizuki

Materials

- Chart paper or notecards
- Sticky notes
- Paint strips

Teach It

1. Begin by reading one of the books on the anchor text list, or any mentor text that includes facts and ideas about a concept or figure. This is especially important when considering student interests as you may find your students like different books than the ones listed above.

2. After reading, have students recall facts from the book.
3. Record these on chart paper or notecards in list format.
4. Discuss how each of these facts contributes to the overall meaning of the text.
5. Work as a class to rank them in order from most important to least important, working to compile a Top Ten list.
6. Divide students into small groups or partners.
7. Provide students with a new text related to the original anchor text or have them use a text of their choice.
8. In their group, have students make a list of facts they learned from this book. Then, have students rank the facts in order from most important to least important.
9. Have groups share their top ten facts with the class.

Try It

- Use this as a low-stakes research or informational writing task where students warm up by collecting information in list format.
- Try this when you want to check students' comprehension without a formal assessment.
- Use this for a real-world connection (Top Ten lists are popular in multiple venues) between the academic and personal.

> **Quick Tip!**
>
> Think ahead by having students check out books in this genre on their library visits. Then use those books for this activity. That way, you can ensure that students are writing about a topic they have selected on their own.

Extensions

- Have students use their lists as their brainstorming for a research paragraph or essay.
- Connect this to I Bet You Didn't Know . . . (p. 120).
- Use the Top Ten lists as a brainstorming activity for writing a summary on a topic or concept.
- Connect this to the Summary Sweep strategy (Harper, 2021).
- Have students draw a picture that corresponds with one of the list items.

Modifications

Emerging Writers

- Use paint strips for this activity, but instead of ten items, use the paint strips divided into three sections and have students identify the top three pieces of information about a concept or idea.
- Instead of conducting research on a topic, have students create a Top Ten list about themselves, a classmate, or a character.
- Use the list format for other topics including classroom procedural items, Top Ten Ways to say something, or Top Ten Synonyms for a word.

Proficient Writers

- Have students create their own lists based on their independent reading and present to the class.
- Instead of completing traditional research projects, have students develop lists around an individual or concept of their choice.
- Use paint strips to color code different aspects of their research. For example, use a specific color for a figure's accomplishments and another color for biographical information.

See It Sample

Crossover
by Kwame Alexander

Top Ten Plays

Play/Event	Description	Justification
1. Josh's hair gets cut	He + Jordan bet and he loses.	Josh is obsessed w/ his locs.
2. Chuck 'Da Man' Bell is their Dad.	He is a famous basketball player.	He influenced the boys to play.
3. Their dad isn't eating healthy.	They go to the Chinese Restaurant + Krispy Kreme.	This leads to his death.
4. Chuck has high blood pressure.	He goes to dr and gets diagnosed.	This leads to his death.
5. Jordan dates Miss Sweet Tea.	Josh sees them kissing in the library	Josh had a crush on her and he's mad his brother is with her.
6. Josh does play by plays of his game.	He goes through all his moves.	It shows he is confident + obsessed with bb.
7. JB's nose is busted by Josh.	Josh throws a hard pass at his brother's face.	He is angry that he's dating Miss Sweet Tea.
8. Josh is suspended.	He gets in trouble for hitting his brother.	BB is everything to Josh.
9. Josh's dad has chest pains playing bb.	They are shooting free throws & he clutches his chest, but then he's ok.	This is foreshadowing his death.
10. Chuck Bell dies.	He has complications from a massive heart attack.	Their dad is everything to them so losing him is tragic.

I BET YOU DIDN'T KNOW . . .

Recently when I was teaching one of my doctoral classes, one of my students (who is a teacher) mentioned something about her elementary school's mascot being the koala. Before anyone could say anything, another teacher piped up and said, "Fun fact about koalas. Did you know that eucalyptus is toxic and koalas often have diarrhea from eating this plant?" Of course, no one knew this, and we were surprised to hear some new and random information about koalas. This lesson focuses on something similar because in this writing, students research a topic, figure, character, or event and write about a little-known fact.

Focus Genre: Informational

Target Grade Level: K–2

Standards

Develop a topic with facts, definitions, or details.

Write informative/explanatory texts to examine a topic and convey ideas and information.

Recall key details from a text.

Anchor Texts

Don't Believe It: Facts and Fibs About Animals by Melvin Berger

Learn With Facts series by Isis Gaillard

Give Bees a Chance by Bethany Barton

Shark Lady: The True Story of How Eugenie Clark Became the Ocean's Most Fearless Scientist by Jess Keating

Gregor Mendel: The Friar Who Grew Peas by Cheryl Bardoe

The Crayon Man: The True Story of the Invention of Crayola Crayons by Natascha Biebow

Materials

- Sticky notes
- Chart paper
- Paint strips
- Notecards
- I Bet You Didn't Know . . . template (p. 248)

Teach It

1. Begin by reading a couple of pages from one of the anchor texts. I suggest starting with the *Don't Believe It: Facts and Fibs About Animals* by Melvin Berger.

2. Have students brainstorm a list of animals (or other topic the class is interested in) they might want to research.

3. Discuss where you might look to find information about the topic. Suggestions might include other books, videos, the internet, etc.

4. Together as a class, practice finding one new or random fact about an animal on the class list.

Because this book is laid out in a one-page format, it works best if students have heard a few samples from the book before. In fact, you might think about using it as a read aloud for several days prior so students get used to the text and the overall structure.

5. After you have located a new fact about one of the animals on the class list, have students work with a partner to choose a new animal to research.

6. Using digital or print sources have students locate one new fact about their animal.

7. Record this new fact on the I Bet You Didn't Know . . . template (p. 248).

Try It

- Use this as a way to get students to collect different facts about an animal or idea or concept.
- Try this when you want students to practice research in an unimposing setting.
- Use this as a quick way to incorporate the research and informational genre into teaching.

Extensions

- Use this as a review game and have students quiz the class by having them guess their animal or topic they researched.
- Incorporate another one of the anchor texts and have students choose a new topic or concept to locate facts.
- Connect this to the Textual Evidence Scavenger Hunt (p. 113) by having students look for specific facts about an animal or concept.
- Instead of finding just one fact, have students connect this to the Top Ten Lists (p. 117) and locate multiple facts.

- Connect this to Two Truths and Lie (Harper, 2021).
- Compile all the different facts into a class book about different animals or other topics.

Modifications

Emerging Writers

- Instead of having students come up with their own animals to research, have a list made ahead of time for them to choose from.
- Have students draw a picture of their animal or concept or item or use a photograph or image and then have them affix address labels or post its to the picture with facts describing it.
- Use animal crackers as a way for students to select their research animals.

Plan ahead and use the leftover animal crackers for the Who Would Win? lesson (p. 142) or the Animal Problems lesson (p. 109).

- Have students draw a picture of their animal on a notecard and record their fact on the back of the card.

Proficient Writers

- Use these interesting facts as a way to hook a reader when writing an extended composition.
- Have students start a larger research writing engagement with this lesson and build on it to create an extended writing.
- Have students continue their research with the Label This! strategy (p. 130).
- Use paint strips to record multiple facts on their animals.

See It Sample

Photo by Alfred Cain

BODY BIOGRAPHY

Because reading is about making meaning and writing is a form of communication, engagements that capitalize on both of those tenets can be beneficial for students. While the informational genre tends to often focus on research and fact-finding, some of these same skills and practices can be used when completing writing engagements that demonstrate reading comprehension and written expression. While Body Biographies are often used with literary text, they can also be used when researching historical figures or when writing autobiographic texts.

Focus Genre: Informational/Narrative

Target Grade Level: 3–5

Standards

Write informative/explanatory texts to examine a topic and convey ideas and information.

Recall key details from a text.

Students apply a wide range of strategies to comprehend, interpret, evaluate, and appreciate texts.

Anchor Texts

Before She Was Harriet by Lesa Cline-Ransome

Fauja Singh Keeps Going: The True Story of the Oldest Person to Run a Marathon by Simran Jeet Singh

Goodnight Stories for Rebel Girls by Ellen Favilli, Francesca Cavallo, and Rebel Girls

A Is for Awesome! 23 Iconic Women Who Changed the World by Eva Chen

One Plastic Bag: Isatou Ceesay and the Recycling Women of Gambia by Miranda Paul

Magic Ramen: The Story of Momofuko Ando by Andrea Wong

Jimi: Sounds Like a Rainbow by Gary Golio

Materials

- Bulletin board paper
- Markets, colored pencils, crayons
- Body Biography Checklist (p. 250)
- Body Biography template (p. 249)

Teach It

1. For this lesson, the first step is determining whether your students will be completing this activity on a character from a literary work or from their research. You can start with one of the anchor texts, use a novel as the focus, or have students choose their own nonfiction book or novel.

Make sure you complete this activity either after students have completed their reading and/or research or throughout the research and/or reading process with them adding information as they collect it over time.

2. Divide students into collaborative groups.
3. Distribute chart paper and markers to each group and have one volunteer from each group lay down on the bulletin board paper so the group members can trace their outline on paper. You can always do this ahead of time, if needed.
4. Have students use the Body Biography Checklist (p. 250) to help them either collect new information about a figure they are researching or to collect information about a character from a literary work.
5. Have students display their completed work and share with the class.

Try It

- As a new way to get students thinking about a historical figure or characters.
- When you want to assess students' comprehension in a nontraditional manner.
- As a way to incorporate a collaborative writing engagement that is hands on.

Extensions

- Compare characters or figures after they complete the project and discuss how characters are similar or different.
- Have students choose additional prompts or questions they might use to locate different information about their research subject.
- Use Body Biographies throughout the year to record important historical figures addressed in social studies.

Modifications

Emerging Writers

- Have students complete the Body Biography template (p. 249) with a partner.
- Instead of writing about a person as the topic, students could do an Animal Biography where they include information about an animal they researched.
- Instead of requiring students to use all the materials in the checklist, have students choose a specific number and include those in their Body Biographies.
- Determine which characters or figures the students will work with. Divide students into groups. Assign one aspect of the Body Biography Checklist to each group and have them rotate from station to station adding their information to each of the characters or figures until each Body Biography is complete.

Proficient Writers

- Using samples created in class, have students compare and contrast characters or figures based on what they see in the Body Biographies.
- Have students add additional information to the Body Biography checklist that pertains to their selected person.
- Use the material collected in the Body Biography to write a traditional biography on the same person.

See It Sample

WOULD YOU RATHER?

Across genres and disciplines, students are often tasked with comparing and contrasting items, individuals, and places. To practice this type of skill, we often use graphic organizer maps such as a Venn diagram or a Double Bubble map. While those tools are helpful when organizing facts and details, the next logical step in this skill acquisition is composing a compare and contrast piece of writing. By incorporating engaging mentor texts, compare contrast writing can be fun and engaging, and easily accomplished with young writers.

Focus Genre: Informational; Compare/Contrast

Target Grade Level: K–2

Standards

Write informative/explanatory texts to examine a topic and convey ideas and information.

Compare and contrast multiple texts, perspectives, and characters.

Recall key details from a text.

Anchor Texts

About Habitats series by Cathryn Sill

You Wouldn't Want to Be . . . series

Who Would Win? series by Jerry Pallotta

Animal Battles series

Compare and Contrast series by Kevin Kurtz

Materials

- Notecards
- Paint strips
- Sticky notes
- Would You Rather? template (p. 251)

I would suggest sticking with a specific series. For example, you might read several of the *About Habitats* series so that students can learn about several habitats before beginning this lesson.

Teach It

1. Begin by reading some of the anchor texts listed above.
2. As a recap to reading, record some of the facts learned about each concept (habitat, animal, person, etc.) on chart paper.
3. Ask students which habitat they would rather live in. Have them orally share their reasons.
4. Explain to students that they are going to choose two habitats to compare.
5. Since the chart paper has recorded facts, their textual evidence needed is already on display.
6. Provide students with the Would You Rather? template (p. 251).
7. Model how to incorporate the information from the charts to complete the template.
8. Have students share their completed work with the class.

Try It

- Use this when you want to practice the skill of compare and contrast.
- Try this when you want to have students examine multiple perspectives or texts.
- Use this as a way to incorporate a collaborative component in writing.

Extensions

- Expand this to a multisentence or paragraph research writing on the topic of choice.
- Have students create an infographic with the same information just presented in a more visual format.

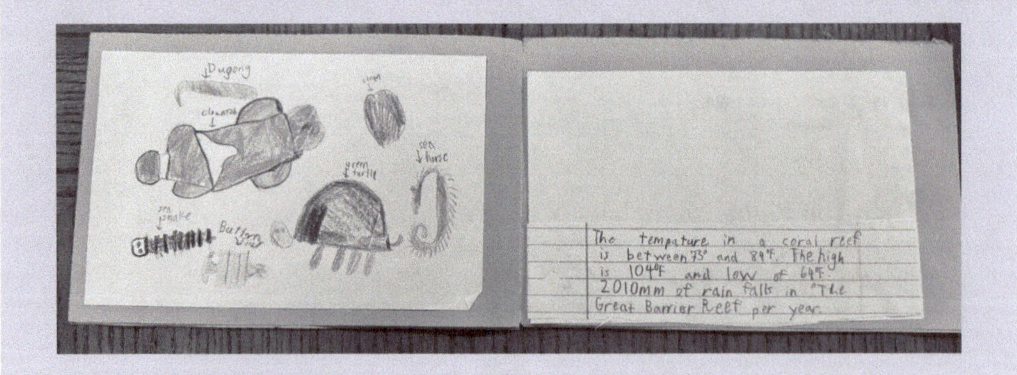

- As a class, take a vote on the two things compared and record the results.
- Compile the completed templates into a class Would You Rather? book.

Modifications

Emerging Writers

- Connect this to other writing lessons like Who Would Win? (p. 142) and have students use the information they learned in that research to draft questions with supporting facts.
- Let students complete the template with a partner so that each individual focuses on a specific topic (e.g., animal or person).
- Have students draw pictures of their topic and use address labels or post its to include their facts.

Proficient Writers

- Teach students how to cite their evidence by adding page numbers from the text next to their facts.
- Have students use multiple sources to compile their information and color code the information based on source.
- Connect this to a persuasive writing task by having students continue their research into a persuasive composition.

See It Sample

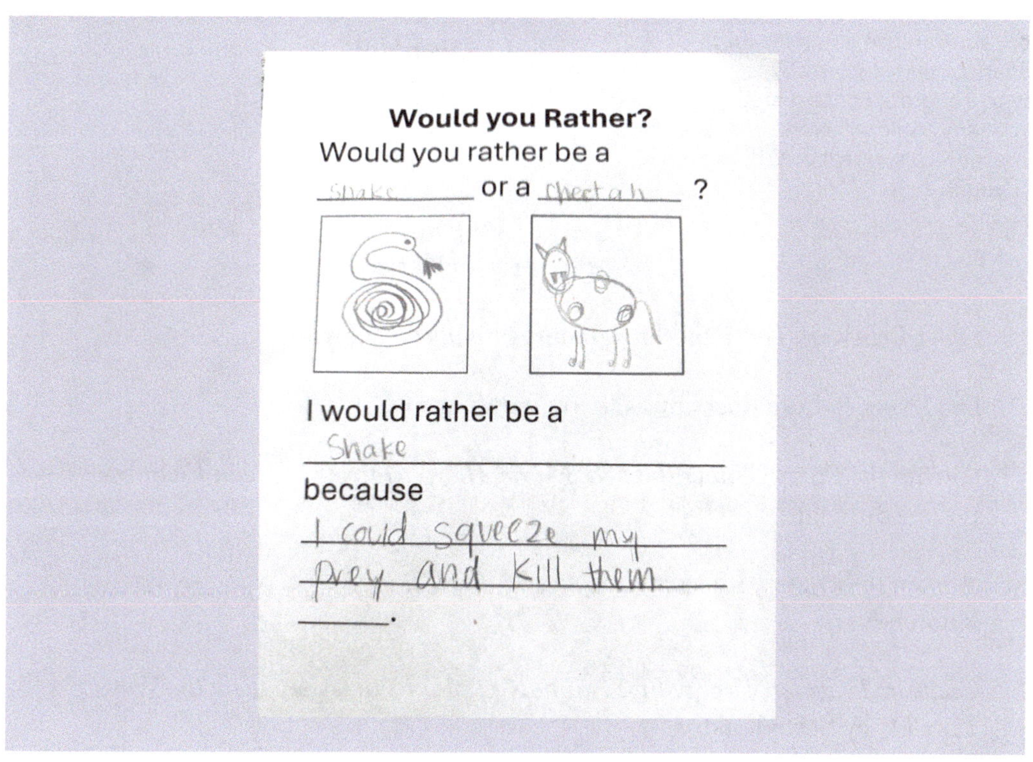

Would you Rather?

Would you rather be a snake or a cheetah?

I would rather be a Snake

because I could squeeze my prey and kill them.

LABEL THIS!

When students read informational texts, many include several text features like headings, text boxes, captions, bold words, and more. This is significantly different than the structure and organization narrative text. Part of understanding the unique features of informational texts involves identifying and explaining how text features help convey meaning and content. In many cases, readers gain significant information to add to their understanding of the overall text through a solid understanding and utilization of these key features. The Label This! lesson helps students practice this skill.

Focus Genre: Informational/Text Features

Target Grade Level: K–2

Standards

Write informative/explanatory texts to examine a topic and convey ideas and information.

Recall key details from a text.

Identify text features and develop an understanding of text features.

> **Quick Tip!**
>
> For this lesson, you can use any texts that contains a variety of text features. This is a great way to integrate content area information, but any topic will work. I have provided a few mentor suggestions, but use any texts that you like!

Anchor Texts

You Wouldn't Want to Be . . . series

Who Would Win? series by Jerry Pallotta

Animal Battles series

Compare and Contrast series by Kevin Kurtz

Don't Believe It: Facts and Fibs About Animals by Melvin Berger

I'm Trying to Love Rocks by Bethany Barton

Solving the Puzzle Under the Sea: Marie Tharp Maps the Ocean Floor by Robert Burleigh

Women in Science: 50 Fearless Pioneers Who Changed the World by Rachel Ignotofsky

Creature Features: Twenty-Five Animals Explain Why They Look the Way They Do by Steve Jenkins

Materials

- Address labels
- Sticky notes
- Sticky note flags
- Blank paper
- Highlighters
- Highlighter tape

Teach It

1. Before beginning the lesson, select a character or animal from the chosen anchor text and place it in the middle of a sheet of chart paper or Google slide.
2. Begin by showing students a variety of text features from some of the anchor texts. This will build their background knowledge and help them get an idea of what types of text features they might include in their own work later in the lesson.
3. Read aloud the selected anchor texts.
4. After reading, show students the chosen character or animal and have them recall facts they heard from the read aloud about that character or animal. Record those facts on a separate sheet of chart paper.
5. As a class, decide which facts from the class list should be add to the prepared chart paper or Google slide with the image or drawing. Also discuss which types of text features you may want to create using the facts and how to design the page. For example, discuss which facts should be in bold print, which ones need to be written in complete sentences, and where each should be placed. You might also introduce directional arrows pointing to the feature that the text is describing.
6. Distribute a sheet of paper to students and have them begin their own composition. They should include a drawing or image in the center of the paper, and then use sticky notes or address labels to label the drawing.
7. Have students share their completed work with the class.

Try It

- Use this as a way for students to conduct research but focus on the visual elements and text features.
- Try this when you want students to practice adding more information and details to their writing while focusing on different components such as vocabulary and key facts and details.
- Use this as a bridge to research writing. Since this strategy focuses on abbreviated information (not necessarily complete sentences), it can help students build confidence in writing.

Extensions

- Use this lesson as an included graphic or figure in a larger research writing project. For example, you might have students start by completing this activity, but then write an extended piece building on their initial brainstorming.
- Have students generate questions based on the information presented in the Label This! lesson. Students could pose questions for their classmates and then revise their own writings based on what questions were posed.
- Use this as an extension to the Would You Rather? lesson (p. 127) and have students include the Label This! strategy as an added visual aid or component.
- Use the information from the Top Ten Lists lesson (p. 117) as a starter for this lesson.

Modifications

Emerging Writers

- Have vocabulary and key details and facts already printed on labels. Let students choose the ones that apply to their topic and include them in their writing.
- Put several facts or vocabulary on sticky notes and display them around the room on pieces of chart paper. For example, you might have a chart paper display of different types of habitats, another focused on food animals eat, and another focused on adaptations. Have students complete a gallery walk and choose the sticky notes they want to include in their writings.
- Begin by completing a whole class Label This! writing on chart paper. Have students use sticky notes or labels to add their own information to the class created chart.

Photo by Alfred Cain

Proficient Writers

- Have students conduct research online to locate little known facts about their topic.
- Encourage students to employ different sentences stems when including facts so they can practice sentence variety.
- Have students draft a sample question that could be answered simply by viewing their graphic.

See It Sample

BEFORE THEY WERE . . .

After reading the book *Before She Was Harriet,* by Lesa Cline Ransome, I was immediately drawn to the craft and style of this book. The author does a beautiful job of starting with the end in mind, the Harriet Tubman of the Underground Railroad, and worked backward to tell the story. Thus, she starts at the end with Tubman's most well-known accomplishment, and then traces her story back to her life as a young child. I loved the structure and craft and began to look for ways to mimic this with other historical figures. To practice this we use a repeated line, "Before he/she was . . ." in our own writing about another historical figure.

Focus Genre: Biography

Target Grade Level: 3–5

Standards

Read a wide range of print and nonprint texts to build an understanding of texts.

Apply a wide range of strategies to comprehend, interpret, evaluate, and appreciate texts. Use knowledge of word meaning and of other texts, word identification strategies, and understanding of textual features (e.g., sound–letter correspondence, sentence structure, context, graphics).

Recall details from texts.

Anchor Texts

Before She Was Harriet by Lesa Cline-Ransome

Other biographical texts, such as

My Brother Martin: A Sister Remembers Growing Up With Rev. Dr. Martin Luther King, Jr. by Coretta Scott King

The Poppy Lady by Barbara E. Walsh

I Dissent: Ruth Bader Ginsburg Makes Her Mark by Debbie Levy

It Began With a Page: How Gyo Fujikawa Drew the Way by Kyo Maclear

Who Was? series

Materials

- Sentence strips or notecards
- Chart paper
- Before he/she was cards

Teach It

1. Begin by reading *Before She Was Harriet* since the writing composition will utilize the Before he/she was . . . frame.
2. Ask students what they noticed about the sentences used. (They should be able to tell you that most of the sentences start off with "Before she was . . . ")
3. Read students a new anchor text. Make sure students have heard the new anchor text at least once before since you are going to ask them to recall details from the book.
4. Have students recall details from the book after reading. Record these on chart paper.
5. As a class, work to put the details in chronological order.
6. Determine which detail is the last one. Record this detail on a notecard or sentence strip. Have one student come and hold the sentence for the class to see.
7. Work backward with the details until you get all the way to the first chronological detail.
8. Insert the opening clause of the sentence, "Before he/she was . . ." in front of each of the details. To do this, give ready-made Before he/she was . . . cards to some students and detail sentence cards to others. Make sure that there is one of the Before he/she was . . . cards posted in front of every single detail sentence card.
9. Have students orally share their sentences in reverse chronological order and complete this modified retelling.

Essentially, you are building a living retelling in front of the class that engages students, gets them out of their seats, and gets them involved in building the story. Each student reads their sentence aloud and builds the story in reverse chronological order.

Try It

- Try this when you want students to mimic a particular author's craft.
- Use this as a way to incorporate biographical writing along with sequential event writing.
- Use this when you want students to conduct a collaborative retelling that gets students physically engaged.

Extensions

- Connect this to the Top Ten list activity (p. 117) and have students use it as a springboard for writing.
- Have students draft this writing in a comic strip or graphic novel format with each sentence functioning as a pane in the comic strip.
- Have students take two characters or historical figures and perform the writing like they would a poem in two voices so that it becomes more of a call and response performance.

Modifications

Emerging Writers

- Have sentences already written on notecards or sentence strips and have students build the story from the created sentences.
- Break this lesson down into two days. On day one, have students recall details in order from the book. On day two, have students use that material to draft their class story in order.
- Instead of using sentences on cards, use picture cards instead.

Proficient Writers

- Use this as an option for writing an independent research composition. Students use this whole group activity as a model for their own independent research.
- Play around with different sentence frames and have students come up with alternative repeated beginnings.
- Instead of focusing on historical figures, have students write about characters from literary texts.

See It Sample

Before He Was Martin Luther King, Jr. (MLK,Jr.)

Before he was the Martin Luther King, Jr who gave his I Have a Dream Speech, he was M.L. who slept in a hand me down crib.

Before he was the Martin Luther King, Jr who gave his I Have a Dream Speech, he played pranks on the people in the neighborhood.

Before he was the Martin Luther King, Jr who gave his I Have a Dream Speech, he made his piano teacher fall off the stool.

Before he was the Martin Luther King, Jr who gave his I Have a Dream Speech, he went to church where his daddy preached.

Before he was the Martin Luther King, Jr who gave his I Have a Dream Speech, he played with the white boys across the street.

Before he was the Martin Luther King, Jr who gave his I Have a Dream Speech, his momma explained the laws that said, "Whites Only."

Before he was the Martin Luther King, Jr who gave his I Have a Dream Speech, he listened to stories from his momma and daddy at the kitchen table.

Before he was the Martin Luther King, Jr who gave his I Have a Dream Speech, he dreamed a dream that turned the world upside down.

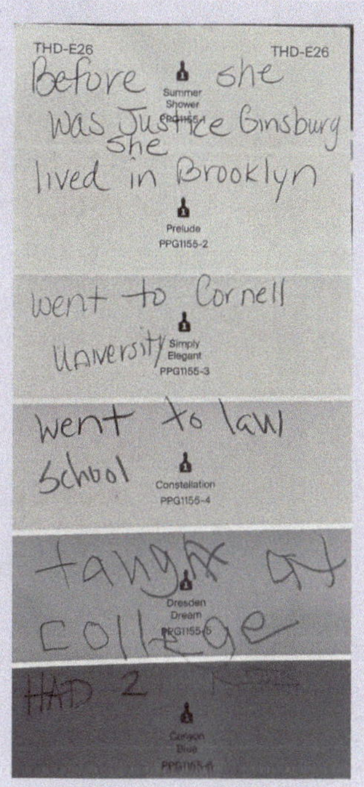

TEXT MAPPING

Text mapping is a great strategy that can be used for annotating a text, highlighting text features, and responding to texts. Often textbooks and informational texts include a number of text features such as diagrams, charts, and graphs, along with content-rich vocabulary. In certain cases, students read in their textbooks and are asked to refer back to a graph explained on prior pages. For some students, this causes confusion, as the entire text is not in front of them at once. Text mapping allows students to see the entire text at once so that they can refer to any diagrams, charts, vocabulary, etc., right in front of them.

Focus Genre: Informational

Target Grade Level: 3–5

Standards

Read a wide range of print and non-print texts to build an understanding of texts.

Apply a wide range of strategies to comprehend, interpret, evaluate, and appreciate texts. Use knowledge of word meaning and of other texts, word identification strategies, and understanding of textual features (e.g., sound–letter correspondence, sentence structure, context, graphics).

Anchor Texts

For this lesson, the types of texts that work best are nonfiction articles or textbook excerpts that incorporate figures, charts, and diagrams. I often use samples from science, social studies, or math textbooks. Just make sure you do not use a narrative; this strategy won't work with that genre. Make sure that the nonfiction sample you choose has several text features including charts, images, or diagrams, captions, bold words and headings, text boxes, or other pertinent text features.

Materials

- Sticky notes
- Highlighters
- Clear tape
- Scissors
- Sticky note flags
- Paint strips
- Text Mapping Slips (p. 252)

Quick Tip!

I typically keep items such as pencils, scissors, tape, highlighters, sticky notes, etc. in sets of pencil boxes. That way, each group has their own set of supplies.

Teach It

1. Make copies of the text you want the students to read. The copies should be single sided since students will tape them together so that the entire article is put together in front of them. The text you select should be no longer than 5 to 6 pages, or else it's too much for students to put together and analyze in this format. (Remember to use texts that have reproducible permissions.)
2. Have students tape the entire article together in a horizontal line.
3. Provide students with a list of tasks to complete along with the text. (Use the Text Mapping Slips on p. 252.)
4. Have students complete the tasks then share their work with the class.

Plan time for this activity directly related to the kind of task(s) you want students to complete. For example, if the objective is for students to highlight and notice specific text features less time should be allotted than if students are expected to answer and draft questions about the reading.

Try It

- Try this when you want students to take a deep dive into informational texts.
- Use this to introduce and reinforce the skills of close reading, skimming and scanning, and highlighting text features.
- Use this when you want students to pay specific attention to the structure of a textbook or piece of text.
- Use this when you want students to practice finding specific evidence from a piece of text.

Extensions

- Use this lesson as a connection to the Textual Evidence Scavenger Hunt lesson (p. 113).
- As a ticket in the door, have students answer a question based on the text that another group developed from their list of prompts.
- Use Text Mapping to help students analyze written primary sources in social studies lessons.
- Have students draft a question that could be answered from their article and have them draw an arrow to the section in the text that answers the question.

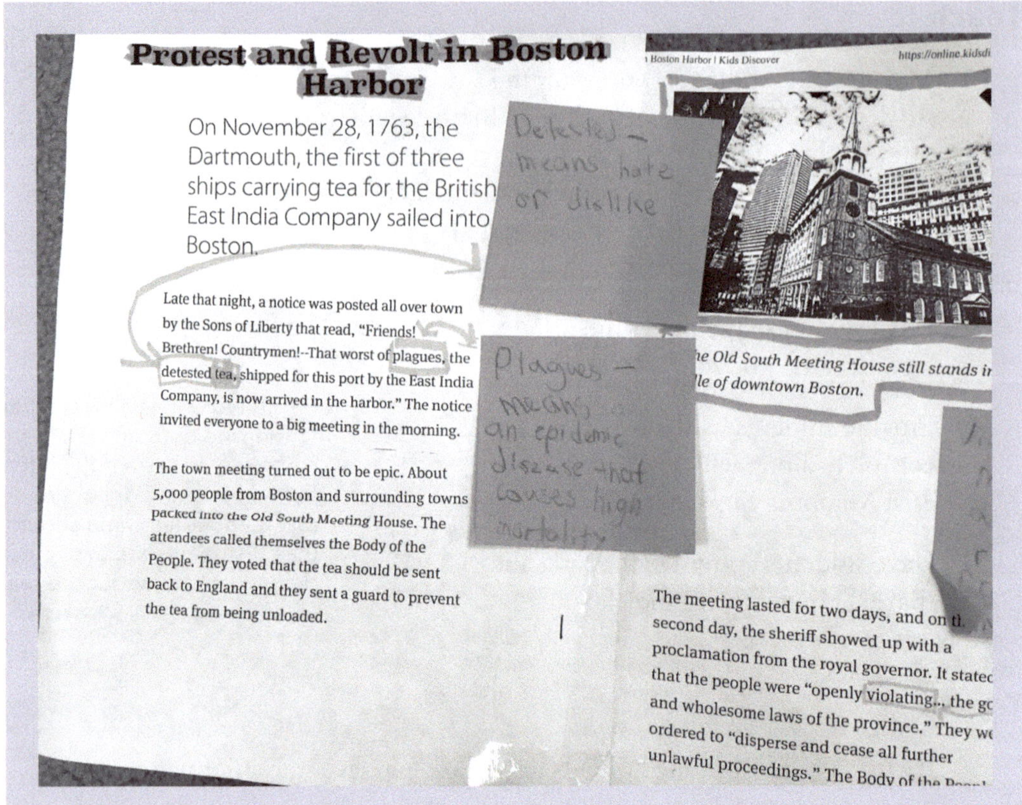

Boston Harbor | Kids Discover https://online.kidsdi

Protest and Revolt in Boston Harbor

On November 28, 1763, the Dartmouth, the first of three ships carrying tea for the British East India Company sailed into Boston.

Late that night, a notice was posted all over town by the Sons of Liberty that read, "Friends! Brethren! Countrymen!--That worst of plagues, the detested tea, shipped for this port by the East India Company, is now arrived in the harbor." The notice invited everyone to a big meeting in the morning.

The town meeting turned out to be epic. About 5,000 people from Boston and surrounding towns packed into the Old South Meeting House. The attendees called themselves the Body of the People. They voted that the tea should be sent back to England and they sent a guard to prevent the tea from being unloaded.

he Old South Meeting House still stands i
le of downtown Boston.

The meeting lasted for two days, and on t
second day, the sheriff showed up with a
proclamation from the royal governor. It statec
that the people were "openly violating... the gc
and wholesome laws of the province." They w
ordered to "disperse and cease all further
unlawful proceedings." The Body of the Peo

Photo by Shelly Tanner

- Collect the articles and then redistribute them to different groups. Have these new groups answer the questions posed by their classmates. This could be completed as a bell ringer the next day or as a ticket out the door.

Modifications

Emerging Writers

- Utilize prompts that focus on text features and structure to support striving readers and writers.
- Provide English learners with address labels to translate key vocabulary into their native languages or to draw small visual representations of the words to support their understanding.
- Develop a list of possible prompts or tasks that can be completed with the text and have students choose the tasks they want to complete.

Proficient Writers

- Cut out the images and graphs included in the text and have students either draft or draw replacements or fill in the spots with the missing images that you cut out.
- Have groups map different articles on a related topic and then jigsaw in groups to share.

See It Sample

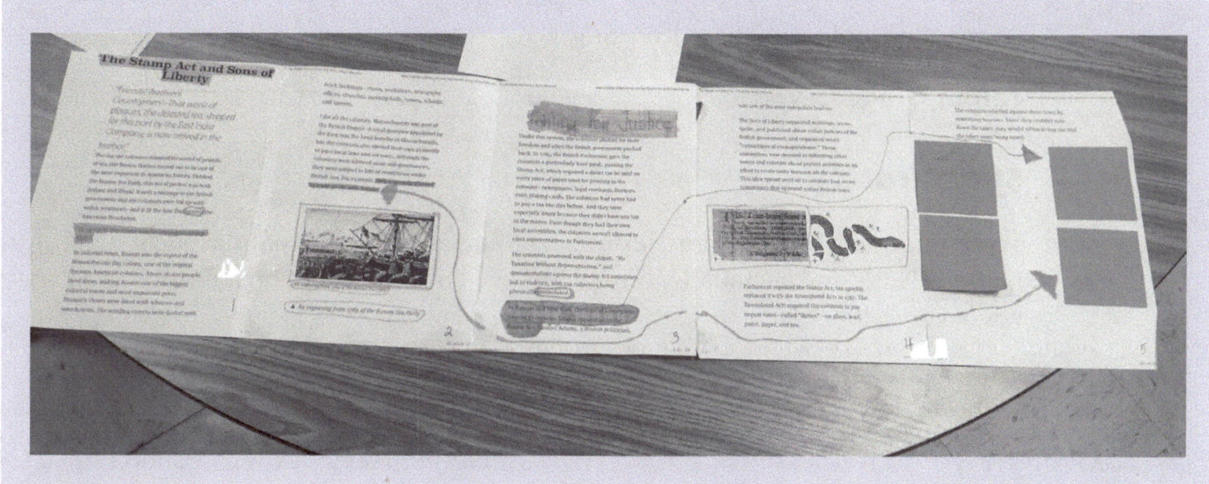

Photo by Shelly Tanner

WHO WOULD WIN?

In this lesson, students read and respond to high-interest, engaging informational text through a quick lesson that introduces them to research and textual evidence. Using the *Who Would Win?* series as a guide, students draft their own animal match-up which can easily be extended into a longer research piece. Plus, because the series employs a variety of text features, students can practice integrating these text features in their own writing.

Focus Genre: Informational Writing

Target Grade Level: K–5

Standards

Write informative/explanatory texts to examine and convey complex ideas and information clearly and accurately through the effective selection, organization, and analysis of content.

> *Quick Tip!*
>
> There are a wide variety of books in this series that include several different wildlife matchups including bugs, spiders, ocean animals, lions, tigers, dinosaurs, and more. Choose the ones that are most representative of your students and their interests or your science standards.

Anchor Texts

Who Would Win? series by Jerry Pallotta

Materials

- Animal crackers or slips of paper with animal names written on them
- Sticky notes or large address labels
- Who Would Win? template (p. 253)

Teach It

1. For about a week prior to this lesson, integrate a variety of the *Who Would Win?* titles in classroom read aloud and instruction. After students have seen a few of the books, ask them what types of information the author includes in the books about each animal. (Information such as size, habitat, food, etc., should be listed.)

2. Display the Who Would Win? template (p. 253) for students to see. Ask for a volunteer to come to the front of the room and have them choose an animal cracker (or slip of paper with an animal name written on it) from the container. Ask them what animal they chose. On the class template, have the student draw a picture of the animal chosen and label it.

3. Have a new volunteer to choose a second animal cracker (or animal name slip) and repeat the task.

4. Ask the student volunteers which of the animals chosen would win if they got in a fight. The students should provide one specific piece of evidence that supports their statement. (If needed, they can get assistance from their classmates.)

5. Record this on the template displayed for the class. Ask students if they know of any unique facts or information about each animal. Record this information on sticky notes or on large address labels. Attach these to the template next to the appropriate animal.

6. For independent writing, provide each student with a pile of animal crackers (or slips of paper with animal names on them) and their own Who Would Win? template. Have them choose two animal crackers and repeat the same activity from the whole group demonstration. Once they complete their template, they can eat the animal crackers.

If students don't know specific evidence that supports their choices or have difficulty finding extra facts and information to include on the sticky notes and address labels, provide them with additional nonfiction books on their topics or allow them to use their digital resources for research.

You can also use the individual snack size packages of animal crackers for easy distribution.

Try It

- Use this lesson as an introduction to informational writing.
- Try this lesson to ease students this genre, since research can be intimidating for some students.
- Use this as a quick and easy way to incorporate science content into the language arts classroom.

Extensions

- Have students choose one main animal that they match up with several different opponents. Discuss what factors affected the win or loss depending on who the animal was matched with.
- Focus on specific aspects of each animal and have students research these components. (These might include habitat, behavior, food, etc.)
- Have students extend this into the entire class comparing different animals. Divide the task into sections and have groups of students research different parts related to the topic. Reconvene as a class and combine the research into a new student created Who Would Win? book.

- Use this in social studies for battles between historical figures or in language arts for battles between characters from different literary works.

Modifications

Emerging Writers

- Before students begin writing, have them orally explain their choices and ideas. Dictate their stories or have them record on their templates.
- Give each student one animal cracker. Place students with a partner and have them collaboratively complete the task.
- Use fact cards as a way to assist students with the task. Create fact cards on each animal possibility so that if students get stuck, they can refer to the fact card for assistance when determining which animal might win.

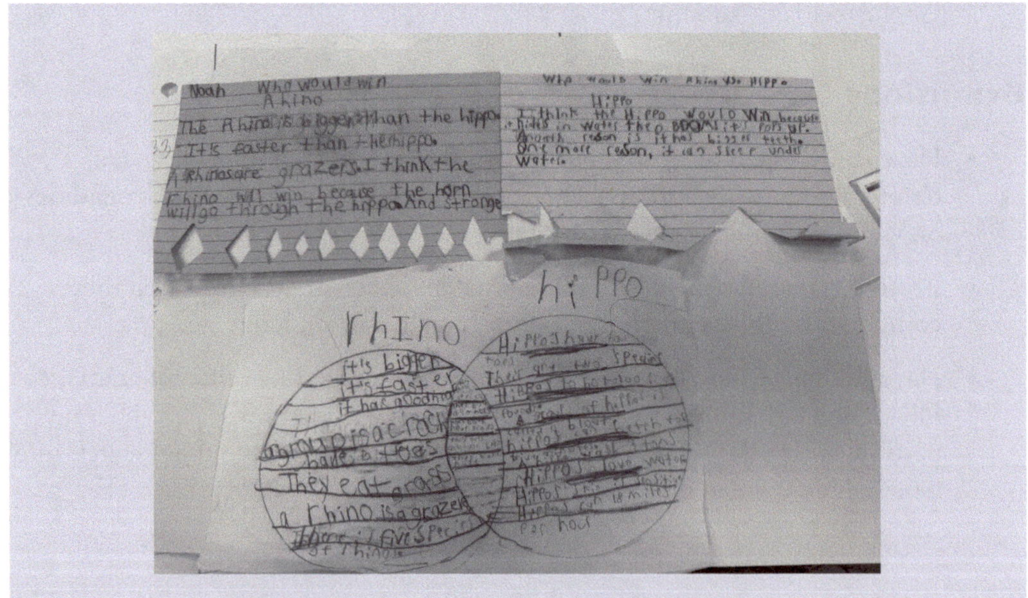

Proficient Writers

- Create an extended piece of writing by conducting research on additional aspects of the animal.
- Have students work with a partner to create a collaborative extended writing. To do this, each student researches their animal and then works with their partner to draft the battle scene where they determine who will win.

See It Sample

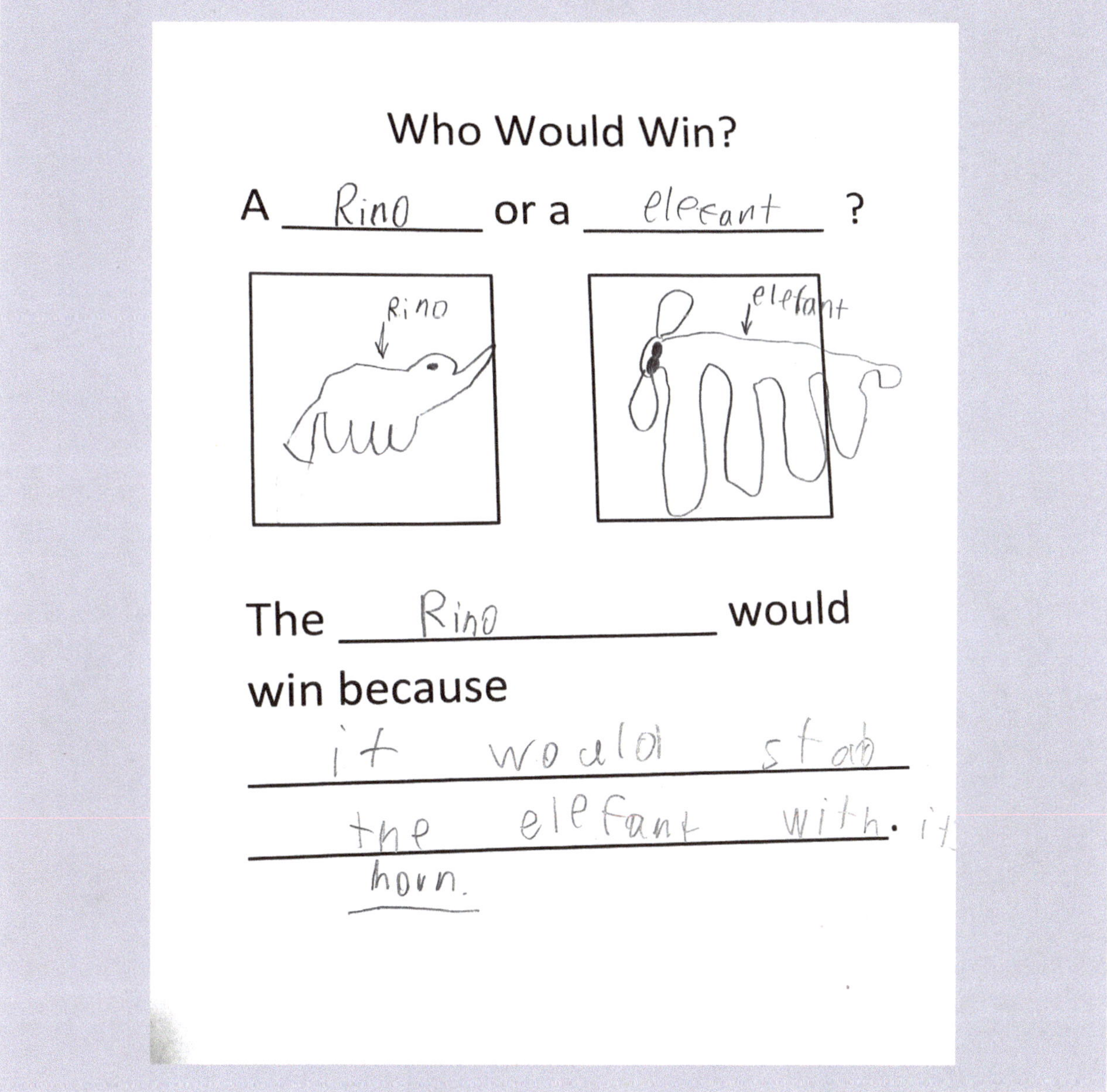

Who Would Win?

A Rino or a eleeant ?

The Rino would win because it would stab the elefant with. it horn.

Chapter 5

FINDING YOUR VOICE

As a writing teacher, one of the most difficult components of teaching writing, I think, is the notion and conceptualization of voice. In fact, the only way I really know how to adequately describe or define voice in writing is to simply say, "You know it when you hear it." Unfortunately, that kind of nebulous explanation does not bode well with most writers, especially for emerging writers. Of course, there are textbook definitions of *voice* that sometimes are just as confusing. Take the definition of *voice* from Master Class: "In literature, "voice" refers to the rhetorical mixture of vocabulary, tone, point of view, and syntax that makes phrases, sentences, and paragraphs flow in a particular manner. Novels can represent multiple voices: that of the narrator and those of individual characters." I am not sure if I understand voice better now or not! While that definition gives is the specific composition-based terminology needed to describe this concept, but it does not necessarily make the understanding any clearer.

Voice is not as simplistic as other writing-related concepts, such as plot or setting, but rather it contains a number of subtle nuances and characteristics that are unique to each individual writer. Part of finding one's own voice in writing requires something many students may have not done on a consistent basis: write. Now, it might seem like this is an oversimplification, but in reality, when students are given the opportunity to practice a skill—whether it is academic, athletic, social, or something else—their performance can improve. Writing is no different.

We know that literacy engagements, including writing activities, are most successful when they are relevant and authentic. Plus, writers improve their ability and competency in different aspects of writer's craft when there are authentic opportunities for practice and immersion. Writers can learn how to develop and cultivate their own voices when they are able to do things such as construct narratives, craft characters and problems, and experiment with word choice and language as they begin to develop and refine how they write and respond through text. When reflecting on myself as a writer and my past instructional experiences, I found that my writing didn't improve when I was shown examples or told how to write; however, my writing did improve when I was given the space and place to explore and craft my own stories. Developing my voice only came after I had multiple opportunities to be immersed in the act of writing and experimenting with language. In fact, we can draw some parallels between the acquisition of language and the way in which we might acquire writing skills. Consider this: We make sense of language through our immersion in the setting and our experiences with the language in our world. That's why you'll often hear young children apply incorrect language rules when speaking until they learn the real rule. For example, young children will often say, "I goed to school," because they are applying the past tense *-ed* rule across the board. In most cases, young children are not explicitly taught grammar rules as toddlers. Hence, I go back to my definition of knowing it when I see it or when I hear it.

Part of my definition works because it capitalizes on experience (seeing/hearing), along with encountering multiple models of what voice sounds like. Without that experience, or without tangible examples, it becomes much more difficult to teach this concept. The deliberate integration of quality mentor texts across genres, along with writing tasks that help students explore their own voice can aid students in developing a solid understanding. That's why no matter the genre or purpose, voice is always important to include and should be explored in multiple settings.

Despite the fact a succinct definition of voice might be difficult to develop, writing engagements that can help students find their own voice are beneficial and can help them conceptualize what is often a nebulous concept. As we've discussed earlier, part of becoming a proficient writer involves taking the time to practice and hone this skill through experience. If we allow students opportunities to engage with voice through a variety of authentic writing engagements, along with the integration of quality mentor texts across genres and mediums, they can become competent in this important aspect of writing.

Stop & Think

It is important for students to see that voice does not always reside in a narrative. Some informational texts that incorporate vignettes or stories utilize voice just as often and effectively. Think about Jerry Pallotta's *Who Would Win?* series, or Melissa Stewart's *Mega Predators of the Past*. Each of these has a distinctive voice even in the informational, nonfiction genre.

There are many authors who have a distinctive voice in their writing. Here are a few examples:

- *We Had a Picnic This Sunday Past* by Jacqueline Woodson
- *Ungifted* by Gordon Korman
- *The Day the Crayons Quit* by Drew Daywalt
- *Spoon* by Amy Krouse Rosenthal
- *Memoirs of a Hamster* by Devin Scillian
- *Be Quiet!* by Ryan T. Higgins

Every time I read a book like those listed above, I file them away as mentor texts that can be used for teaching voice. However, I rarely focus exclusively on voice because I find that I can integrate it into other writing lessons with much more success. In fact, I have found that in most instances, wrap around writing lessons—ones that address a number of writing component—are most effective. Now granted, some types of writing do have specific characteristics based on the genre—think about the genre of argument and the inclusion of a counterclaim—but many have characteristics that transcend genres and purposes. Those types of writings (narrative, informational, persuasive) allow for a myriad instructional purposes and lessons due to their structure and format. Within these genres, along with other writing opportunities like quick writes, writing to learn engagements, and process writing, writers can practice a variety of aspects of writer's craft all while gaining more experience with the act of writing. Even our youngest readers and writers can pick up on the exasperated voice of the crayons in Daywalt's text, the joyful and content voice of Seymour in *Memoirs of a Hamster* (until he learns cats are big fat liars), and Gary Paulsen's wit and humor in *How Angel Peterson Got His Name*.

Yagoda (2005) reminds us, "It is frequently the case that writers entertain, move, and inspire us less by what they say than by how they say it. *What* they say is information and ideas and (in the case of fiction) story and characters. *How* they say it is style." Getting our students to write with their own style and voice can help them create unique and powerful compositions that celebrate who they are as writers by the manner in which they say it.

I wonder if our students were able to see how the words they put on the page are not just another means for expression and communication of ideas, but are another means for expressing *themselves*. How powerful might that become? These next few strategies focus on just that: helping students develop and nurture their unique voices through their own writing.

CHAPTER 1 In the Beginning, We Write
CHAPTER 2 Breaking Into Story
CHAPTER 3 Tell Me More
CHAPTER 4 Learning Through Writing
CHAPTER 5 Finding Your Voice
CHAPTER 6 The Art of Persuasion
CHAPTER 7 The Measure of Success

WHOSE LINE IS IT ANYWAY?

In order for students to develop dynamic characters, and analyze, critique, and compare characters, students need to have multiple chances to practice these skills and explore the subtle nuances of characters in literature using a variety of strategies. In fact, strategies that help students practice different skills that address multiple aspects of character development, including dialogue construction, character traits, and character evolution can aid students as they complete character analysis writing tasks. Plus, when students focus on what a specific character has said, they can use those dialogue snippets as examples of a particular character's voice. Think about it. In order for students to determine who might have said a particular line out of context, they have to possess a solid understanding of who that character is and what traits and personality they have. Using that information, they can connect the dialogue with the best character based on the examples from the text and the character's voice.

Focus Genre: Narrative/Dialogue Focus

Target Grade Level: K–5

Standards

Apply a wide range of strategies to comprehend, interpret, evaluate, and appreciate texts. Draw on prior experience, interactions with other readers and writers, knowledge of word meaning and of other texts, word identification strategies, and understanding of textual features (e.g., sound–letter correspondence, sentence structure, context, graphics).

Anchor Texts

Any narrative text works in this lesson as long as it includes a significant amount of dialogue from multiple characters. However, here are a few of my favorites.

If using a picture book, make sure it is one that students have read or heard a few times. If you are using a novel, try this activity no sooner than midway through the reading. Ideally, this would be a good activity to use at the end of a novel.

The Ghost of Tupelo Landing by Shelia Turnage

Smack Dab in the Middle of Maybe by Jo Watson Hackl

Supergifted by Gordon Korman

Wishtree by Katherine Applegate

The Day the Crayons Quit by Drew Dawalt

Voices in the Park by Anthony Browne

Beach Party Surf Monkey by Chris Grabenstein

The Investigators series by John Patrick Green

I Want My Hat Back by John Klassen

The Very Impatient Caterpillar by Ross Burach

Familiar Fairy Tales

Materials

- Sentence strips or notecards with quotes from characters
- Chart paper
- Sticky notes
- Whose Line Is It? template (p. 254)

Teach It

1. When finishing up a book, novel, or other extended work, make a list of the characters on a sheet of chart paper and display the list.
2. Have students brainstorm character traits for each of the characters. Record the character traits on sticky notes and then place them next to their corresponding characters on the chart paper.

Photo by Alfred Cain

3. Discuss each of the characters and their character traits.

4. Display a quote or piece of dialogue from text that one of the characters said.

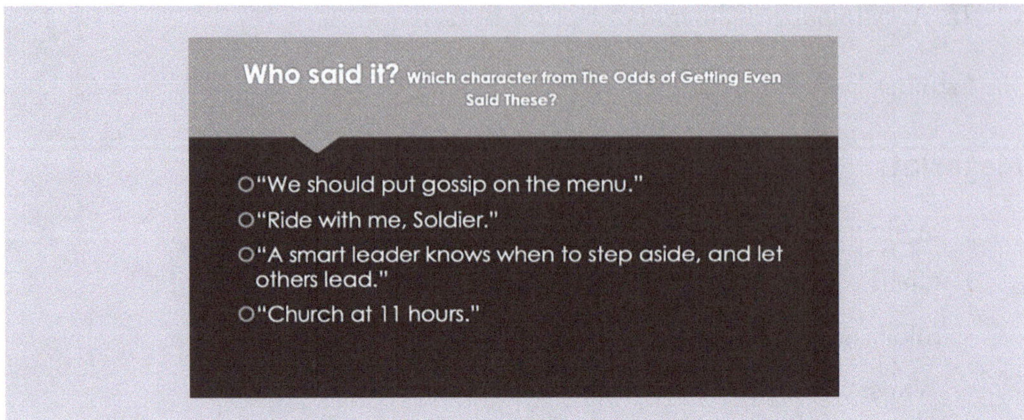

5. Using the list of characters and their character traits, have students determine which character from the list is the speaker of the line.

6. Have students use notecards or sticky notes to record their ideas. Instruct them to use evidence from the brainstorming session to support their inferences.

7. Have students share their ideas and evidence with the class.

8. Provide students with a list of five to ten additional quotes from the text that can be attributed to different characters.

9. Have students refer back to the brainstorming information to complete the activity independently or with a partner. Record their answers on the Whose Line Is It? template.

Try It

- Use this when you want students to interact and engage with character dialogue in a different way.
- Try this as a way to review the important characters in an extended work or novel.
- Use this if you want students to consider a character's words and dialogue when they complete a character analysis.
- Use this as a way for students to bridge between character analysis and voice.
- Try this when you want to check students' comprehension but not necessarily with a formal assessment.

Extensions

- Have students use the direct quotes as a frame for them to write new dialogue that their selected character might say.
- Use the dialogue to make inferences about what is happening with that character at that time.
- Divide students into pairs or small groups and have them make connections between characters in multiple books or other texts.
- Have students choose dialogue that could be part of a conversation between characters and perform that for the class.

Modifications

Emerging Writers

- Post each character and their traits on large pieces of chart paper around the room to create character stations. Have students partner up and give them a few sample quotes. Instruct them to rotate around the room to each character station and determine where their quotes should be placed.

Photo by Alfred Cain

Quick Tip!

You might also break this lesson up by having students brainstorm about the characters on Day 1 and then match the dialogue to the character on Day 2.

- Create a matching center or station where students use character cards and dialogue that they sort and connect. Use this as one of the centers or stations during your small-group instruction rotations.
- Have students perform the dialogue and have classmates guess their character. This could easily be connected to Readers' Theatre.
- Instead of using material from literature, have students draft dialogue that they might use it they were feeling specific emotions or in specific social situation.

Proficient Writers

- Instead of focusing on characters in one novel, use characters from multiple novels as a more comprehensive review.
- For a cross-curricular connection, have students focus on historical figures instead of fictional characters.
- Connect this to the Tweets Like/Posts Like activity in *Writing Workouts* (Harper, 2023).

See It Sample

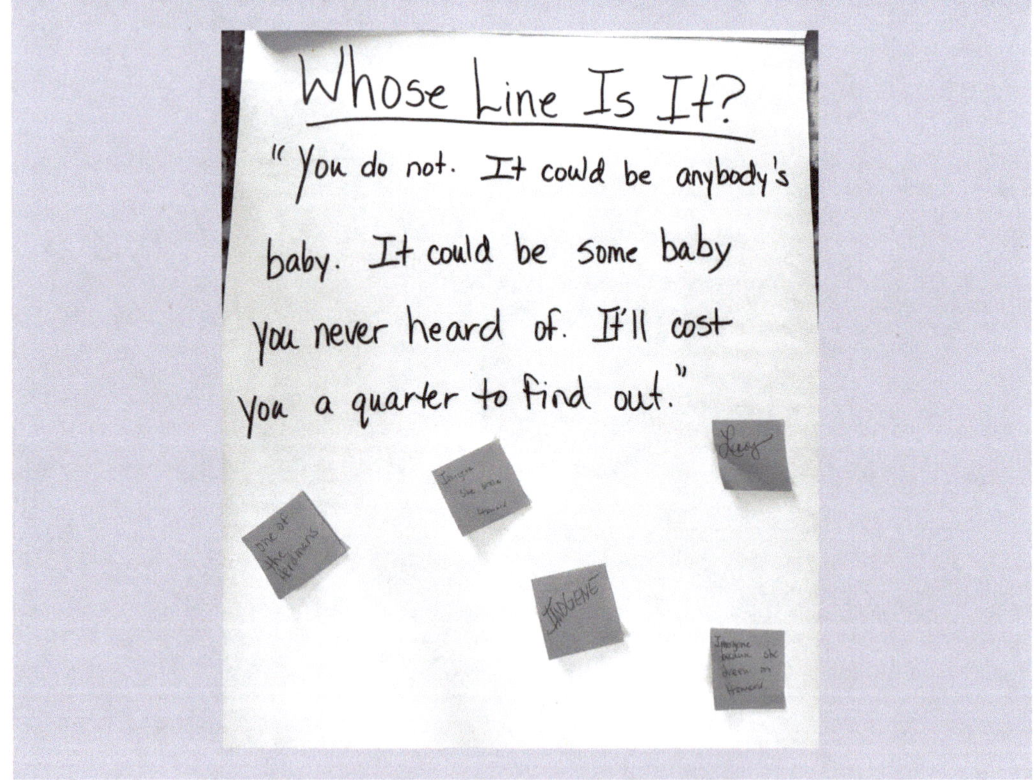

VOICE OVER

For writers, sometimes finding their voice can be intimidating. However, there are multiple real-world examples that can aid students in experiencing the different voices of characters which can aid them in developing and constructing their own. For example, on social media, there are popular users who use videos of animals, people, cartoon characters, etc. and create hilarious voiceovers based on these short clips of film. Often some of the most entertaining ones are the voiceovers created for short films or clips with animals as the main characters. Using short visual film clips can help students see how to create words based not only on a character's actions, but by using their traits and voice as well.

Focus Genre: Narrative/Dialogue Focus

Target Grade Level: 3–5

Standards

Apply a wide range of strategies to comprehend, interpret, evaluate, and appreciate texts. Draw on prior experience, interactions with other readers and writers, knowledge of word meaning and of other texts, word identification strategies, and their understanding of textual features (e.g., sound–letter correspondence, sentence structure, context, graphics).

Adjust use of spoken, written, and visual language (e.g., conventions, style, vocabulary) to communicate effectively with a variety of audiences and for different purposes.

Anchor Texts

The Wishgranter produced by Ringling College of Art and Design

La Luna produced by Pixar Animation Studios

Presto produced by Pixar Animation Studios

Tom & Jerry produced by Hanna Barbera and MGM Television

Partly Cloudy produced by Pixar Animation Studios

Bao produced by Pixar Animation Studios

Materials

- Notecards
- Sticky notes
- Paint strips

CHAPTER 1 In the Beginning, We Write
CHAPTER 2 Breaking Into Story
CHAPTER 3 Tell Me More
CHAPTER 4 Learning Through Writing
CHAPTER 5 Finding Your Voice
CHAPTER 6 The Art of Persuasion
CHAPTER 7 The Measure of Success

Teach It

1. Before you share the mentor film text, watch the clip to determine exactly how many characters are in the film. This is important as it will determine how you will instruct the students in the lesson and plan the activities in the lesson.
2. Start by playing one of the mentor texts listed above. You may find that you have a video or film clip that you want to use instead. Just make sure that the clips you use have multiple characters in them and that there is no existing dialogue, since the goal of the activity is to have the students construct their own.
3. Have students watch the clip first without writing anything. This is important because the students need to have a basic understanding of the entire clip before they begin the written task.
4. After students have seen the clip at least once, explain that students will each be assigned a specific character, and they will be responsible for writing that character's dialogue. First, they need to write down details about their character based on their observations so they can begin to understand that character's personality and nature. Explain that his will help them write and speak in that character's voice.
5. Distribute different colored sticky notes to students. Create a sticky note key where students can see which character their color sticky note corresponds with. This will ensure that multiple students will observe the same character, as this is important for the next steps in the strategy.

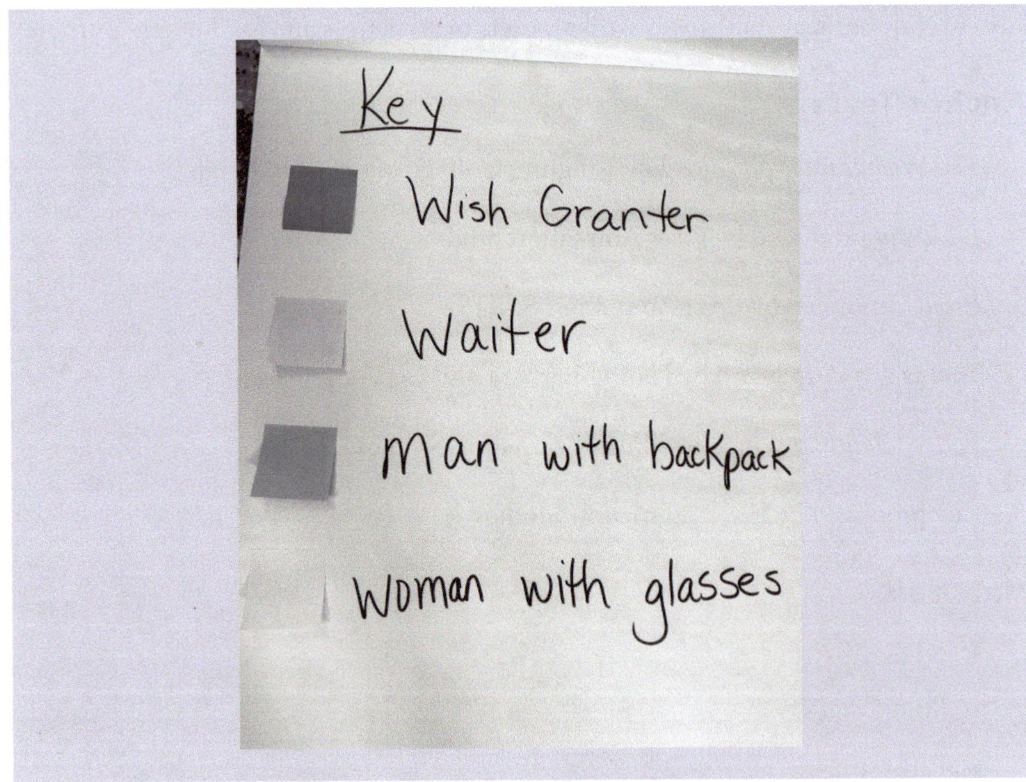

6. Play the video clip again.
7. Have students write down their observations of their characters.
8. After the second viewing, have students get in groups based on the characters they were assigned. In those groups, have them discuss what they noticed about their character and any observations, ideas, or facts they gathered during the second viewing. Have students record their ideas on large sheet chart paper in order to build an overarching description of their assigned character.

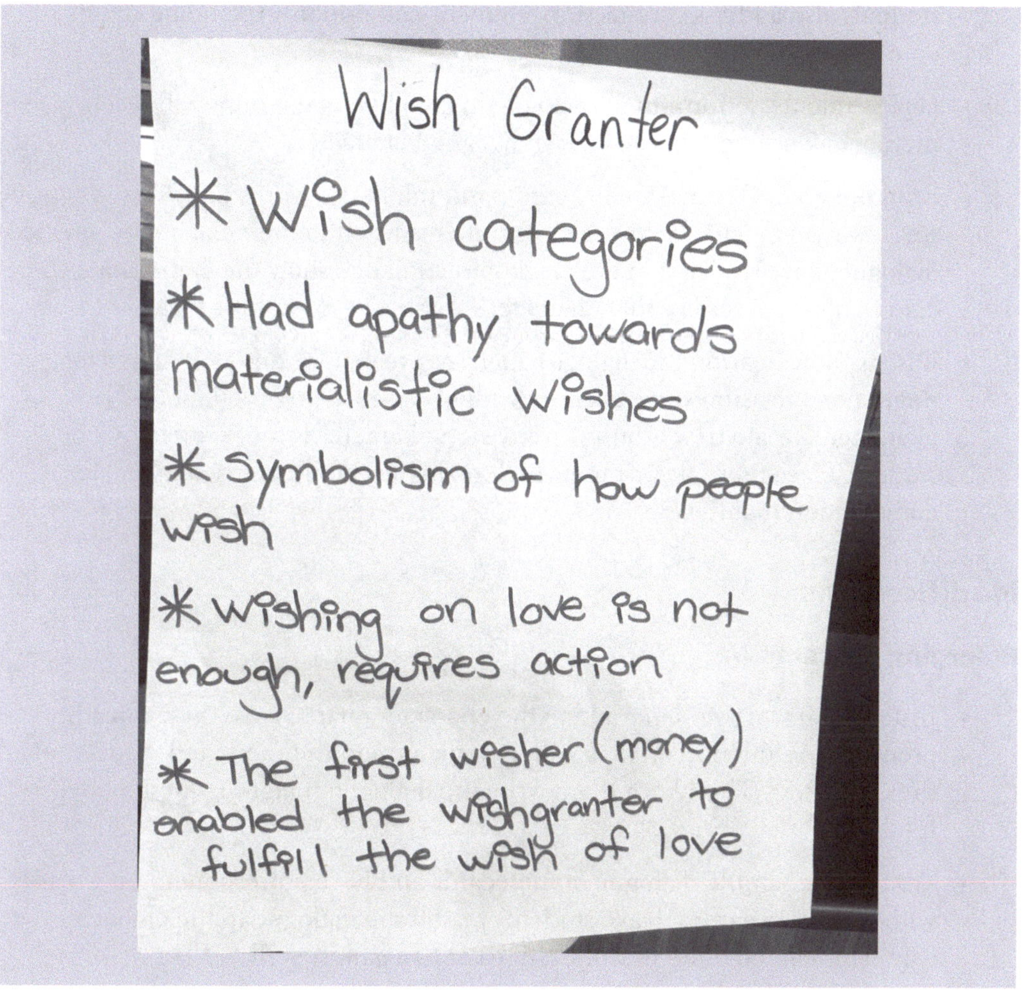

9. Play the video clip a third time.
10. Have students record or write the dialogue for their assigned character using their observations and collaborative discussion as a frame for writing in that character's voice. You can choose to have students do this individually or in partners.
11. Once students have finished writing their dialogue, have students share it with the class.

CHAPTER 1 In the Beginning, We Write
CHAPTER 2 Breaking Into Story
CHAPTER 3 Tell Me More
CHAPTER 4 Learning Through Writing
CHAPTER 5 Finding Your Voice
CHAPTER 6 The Art of Persuasion
CHAPTER 7 The Measure of Success

Try It

- Use this as a low-stakes and fun way to practice dialogue.
- Try this when you want students to take part in a collaborative engagement.
- Use this as a way to get students thinking about character development and analysis.

Extensions

- Instead of simply focusing on the dialogue and character aspects, have students also address various story element components including setting, conflict, etc.
- Have students perform their dialogue in collaborative groups with each member assuming the role of their assigned character.
- Print out character personality cards. You might use words like *bossy*, *angry*, *shy*, *sassy*, *confident*, *excited*, etc. As students listen to their classmates' created dialogue, have students in the classroom audience show the appropriate voice card that best describes that character's voice.
- Discuss how hearing the dialogue that was created for different characters might need revision since each individual was focusing on their one character. Create new groups where each character is represented by one student. Have them determine which dialogue should be used to create a conversation that flows.

Modifications

Emerging Writers

- Instead of having students add to the character charts, have these already premade so students can do a gallery walk around the room and read about the characters. Then have them write the dialogue matching these posted traits.
- Write some sample dialogue on notecards and have corresponding notecards with character names. Have students match the dialogue to the character that way. This can be done in workstations or as a gallery walk.

Proficient Writers

- Have students craft a new piece of dialogue that one of the characters might have said and add it to their classmates' ideas.
- Take some of the sample dialogue ideas the students created and draft new ways that character might say the same statement but with different words, phrases, and examples.

- Have students brainstorm a potential part two for their video clip. Ask them to consider what might happen in the next part of the story? What is next for the characters? What might they say? You could also pause the video clip at a pivotal moment in the clip and have students draft their own ending or continuation. Then, play the full clip and have students compare their ideas to the video.

See It Sample

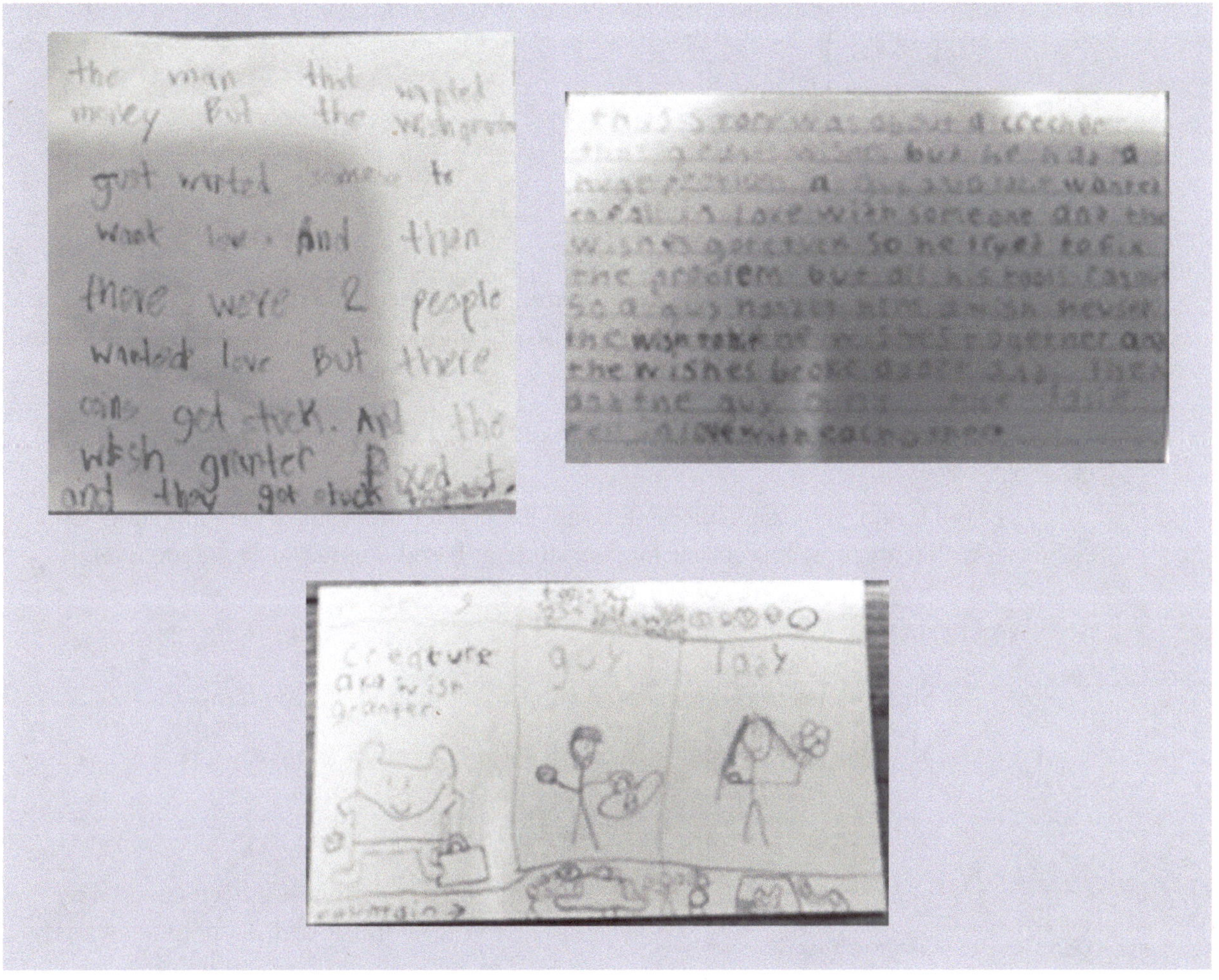

Photos by Shelly Tanner

SONGS FOR VOICE

Because voice is hard to define, this can make it difficult for writers to use in their written compositions. While picture books, novels, and poetry can serve as excellent examples of voice in writing, music can offer another layer of understanding and explanation. In fact, giving students examples of how voice *sounds* can help them develop their own voice when writing.

Focus Genre: Narrative

Target Grade Level: 3–5

Standards

Apply knowledge of language structure, language conventions (e.g., spelling and punctuation), media techniques, figurative language, and genre to create, critique, and discuss print and nonprint texts.

Anchor Texts

For this lesson, your main anchor texts are the different versions of the same song. Choose songs that are most appropriate for your students based on interest and grade level.

Materials

- Sticky notes or index cards (if you do not plan to use the template)
- Musical Voice template (p. 255)

Teach It

1. Find a song that has been covered by multiple music artists. Include a variety of covers, but no more than five.
2. Make a copy of the lyrics (these will all be the same no matter who the artist is covering the song.)
3. Provide students with the Musical Voice template (p. 255) and a copy of the lyrics.
4. Play a portion of one of the songs. Encourage students to follow along with the lyrics as they listen. Have students make notations of their observations on the template. Encourage them to consider the following:

Quick Tip!

It's a good idea to make sure that the covers vary in musical genre. For example, you might include a rock and roll, blues, country, ballad, etc. since each of those has a distinctively different style. My absolute favorite to use is Michael Jackson's *Billie Jean*. However, this may not be appropriate for your grade level. You might use covers of Taylor Swift's *We Are Never Ever Getting Back Together,* Elvis's *Hound Dog,* Dolly Pardon's *Jolene,* The Beatles's *Twist and Shout*, or even familiar kids' songs like *Mary Had a Little Lamb.*

- How does this song make you feel?
- What is the overall mood?
- What do you notice about the singer's performance?

5. Repeat step four with each sample cover. Make sure you play the most famous cover last.
6. After students have listened to each cover song, have students discuss the differences in each version. Make sure to draw attention to how the lyrics were the same for all the versions instead of how the tempo, key, style, and artist changed.

Songs for Voice

Song Title	Noticings *(mood, feeling, tempo, etc.)*
Billie Jean SONG 1	Blues nostalgic sad Soul melancholy missing guitar
SONG2	rock ballad like Coldplay passion hard times blames himself bluesy
SONG3	upbeat her fault irritated denying trifling don't know her fast beat

7. Have students discuss how each artist's individual performance affected the overall message of the song.
8. Connect this concept back to writing by explaining that individual authors use certain words and phrases that create their individual voices. Explain that how words are used and in what context affects voice along with perspective and point of view.

A great picture book to use for this is *Mirror Mirror: A Book of Reverse Poems* by Marilyn Singer. In this book, the author uses the same words and phrases but in a different order which completely changes the meaning of each poem. Some of her other titles include: *Echo Echo: Reverse Poems About Greek Myths* and *Follow Follow: A Book of Reverse Poems.*

Try It

- Use this when you want students to have a tangible example of what voice sounds like.
- Try this as a way to connect music to writing.
- Use this when you want to help students make real-world connections between writing in the world and writing in the classroom.
- Try this as a way to also address the skill of comparison and contrast indirectly.

Extensions

- Have students use descriptive words to describe each song and draft a persuasive paragraph about why a certain version or cover is the best performance.
- Have students locate images that match the overall mood and voice of each version of the song.
- Connect this to a lesson on characters or for a connection to a novel study by having students choose which cover would best fit the voice of a specific character.

Modifications

Emerging Writers

- Provide students with a word bank to use when describing each of the songs.
- Instead of having students listen to all the songs, make this a station activity with one song version at each station. Only do this if you have headphones because otherwise there will be too much noise overlap with the different songs and it won't be effective.
- Instead of having students record words on the template, have them record their moods and thoughts using emojis. You could also have students create notecard emojis by drawing different mood emojis on notecards which they can hold up when a specific song is played.

Proficient Writers

- Have students locate a new cover of the main song and share it with the class.
- To add further support for the descriptions, have students include lyrics as the textual evidence that supports their descriptions.
- Have students extend the activity by comparing and contrasting each of the songs.

See It Sample

Songs for Voice

Heartbreak HOTEL

Song Title	Noticings *(mood, feeling, tempo, etc.)*
Song 1	Slow, rock, sad missing girl crying Band
SONG 2	Kind of slow, upbeat Guitar
Song 3	Dancing fast Happy - Glad she's gone
Song 4	Too slow Girl singing really sad lots of drums
Song 5	Country Western Cowboy

Character Playlist Template

Character: Roseuro

Song and Artist	Justification for Inclusion
perfect reveng	because he wants reveng
fight of our lives	because he dose not know were he belongs
life is sweeter	when he is in the life
shuffle of love	when he walks to the banquet hall
get your hands dirty	when he is chosing to go to the light or to stay

CHARACTER PLAYLISTS

With the wide range of reading material available in language arts classrooms, students are able to meet an infinite cast of characters from a number of backgrounds. Character analyses are frequent residents in the language arts classroom, and for good reason, as these engagements give students the opportunities to critically analyze a character's actions, dialogue, and thought process in a work. While this becomes more of a focus in the upper grades, giving students opportunities to write about a variety of characters can help them with their comprehension as well as with the creative construction of their own characters when they are charged with writing stories. When writing, developing and creating authentic and dynamic characters can be challenging, but character development is key when crafting narratives and other fictional stories. Building an authentic character means going beyond a vivid physical description, and in reality, some of the best novels leave those physical details up for the reader to fill in. Rather, rich characters are developed through their actions, dialogue, thoughts, mannerisms, likes, and dislikes. One way that students can start thinking about their own characters and analyze characters from novels is through the creation of Character Playlists.

Focus Genre: Narrative

Target Grade Level: 3–5

Standards

Apply a wide range of strategies to comprehend, interpret, evaluate, and appreciate texts. Draw on prior experience, interactions with other readers and writers, knowledge of word meaning and of other texts, word identification strategies, and understanding of textual features (e.g., sound–letter correspondence, sentence structure, context, graphics).

Anchor Texts

This activity works best with novels because readers are able to get more reading time with each character. While you can pretty much use this strategy with just about any novel, here are a few of my favorites.

Marcus Vega Doesn't Speak Spanish by Pablo Cartaya

Paper Things by Jennifer Richard Jacobson

The Benefits of Being an Octopus by Ann Braden

Summer of the Gypsy Moths by Sara Pennypacker

Crenshaw by Katherine Applegate

The Odds of Getting Even by Sheila Turnage

Materials

- Sticky notes
- Chart paper
- Character Playlist template (p. 256)

Teach It

1. Determine which characters from the text will be the focus for this engagement. Display the list of characters.

This makes a great culminating activity for a novel.

2. Talk to students about song playlists. Ask them if they have certain playlists for specific activities or times of the day. Invite students to share what makes those playlists unique. (Even if your students don't have their own playlists, they can probably tell you about their favorite songs or maybe about the songs they listen to with their friends, coaches, and families.)
3. Choose one character to work through as a class example. Write the character's name at the top of a sheet of chart paper.
4. Brainstorm some character traits that could be used to describe that character. Record the character traits on sticky notes and put them on the chart paper.
5. Based on these traits, discuss what types of songs this character might like. For example, if the character is more solemn and reflective, songs with a slower pace such as ballads, might be good starting points.
6. As a class, collaboratively develop a five to seven song playlist, discussing the songs and giving evidence for their selections throughout the discussion.
7. Go back to the original list of characters from step one and display the list again.
8. Have students work in pairs and choose one character from the list.
9. In pairs, have students develop a playlist of five to seven songs that their character might listen to along with a justification of each song choice. Instruct students to use the Character Playlist template (p. 256) to record the playlist.
10. Have students share their playlists with the class when they are finished.

Try It

- Use this when you want students to utilize their personal interests and knowledge in academic lessons.
- Try this as a way to connect music to literary works.
- Use this when you want students to review multiple characters from a literary work.

Extensions

- Once students have created their playlists, use them as the ticket in the door on the following day. Show the students an individual list of songs and have them guess which character's playlist is displayed.
- Have students choose one of the songs from the list as the character's "Theme Song." Have students justify and explain their choice.
- Extend this into creating an entire soundtrack for a novel or extended literary work like the one shown on page 170. With a novel soundtrack, you can include songs from across characters to create a more comprehensive musical representation of the text.
- Have students create a companion list of character favorites that goes along with the playlist. For example, they might include a character's favorite foods, activities, hobbies, etc.

Modifications

Emerging Writers

- Before students start developing full playlists, have them start with the Walk Out Song (p. 211).
- Instead of a song playlist, have students create a Top Ten List for their character. Ideas might include the Top Ten List of Mistakes a character made, Top Ten Things I Love About This Character, Top Ten Wins, etc.
- Give students a list of multiple characters and have them add one song for each character. Then, regroup the students and have them collect all the songs for character A, B, and so forth in order to create a class-made playlist.

Proficient Writers

- Connect this activity to a persuasive writing lesson by having students draft a persuasive piece for why their playlist best suits the character.
- Have students design an album cover for their playlist using images that best represent their character.
- Encourage students to connect the songs from their playlist to a particular mood of a character or to a specific event that occurred.

See It Sample

Character Playlist Template

Character Big Bad Wolf

Song and Artist	Justification for Inclusion
Hungry like the wolf Duran Duran	The Big Bad wolf was going to eat the girl.
Wolf Moon by Neil Young	The character is a wolf and they howl at the moon.
Lady in Red by Chris de Burgh	Little Red Riding Hood wore red.
Over the River and Through the Woods to Grandmother's House we Go	They went to Grandma's.
Man Eater by Hall and Oates	The wolf wanted to eat her.

NOVEL/BOOK SOUNDTRACKS

Who doesn't love a great movie soundtrack? Think about the powerful songs that came from movies like *The Bodyguard*, *Saturday Night Fever*, *Dirty Dancing*, and *Flashdance*. Even some television shows have amazing soundtracks. *Stranger Things*, *Bridgerton*, and *Sons of Anarchy* billed some great songs in their weekly episodes. Soundtracks for movies and television shows add another layer of meaning to the text. In addition to the acting on the screen, themes, moods, and conflicts get reiterated in the form of a song. Why shouldn't novels, fairy tales, and picture books be given the same attention? Novel/Book Soundtracks allow students the opportunity to engage with the overall theme and plot of a novel by adding another layer of meaning in the form of song. Plus, it capitalizes on student interest since they are able to incorporate songs they listen to in their personal lives, with appropriate justifications of course, into this assignment.

Focus Genre: Narrative

Target Grade Level: 3–5

Standards

Apply a wide range of strategies to comprehend, interpret, evaluate, and appreciate texts. Draw on prior experience, interactions with other readers and writers, knowledge of word meaning and of other texts, word identification strategies, and understanding of textual features (e.g., sound–letter correspondence, sentence structure, context, graphics).

Employ a wide range of strategies as they write and use different writing process elements appropriately to communicate with different audiences for a variety of purposes.

Anchor Texts

Use any novel for this activity. You could also create a playlist for a picture book series instead.

Materials

- Sticky notes
- Chart paper
- Paint strips
- Novel Playlist template (p. 257)

Teach It

1. At the end of a novel unit, recap the novel by reviewing the overall themes, characters, plot, conflict, etc. List these ideas on chart paper.
2. Discuss how songs have moods and also convey messages.
3. Show students some sample movie or television soundtracks. I suggest using soundtracks from family-friendly movies or television shows that your students watch.
4. Discuss how the songs used in the movies help the director and actors add another layer of meaning onto the film.
5. Refer back to the brainstorming list in Step 1. Explain to students that they will create their own soundtrack for the novel using the ideas from the brainstormed list.
6. Have students work with a partner to create their own novel soundtrack using the Novel Playlist template (p. 257). You could also have students add their song ideas on paint strips as well.
7. Have students share their completed soundtracks with the class.

For help about how songs have mood, refer to the Walk Out Songs (p. 211), Character Playlists (p. 164), or Songs for Voice (p. 160).

Try It

- Use this as a culminating activity for a novel study.
- Try this when you want students to review previously studied works of literature.
- Use this as a way for students to connect personal interests to academic demands.

Extensions

- Compile a class songbook of novel soundtracks for all the books read during the year.
- Create a music video that uses one of the songs as a backdrop for the video.
- Play different songs from different soundtracks made during the year. Have students guess which novel they are from.

Modifications

Emerging Writers

- Instead of having students focus on the entire novel at once, take it chapter by chapter as the class is reading. At the end of the chapter, have students pick a song that best supports that chapter.
- Compile a teacher-created song bank that is connected to the novel and have students choose the ones that they think fit best with the novel.
- Have students list the top events that occurred during the novel and then have them choose a song to go with the event instead of the characters.

Proficient Writers

- Have students create a theme song for the novel as a whole.
- Use the Character Playlists strategy (p. 164) as a song bank for choosing songs that should be included in the soundtrack.
- On an assessment, include a few sample soundtrack options and have students choose and defend the one that they believe best fits with the novel.

See It Sample

Charlotte's Web

Novel Soundtrack Template

Song and Artist	Justification for Inclusion
NO Doubt - Spiderwebs	Charlotte wrote messages in the webs.
Old MacDonald Had a Farm	The setting was a farm.
County Fair by The Beach Boys	They take Wilbur to the fair.
See You Again by Charlie Puth	Charlotte dies and Wilbur will see her one day in heaven.
Itsy Bitsy spider	Charlotte was a spider.

CHARACTER PARTNER POEMS

Character Partner Poems have a lot of the same characteristics as the Bio Poem (Harper, 2017) and the Partner Poem (Harper, 2023). You may recall from my first book that my students loved Bio Poems because there was a specific formula and length requirement included. This type of template made it easier for many students because they were able to see exactly what material was needed for completion. The Partner Poems from *Writing Workouts* are similar in the sense that they follow a template, and create somewhat of a checklist or list of ideas for inclusion while performed in two voices, with two students performing their poems together. Partner Poems as getting to know you activities can create a lovely, unique, collaborative writing engagement. In this lesson, we revisit the idea of a Partner Poem but use it to write in the voice of literary characters, thus offering students another opportunities to play around with the concept of voice. Using this retooled Character Partner Poem addresses a variety of literacy standards since it is focused on facts and information about characters in literary works. This strategy serves as a fresh way to address a character analysis and also includes a collaborative component.

Focus Genre: Narrative

Target Grade Level: 3–5

Standards

Employ a wide range of strategies to write and use different writing process elements appropriately to communicate with different audiences for a variety of purposes.

Anchor Texts

The anchor texts in this lesson look at little different since you will be using characters from books your students have already read. Instead, I would suggest poems and books written in different voices to give students a tangible example of different voices.

Joyful Noise: Poems for Two Voices by Paul Fleischman

Voices in the Park by Anthony Browne

The Pain and the Great One by Judy Blume

Messing Around on the Monkey Bars and Other School Poems for Two Voices by Betsy Franco

Boom! Bellow! Bleat! Animal Poems for Two or More Voices by Georgia Heard

I Am Phoenix: Poems for Two Voices by Paul Fleischman

Shh! We Have a Plan by Chris Haughton

Once Upon a Cool Motorcycle Dude by Kevin O'Malley

Math Talk: Mathematical Ideas in Poems for Two Voices by Theoni Pappas

Seeds, Bees, Butterflies and More! By Carole Gerber

Mirror Mirror: A Book of Reversible Verse by Marilyn Singer

Materials

- Chart paper
- Sticky notes
- Character Partner Poem template (p. 258)

Teach It

1. Begin by creating a list of main characters from an extended literary work or brainstorm a list of characters across multiples books that have been read.
2. Write one character's name at the top of each sheet of chart paper and place the chart papers around the room.
3. Have students go a gallery walk and record information about the characters (dialogue, traits, events) on sticky notes and place the sticky notes on the corresponding sheets of chart paper.
4. Provide students with the Character Partner Poem template (p. 258).
5. Explain to students that they are going to choose one of the characters from the gallery walk to draft their poems.
6. As a reminder of how Partner Poems are constructed, compose one about yourself or about a sample character not listed on chart paper. You can also show students a completed poem as an example.
7. Have students complete their own templates. (To modify, this can be done in pairs instead of independently.)

Photo by Shelly Tanner

8. When it is time to share, pick two students to read their poems aloud.
9. Have students alternate their voices. For example, student one reads their first line and then student two reads their first line. This continues until the whole poem is performed. Have their classmates guess which character's voice is represented in each of the poems.
10. Invite another pair of students to perform.
11. Discuss how the poems shifted and changed based on who was paired.
12. Have students circulate the room and find a few classmates to perform their poems with.
13. Give students 5 to 7 minutes to collaboratively perform in small groups.
14. Have students share their noticings with the class.

Try It

- Try this when you want students to practice writing poems.
- Use this as a way for students to develop a collaborative culminating product.
- Instead of a traditional comprehension activity or character analysis engagement, use this as a substitute.
- Use this when you want students to compare multiple characters from a work or characters from across books.

Extensions

- Have students add another sentence starter to the poem template.
- Create a class collaborative poem by combining information from multiple student examples to draft a class poem about characters from an entire novel.

Photo by Shelly Tanner

- Have students form small groups and have them combine their poems into one that they perform in unison.
- Divide students into groups based on the character they chose. Have them pick the best lines from each of their poems to create a new poem.

Modifications

Emerging Writers

- Instead of having students complete all the parts, have them choose a few sentence starters on the poem to complete and then share them with a partner.
- Draft ready-made partner poems for characters and have students guess which character is the focus.
- Change the sentence starters from "I . . ." to "You . . ." or "He/she . . ." and have students write about one of their classmates as a warm-up.

Proficient Writers

- Instead of focusing on existing characters in books, have students make up a character and write from their perspective.
- Use this for writing about historical figures or for a twist on biographies.
- Don't make this exclusive to books or written texts; use this strategy for movies, short films, and images too.

See It Sample

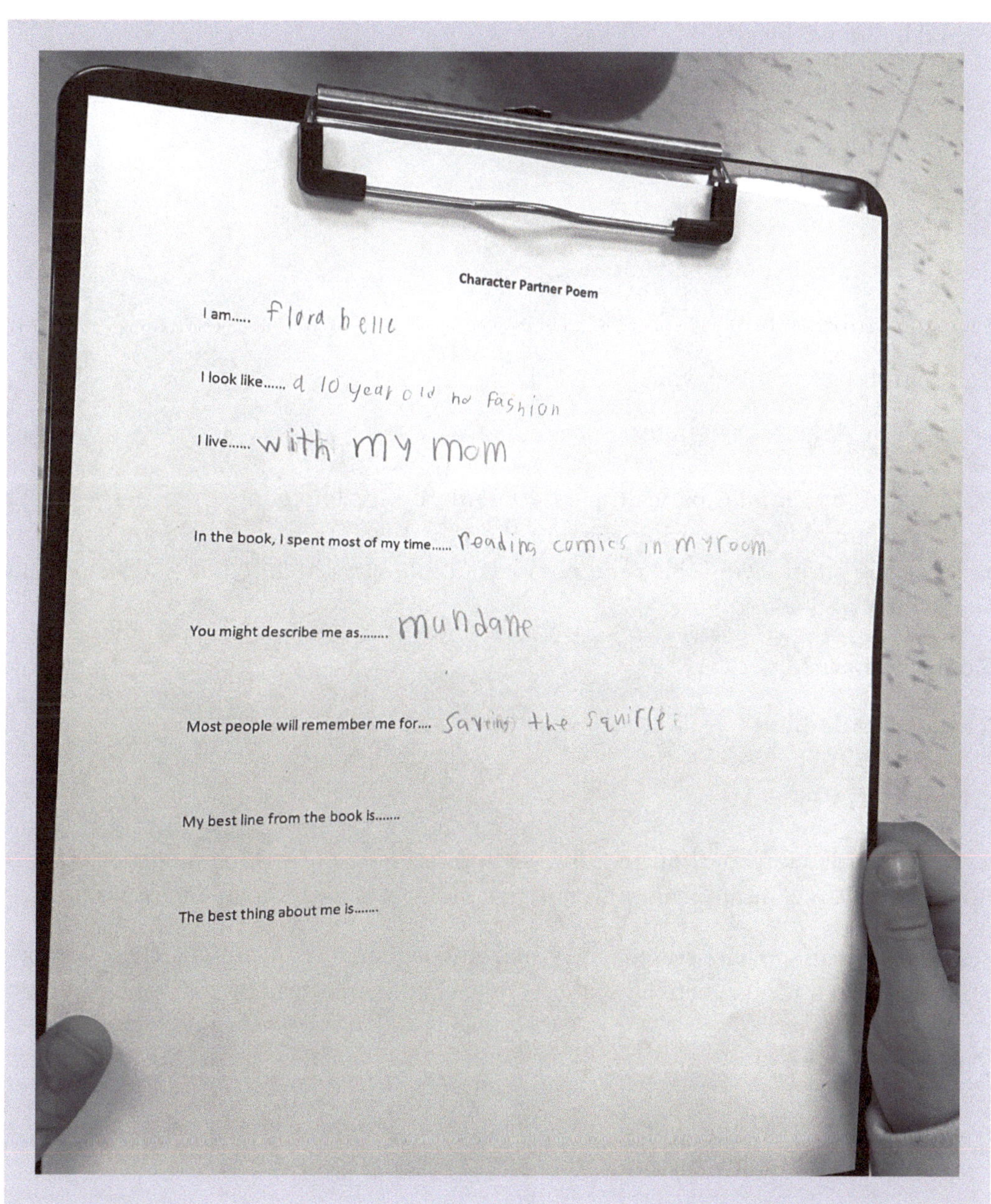

Character Partner Poem

I am..... flora belle

I look like...... a 10 year old no fashion

I live...... with my mom

In the book, I spent most of my time...... reading comics in my room

You might describe me as........ mundane

Most people will remember me for.... saving the squirle

My best line from the book is.......

The best thing about me is.......

Photo by Shelly Tanner

SAY IT AGAIN

Being from the South, I am used to people having all kinds of ways and expressions to say something, myself included. In fact, sometimes it's how we say something that has more impact than what we say. Plus, it's the *how* that helps develop an author's voice, but also that of the characters in works of literature. Our use of phrases, punctuation, and word choice all contribute to an author's voice. Take these examples that mean the same thing:

I'll be home directly.

I'll be home in just a bit.

I'll be there in three shakes of a lamb's tail.

Or

I'm running behind this morning.

I'm coming in hot.

I'm rolling in on two wheels.

I got held up this morning.

Each of these examples basically says the same thing. The content or message isn't really changing, but rather the voice or the way it is said is. In this lesson, students practice the art of saying the same phrase multiple ways in an effort to develop and refine their own voice.

Focus Genre: Narrative

Target Grade Level: K–5

Standards

Employ a wide range of strategies to write and use different writing process elements appropriately to communicate with different audiences for a variety of purposes.

Adjust the use of spoken, written, and visual language (e.g., conventions, style, vocabulary) to communicate effectively with a variety of audiences and for different purposes.

Anchor Texts

This Is How We Do It: One Day in the Lives of Seven Kids From Around the World by Matt Lamothe

See You Later, Alligator by Sally Hopgood

More Than Words: So Many Ways to Say What We Mean by Roz MacLean

My Teacher Likes to Say by Denise Brennan Nelson

Parts by Tedd Arnold

Materials

- Chart paper
- Notecards
- Paint strips
- Sticky notes

Teach It

1. Display a common statement such as, I'm hungry, I am tired, I am excited, or other similar phrases or statements.
2. Discuss the different ways that the phrase can be stated.
3. Make sure that items such as word tiers and levels (the formal or informal/slang tone or use), audience, and person speaking are discussed.
4. Divide the class into pairs or groups. Have each group draft a new way to say the statement. Have students record these ideas on sticky notes or notecards.
5. Have students share their ideas with the class.
6. As a class, determine the three best ways to revise the target statement.

1. I am exhausted to the point I can't even get out of my bed.

2. It feels like all my energy drained out.

3. I'm having a difficult time keeping my eyes open.

Try It

- Use this when introducing or reinforcing dialogue.
- Try this as a way for students to practice constructing dialogue.
- Use this when you want students to practice revising dialogue to make the writing more authentic.
- Use this as a way for students to explicitly see that there are multiple ways to say a phrase.

Extensions

- Have students take their dialogue options and draft character descriptions for the character who might say them. This works especially well with primary students because you can use existing characters from familiar books like fairy tales.
- Continue the engagement by formally punctuating and inserting the dialogue into a written composition.
- Match a character from a literary work to the dialogue that sounds like that character.

Modifications

Emerging Writers

- Provide students with some familiar phrases that they use on a daily basis. Have students give different ways to say those phrases.
- Write different ways to say several phrases on notecards and distribute them to students. Have students circulate the room until they find their match(es).
- Use lines from familiar children's books for students to rewrite.

Proficient Writers

- Instead of using a printed statement, use a video clip of dialogue instead.
- Use clips from a movie that has been remade and compare the differences between the actor's dialogue.
- Take lines from famous speeches and have students complete the same activity.
- Provide students with the modified statements ahead of time and have students choose which statement is best.
- Provide students with a character sketch of the person who might be saying the dialogue. Have them use this information to help them determine what would sound like their assigned character.

- Use paint strips to create a list of possibilities. Draft a sample sentence that you want students to address in the top block of a paint strip. Place the paint strips on the floor in a pile or on a table and have students pick up a paint strip and record one way to say the phrase in the next box. Put that paint strip back and choose another. Have students continue until all the paint strips are full of options for saying a particular phrase. Post these in the classroom for dialogue ideas in the future.

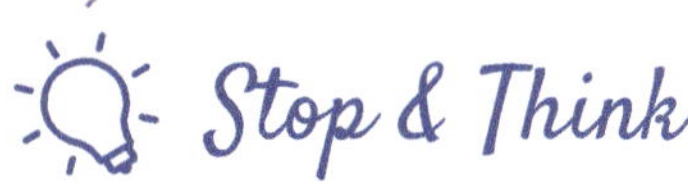

> **Stop & Think**
>
> This is a similar activity to the Yesterday I Had the . . . paint strip lesson (p. 240).

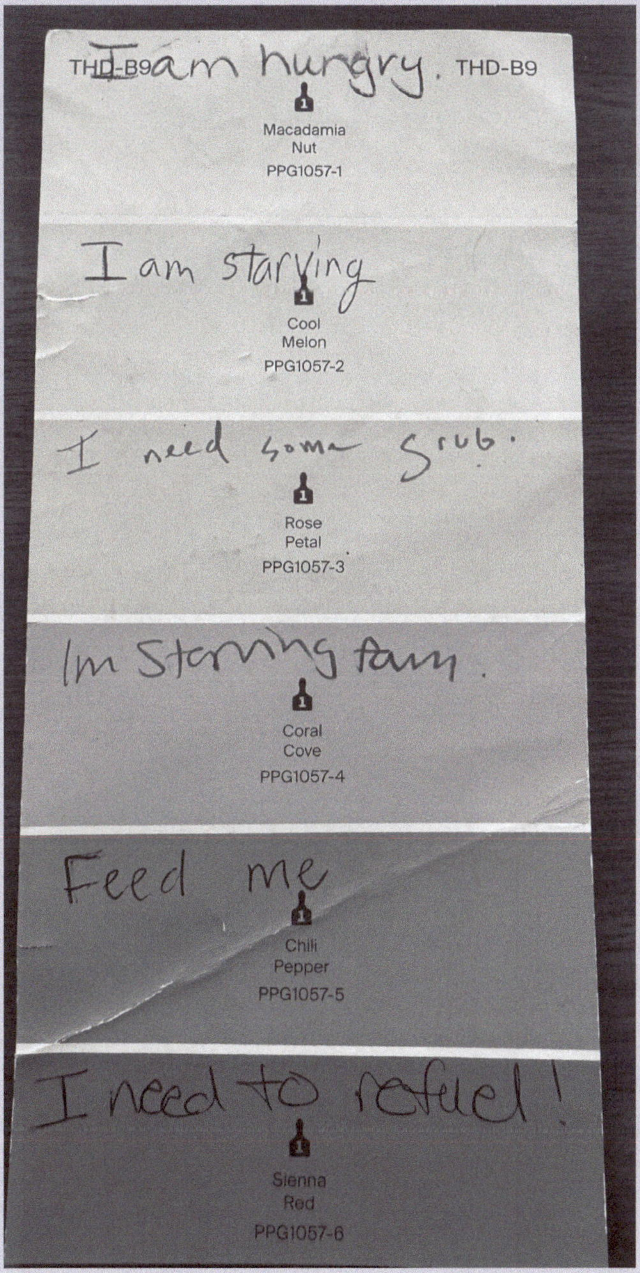

CHAPTER 1 In the Beginning, We Write
CHAPTER 2 Breaking Into Story
CHAPTER 3 Tell Me More
CHAPTER 4 Learning Through Writing
CHAPTER 5 Finding Your Voice
CHAPTER 6 The Art of Persuasion
CHAPTER 7 The Measure of Success

See It Sample

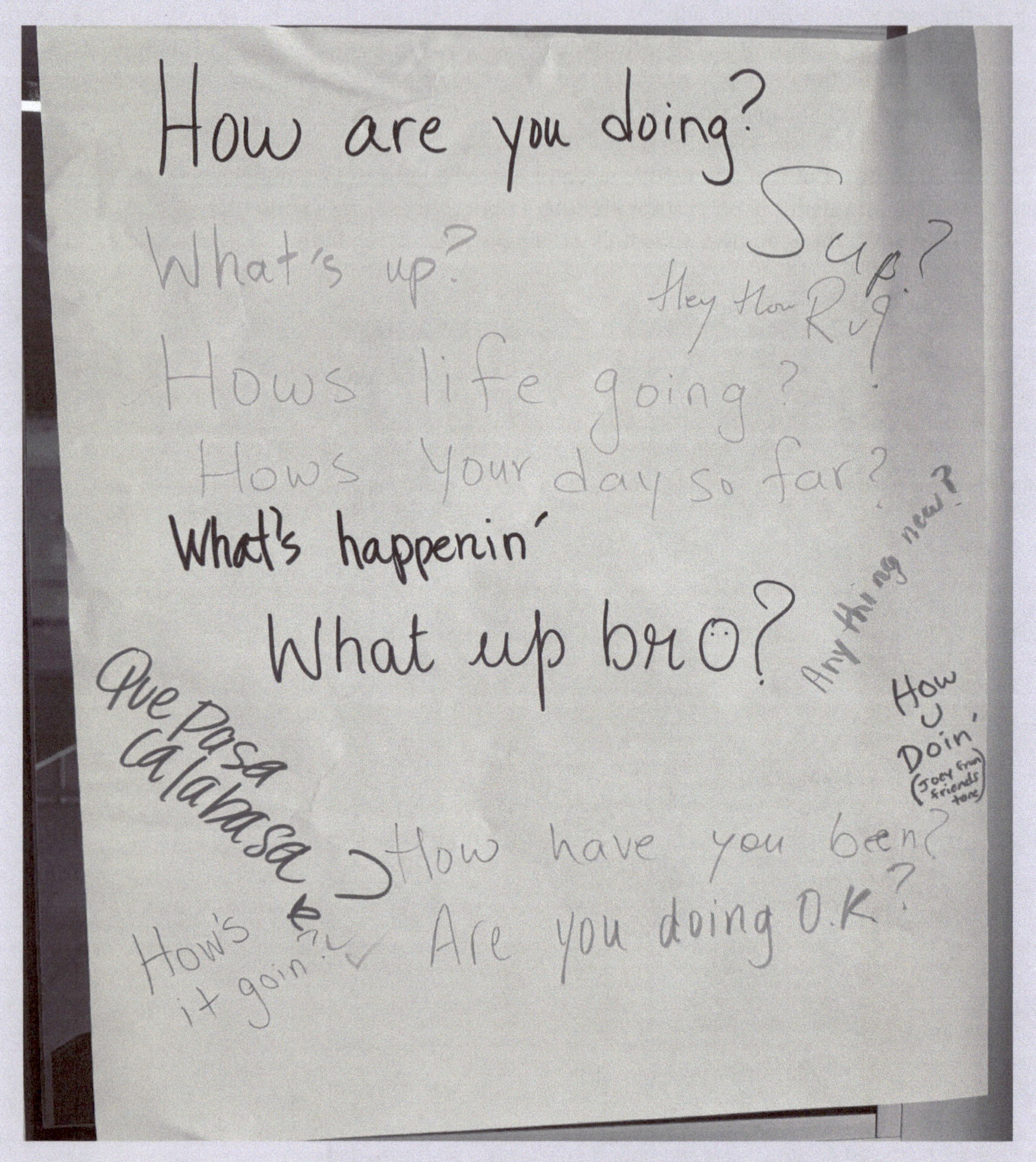

WHAT'S IN A NAME?

In this lesson, students explore the genre of personal narrative by writing about their names. Using the anchor texts as a springboard, students create a three-part composition using the Name Writing Organizer (p. 259, p. 260, or p. 261) as a guide. The organizer is divided into three components for a first, middle, and last name and can be modified as needed. For example, students might want to omit their middle name and include a nickname instead.

Since students are writing about their names, this is a prime opportunity for them to start off with a writing task that capitalizes on something they know a lot about: themselves! Plus, this is a great icebreaker writing that allows them to get to know their classmates in a low stakes engagement. While the focus genre is personal narrative, this lesson is the perfect fit for incorporating elements of voice since word choice, expression, phrasing, and point of view are all part of voice.

Focus Genre: Personal Narrative

Target Grade Level: K–5

Standards

Write narratives to develop real or imagined experiences or events using effective techniques, well-chosen details, and well-structured event sequences.

Anchor Texts

Mommy Doesn't Know My Name by Suzanne Williams

The Name Jar by Yangsook Choi

Quinnie Blue by Dinah Johnson

Your Name Is a Song by Jamilah Thompkins-Bigelow

My Name Is Not Alexander: Just How Big Can a Little Kid Dream? by Jennifer Fosberry

My Name Is Not Isabella: Just How Big Can a Little Girl Dream? by Jennifer Fosberry

My Name Is Maria Isabel by Alma Flor Ada

My Name Is Yoon by Helen Recorvits

You Stole My Name by Dennis McGregor

Namedrop is a great resource that can be used for students who have unique names that might get mispronounced.

Namedrop allows individuals to record their names and create a unique link to the sound recording. Check it out here: https://namedrop.io/

Alma and How She Got Her Name by Juana Martinez-Neal

"My Name" From *The House on Mango Street* by Sandra Cisneros

The Change Your Name Store by Leanne Shirtliffe

My Name Is Elizabeth by Annika Dunklee

Materials

- Blank notecards (lined or unlined depending on the needs of the class)
- Stapler
- Name Writing Organizer (p. 259, p. 260, or p. 261)

Teach It

1. Read aloud one of the anchor texts listed above. Before you begin reading, set the purpose for reading and listening. Remind students to listen for specific items including, but not limited to interesting details about the character's name, stories that are connected to the names, how the character describes his/her name, etc.
2. Show students the Name Writing Organizer (p. 259, p. 260, or p. 261) and model how to brainstorm information about your own name. Brainstorm details that might be included for each section of the graphic organizer. Consider items like nicknames, who you were named after, the meaning of your name, famous people who have the same name, etc.
3. Distribute a copy of the Name Writing Organizer to each student and have them complete the graphic organizer with information about their names.
4. Once students have filled out the graphic organizer, have them tear it into three sections. (This helps remind students of the separation and organization of information.)
5. Model for students how to transfer the writing on the organizer into complete sentences. (Make sure to do this part or you might end up with their short-hand notes copied onto their notecards.)
6. Provide students with three blank notecards. Have them use one notecard to write their information about their first names, one notecard for the information about their middle names, and one notecard for the information about their last names. (Remember, some students will have multiple names, no middle name, or hyphenated last names. Provide them with a notecard for each component of their name.)
7. Staple the three notecards together in a vertical line.

Try It

- Use this as a way to incorporate a lesson about personal narratives on any topic as a warmup for writing in that genre.
- Use this as a way to get to know your students by starting off with this writing early in the year.
- Use this as an opening writing for new students who enter the class throughout the year.
- Try this to encourage English learners to write about their names in their home languages.

Extensions

- Have students complete a Name Writing Organizer on a historical figure, character from a novel, or author in order to add a research component to this task.
- Use this strategy as a unique way to research the names of historical landmarks or other geographic locations.
- Begin a unit on biographies or autobiographies by using Name Writing as a springboard into the extended writing.
- Create a family writing opportunity by sending home blank copies of the Name Writing Organizer for students' family members to complete.
- Encourage students to choose a new pen name that they use when writing. This can be their chance to choose the name they always wanted.

Modifications

Emerging Writers

- Have students use paint strips to compare their names to their classmates'.
- Build up to the culminating product by having students start with their first names and later move on to the other components.
- Have them write one sentence about their names per notecard and staple these together for a three-sentence composition.

Proficient Writers

- Have students write a full paragraph for each part of their name so when stapled together, they have a three-paragraph composition.
- Apply specific transitional phrases between each section to improve the flow of the finished product.

See It Sample

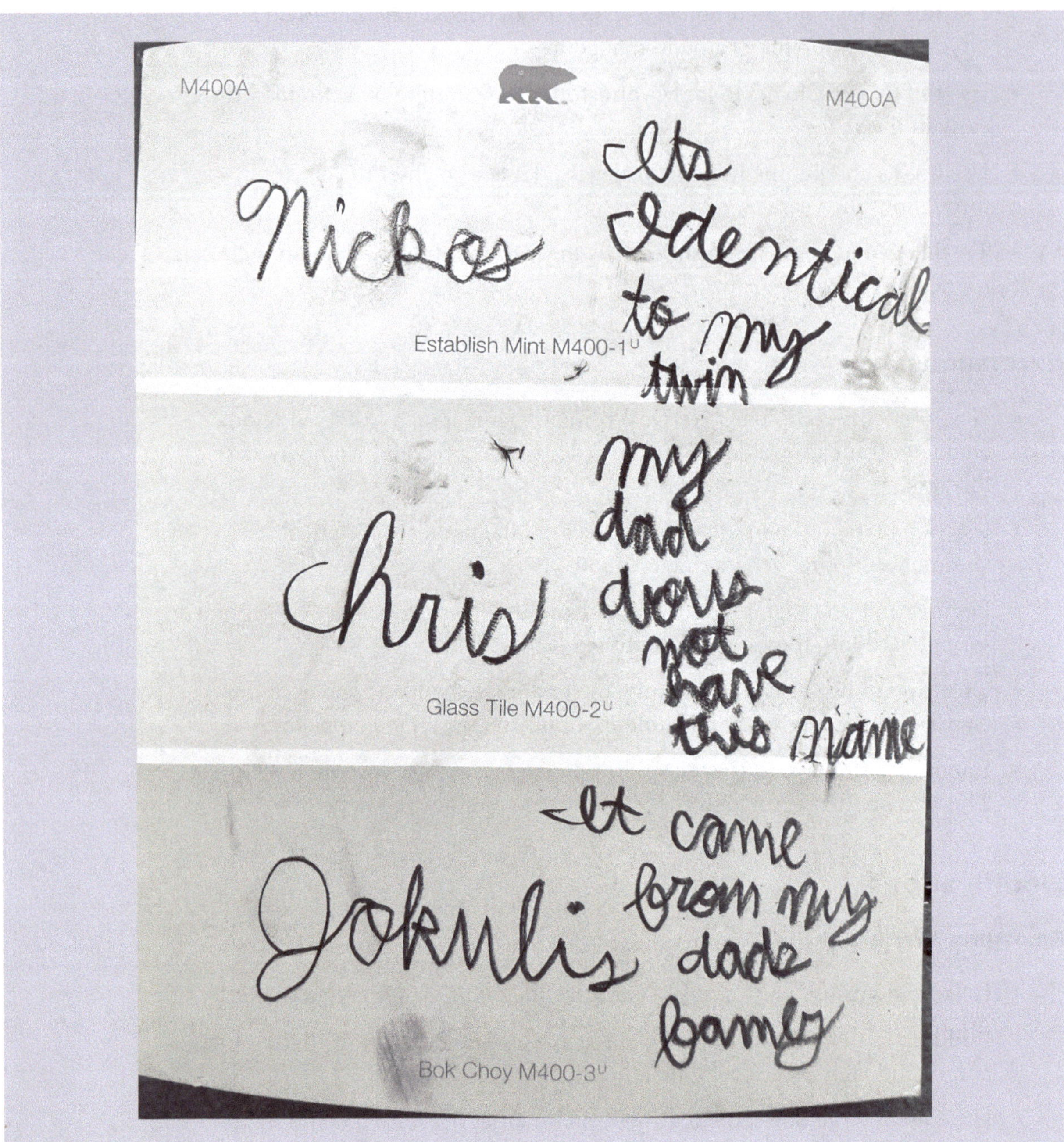

Photo by Nickolas Jokulis and Mickolan Jakulis

Chapter 6

THE ART OF PERSUASION

While we live our lives in story, we also spend a good deal of our lives persuading people for a number of purposes. In fact, one might argue that the persuasive genre, and later the one of argument, are a close second to narrative. Just as we use story to document and make sense of our world experiences, we use the skill of persuasion often as a means for advocacy and the development and enactment of individual and, in many cases, collective agency. We might persuade someone to take our side, get us a present, buy a product, or form a specific opinion on a topic. In our careers, we may write cover letters for jobs we want to obtain, emails to our supervisors with requests for salary increases or leadership opportunities, argue for the best textbook program for the school district, or speak at a faculty meeting or public forum on behalf of students or colleagues. All of those examples are firmly grounded in the persuasive genre. If you think about the conversations you have on a daily basis, I bet you would see that many of them involve some type of persuasive component. Even our work-related interactions are often centered in the art of persuasion. Just in the past week I have

- Received solicitations from credit card merchants enticing me to upgrade or change my current card
- Been asked by administration to provide reasoning for delivering a specific degree program in a face-to-face format
- Reviewed a book on Amazon for a novelist friend regarding his latest book
- Engaged in conversations with my son regarding why he should be able to continue to watch YouTube videos
- Explained to a colleague all the benefits of participation in a National Writing Project Summer Institute and why she should attend

- Wrote a letter of recommendation for a principal encouraging a district to hire him for a position
- Drafted emails to literacy organizations requesting that I be considered as a speaker at their events

In those few examples, notice how many of them, though they might not focus solely on the persuasive genre, include numerous components and features that are informed by or influenced by the persuasive genre. While there are certainly specific features and subtle nuances that are exclusive to persuasive writing, much like other genres, you will often find that there are crossover components.

Mastering this genre is especially important as students get older. Many standard sets in middle grades and high school make an abrupt shift to informational and argument writing. Without a solid understanding and grasp of persuasive writing, mastering the genre of argument may be difficult. In fact, I often use persuasive writing as a springboard into argument writing since much of what is required in arguments is inspired by components of persuasive writing.

Like other types of writing, students will write better compositions when they are asked to write about something they know. When beginning to practice persuasive writing, it is important for students to have an opportunity to begin writing about topics that are familiar to them or are ones they enjoy. Instead of creating prompts and topics that are disconnected from students; daily lives, look for ways to incorporate their interests into this genre as well. When I taught middle school, I often listened to my students' conversations to determine what issues were concerning to them. In most instances, when we tackled the persuasive genre, I asked students for suggestions and topics. This helped me ensure that for the most part, we were writing about topics in which they were vested. For example, in my district, there was no conversation from upper administration about the implementation of school uniforms. Had I chosen the prompt suggested in our curriculum materials centered on school uniforms, there would have been limited relevance since the students knew this was not on the table for discussion. However, the subject of dress code was always a hot topic, so many students chose to write about this because it was relevant. As a result, students wrote better compositions because the topic connected to their personal and academic lives.

While elementary students may be less concerned with the dress code than my middle grade students were, you can bet there are a number of topics that K–5 students are very interested in writing about. In a recent visit to an elementary school, I asked students for some suggestions on what we might write about when we began a persuasive writing activity. Their suggestions were not only authentic, but many of them were downright hilarious.

- We should get more recess time.
- We want to use the parachute in PE every week.
- Could we ask for a class monkey for a pet?

- Could we ask Ms. Bryan to let us play with the instruments in music instead of her hogging them?
- I need to learn how to get a girl to be my girlfriend. Could I persuade the girls in my class?
- My mom won't let me get Snapchat. I'll write and tell her why I need it.

Each of these suggestions could be used when teaching the persuasive genre. Plus, despite the fact that each of those topics is different, some of the same tools and techniques would be used regardless of the topic.

Like other genres and writing ideas, much of what I have included in this chapter has been inspired in some way by a real-life event, text, or scenario. You'll find that the real world is often ripe with writing inspiration. While the world we live in offers endless potential for writing, quality children's literature or elementary novels are excellent sources of inspiration for the persuasive genre. For example, Wendy Vanderlyn's *Flipped* is an excellent book for teaching perspective and point of view. It also is fantastic for persuasive writing since each character, through the telling of their own story, attempts to convince the reader or their position or accounting of events. For example, the book begins with each character's recollection and interpretation of their first meeting when Bryce moves in across the street from Juli. Her version of their first meeting? Love at first sight. His version? Just an annoying girl who unfortunately is also his neighbor. Each chapter follows their experiences and interactions through their individual voices and they could not be more different! Similarly, Judy Blume's *The Pain and the Great One* works well for perspective and point of view also, but has persuasive components. In Drew Daywalt's *The Day the Crayons Quit*, you can't read the letters from Gray, Pink, and Peach crayon and tell me they don't drip with persuasion along with the craft of voice. Those are just a few of the mentor texts that could be used when teaching persuasive writing. Yet don't stop there. Commercials, billboards, video clips, images and more are excellent examples of persuasive writing in the real world. Plus, when you draw attention to these types of real-world examples, it not only shows students relevant instances, but also extends the classroom learning beyond the four walls of your room. Nothing makes me more excited than a student who shows up on a Monday and tells me about a billboard they saw on I-20 that reminded them of our writing lesson!

POST-IT® PERSUASION

Focus Genre: Persuasive Writing

Part of persuasive writing includes the ability to articulate reasons and support for an opinion or position. Not only must these reasons be relevant to the topic, but they also must be well organized so that the reader can follow the thought process and reasoning. Using sticky notes can help students accumulate their support by starting with a list and then grouping and organizing the sticky notes so that the composition flows well. Due to the structure of this strategy, it is easily modified for a variety of learners and content areas.

> **Quick Tip!**
>
> This strategy also works well with narrative and informational writing.

Target Grade Level: K–5

Standards

Develop a composition with a beginning, middle, and end.

Determine the distinction between fact and opinion.

Write persuasive compositions with supporting evidence to convey a position or opinion.

Anchor Texts

Can I Be Your Dog? by Troy Cummings

I Wanna Iguana by Karen Kaufman Orloff

I Wanna Go Home by Karen Kaufman Orloff

I Wanna New Room by Karen Kaufman Orloff

Earrings by Judith Viorst

The Perfect Pet by Margie Palatini

I Will Never Not Ever Eat a Tomato by Lauren Child

Dear Mrs. LaRue: Letters From Obedience School by Mark Teague

Materials

- Sticky notes (variety of different colors)

Teach It

1. Begin by reading one of the titles on the anchor text list.

2. Discuss the book with the class. Make notations of tactics for persuasion or argument the author uses or any specific characteristics they noticed about the read aloud.

I typically start with *I Wanna Iguana* for Grades K–3 and use a book like *The Perfect Pet* or *Dear Mrs. LaRue: Letters from Obedience School* for upper grades.

3. Have students brainstorm something they might like to ask for. This could be a pet, electronic device, bigger room, etc. Model an example for the class. To do this, share with students something you might want. For example, "Boys and girls, have you noticed that our reading rug isn't quite big enough for all our friends to sit on? That is what I am going to write about in my persuasive paper. I am going to ask for a new reading rug."

4. Distribute a sticky note to each student and have them write down what they plan to write about.

5. Once they have made their decision on their topic, have them determine who their audience is. Refer back to the sample you modeled for the class and share who that audience might be. In the example above, I might say, "Now, since I am writing about a new reading rug, who do you think my audience should be? Who would be responsible for giving me a new rug? I think I should use the principal as my audience since they have money to buy classroom supplies." You might even have students record this on a separate sticky note in a different color as a reminder of whom they are writing to.

This is very important because many students tend to write for one audience: the informal one. Or, have you ever noticed that many students seem to write their papers as thought their teacher is the intended audience?

6. Once students have chosen their topic, refer back to the example you shared with the class.

7. Model for students how to draft reasons that support their topic. For example, if a student is asking for a new pet, a sample reason why they should get it might be that they received good grades this month or because they are responsible.

8. Distribute three new sticky notes to each student. Have them record one reason per sticky note that explains why they should receive their ask.

Using sticky notes makes revision so much easier. If you find that students have duplicated information or have irrelevant information, you can simply get rid of them and add new ones. Or if information is not organized clearly, you can easily pick up the sticky notes and move them around.

You may want to provide students with a list of sentence starters to make this process more time efficient or to support English learners.

9. Once students have listed their reasons, you may need to do a quick mini lesson on sentence construction. This is especially important if they wrote down just a word on their sticky note. For example, if they wrote "good grades" on a sticky note, model for the class how you would rewrite that so that it says something like, "I should get a new pet hamster because I get good grades in school."

10. After students have revised their sticky notes into complete sentences, model how to write a generic opening sentence and a generic conclusion sentence, for example, "Hamsters are excellent pets for kids and there are many reasons why I should have one," and "In conclusion, there are many reasons why I should receive a hamster as a pet."

11. Once students have written all their sentences, have them arrange the sticky notes in the correct order so that it reads like a full paragraph.

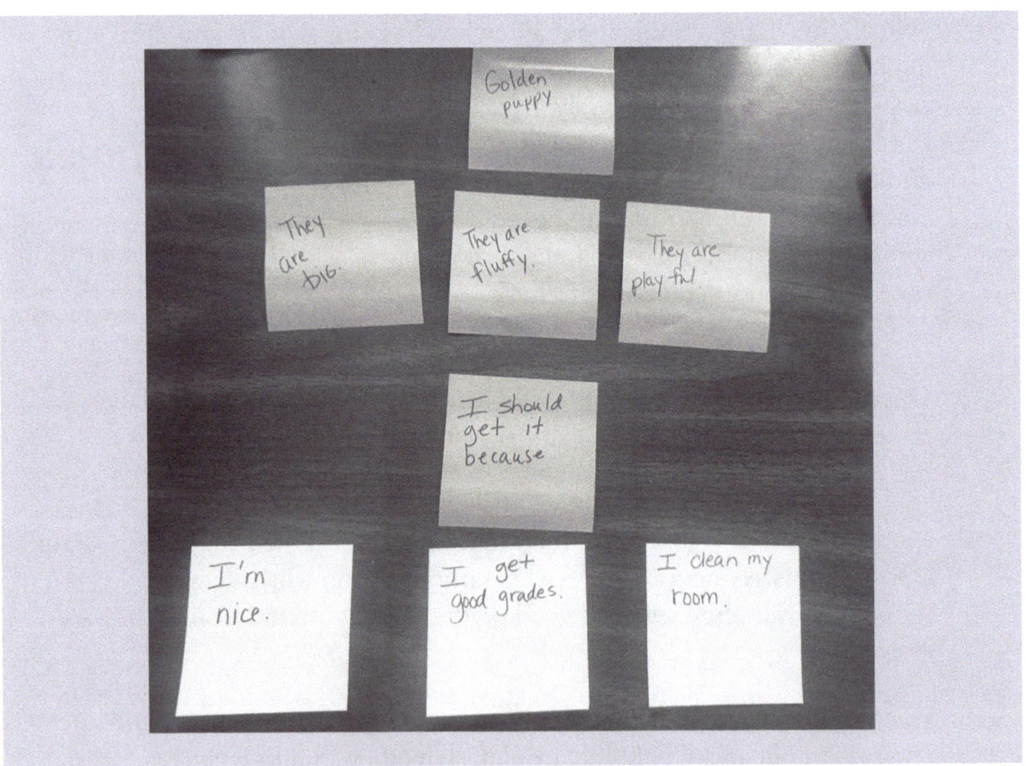

12. Have students share their completed work with the class or a partner.

> **Quick Tip!**
>
> You could have students copy their sticky notes onto regular paper to create a completed paragraph. Or you could have them affix the sticky notes on a sheet of paper and then slide it into a plastic sleeve.

Try It

- Use this when you want students to practice writing in the persuasive genre while also focusing on organizational skills and tactics.
- Try this as a way to get students to expand their writings in an engaging and low-stakes manner.
- Use this as another way to demonstrate and practice revision. This is similar to a traditional graphic organizer, but because it's written on sticky notes, it makes the task much easier because students can move sentences around.
- Use this as a low-stakes and engaging way to get students to write multisentence and paragraph compositions.

Extensions

- Try sticky note paragraphs in other genres. For example, use it when teaching compare contrast lessons and color code the sticky notes based on the topic.
- Have students write a sticky note response to the original writing and determine if the reasons provided in the original writing were convincing.
- Have students extend this from a one-paragraph writing to a multiparagraph composition by having them extend each section with elaborative evidence or other examples that can be used to develop more descriptive and thorough compositions.

Modifications

Emerging Writers

- Have students work together with a partner to create a collaborative writing composition.
- Instead of creating an entire paragraph, have students use sticky notes to construct one sentence. Modify this activity by having students write one word on each sticky note and draft a complete sentence.

Proficient Writers

- Begin introducing the genre of argument by having students include a counterclaim on one of their sticky notes and then respond to it.

CHAPTER 1 In the Beginning, We Write
CHAPTER 2 Breaking Into Story
CHAPTER 3 Tell Me More
CHAPTER 4 Learning Through Writing
CHAPTER 5 Finding Your Voice
CHAPTER 6 The Art of Persuasion
CHAPTER 7 The Measure of Success

- Have students continue expanding on this writing by integrating transition sentences and phrases as they move from paragraph to paragraph.
- Complete this task by extending it to a multi paragraph composition.

See It Sample

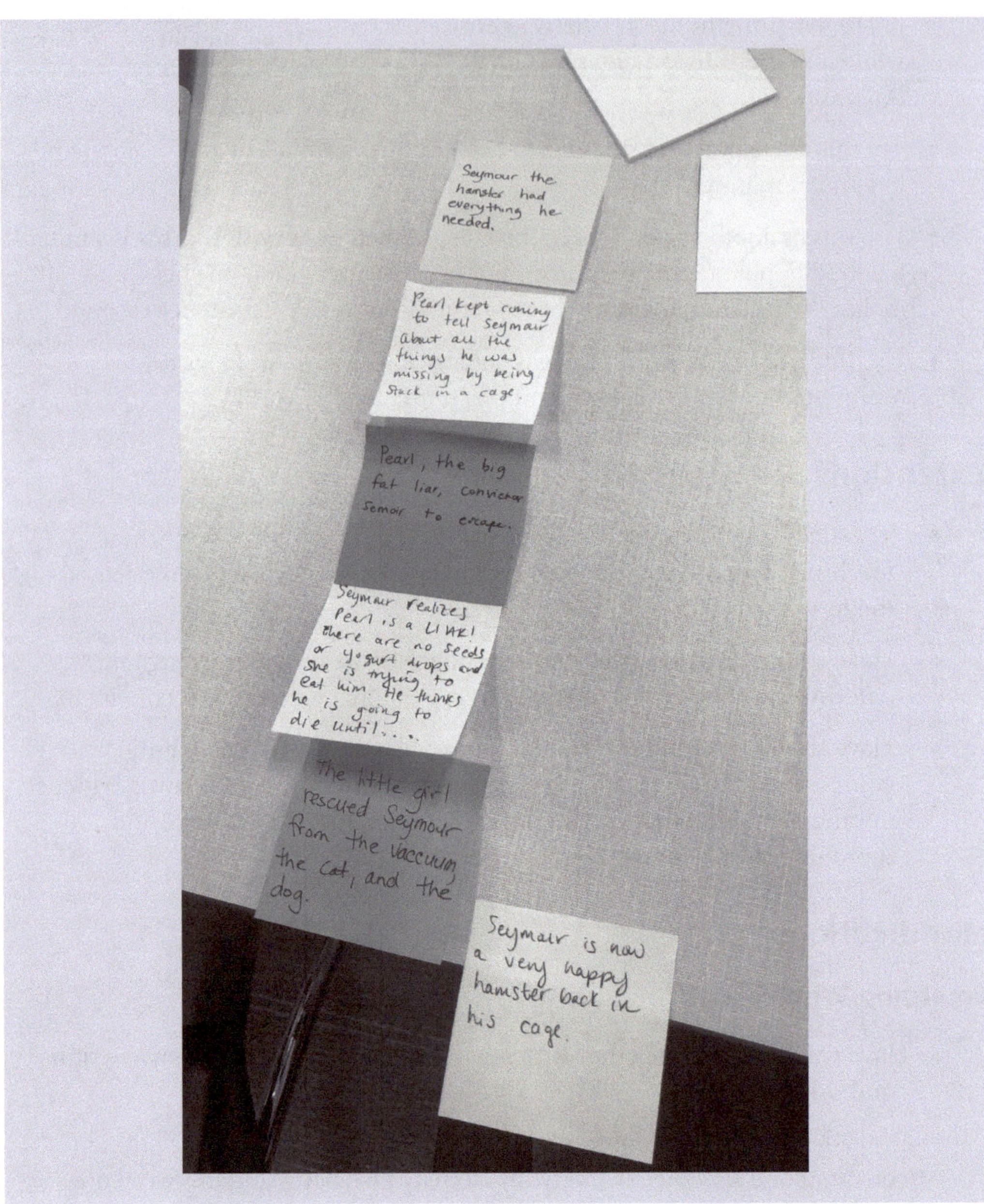

Photo by Alfred Cain

CHAPTER 1 In the Beginning, We Write
CHAPTER 2 Breaking Into Story
CHAPTER 3 Tell Me More
CHAPTER 4 Learning Through Writing
CHAPTER 5 Finding Your Voice
CHAPTER 6 The Art of Persuasion
CHAPTER 7 The Measure of Success

CAST THE CHARACTER

When students read, drawing attention to the mental images and visualization that should occur is key to comprehension and understanding. This is especially important as students advance through elementary school as books shift from a heavy reliance on images to more alphanumeric text. In fact, when done well, students should visualize a running movie or image in their heads about what is happening in the material. One of the best ways to have students focus on visualization *and* use textual evidence is through this strategy, Cast the Character.

Focus Genre: Persuasive/Narrative

Target Grade Level: 3–5

Standards

Apply a wide range of strategies to comprehend, interpret, evaluate, and appreciate texts. Draw on prior experience, interactions with other readers and writers, knowledge of word meaning and of other texts, word identification strategies, and understanding of textual features (e.g., sound–letter correspondence, sentence structure, context, graphics).

Anchor Texts

There are many anchor texts that would work with this lesson, but I have included some of my favorites.

Three Times Lucky by Shelia Turnage

A *Snicker of Magic* by Natalie Lloyd

A *Handful of Stars* by Cynthia Lord

Isaiah Dunn Is My Hero by Kelly J. Baptist

War Stories by Gordon Korman

Pay Attention Carter Jones by Gary Schmidt

Stay by Bobbie Pyron

Materials

- Chart paper
- Sticky notes
- Notecards

Quick Tip!

If you prefer, you can use a picture book for this lesson, but you need to read it aloud without showing students the pictures.

Stop & Think

You do not have to locate images of famous actors. In fact, I often use stock images online or images from my friends and family as casting options. Cole Sprouse may not be available for your classroom novel movie, so you may need a backup!

Teach It

1. Choose a main character from an extended work, preferably a novel. Make sure the students have completed reading the entire work before you start this activity.
2. Based on the textual evidence provided in the text, before the lesson begins, locate images of individuals online who might be possibilities of visual representations of the character. For example, if your novel includes a male character who is a teenager, you might locate multiple images of male teenagers that might look like your character. If there is additional textual evidence in the novel such as height, race, hair color, physical build, etc., include those considerations when you decide which images to include. You can refer to these images as "casting options."
3. Arrange the selected character images into a slide presentation program, such as PowerPoint or Google Slides, starting with a slide that includes the character's name. You will use this slide presentation later in the lesson.
4. Have students brainstorm or recall information about each character in the selected text or novel to activate prior knowledge. Record these on the board or have students record them on a sheet of paper.
5. Show students the first character image from your slide deck. Have them locate textual evidence that supports the character's picture from the novel. You can have students record these on sticky notes and add to their sheets of paper or you can type them on the slide.
6. Display each slide and each character's image, repeating Step 5.

7. Once this is complete, assign each casting option to a small group of students. Using the textual evidence provided, have them draft a persuasive composition in support of their casting option.
8. Have students share their completed work with the class.

Try It

- Use this as a way for students to revisit characters at the end of a novel.
- Try this when you want students to discuss how they visualize what characters look.
- Use this as a way to merge textual evidence with character and visualization lessons.
- Try this when you want students to work on a persuasive engagement that utilizes the inclusion of textual evidence.

Extensions

- Have students visualize multiple parts of the novel including the characters, setting, and specific events.
- Ask students to complete a version of a memory map from *Writing Workouts* (Harper, 2023) where they draw what they remember from a specific part of the story.
- Have students research what materials are included in an actual casting call and draft their persuasive composition in that format.
- Do this with the setting of a novel or a specific event that occurred (e.g., You could focus on the main character's car, referred to as "Pickled Jalapeño" because of its green color in the novel *A Snicker of Magic*).

Modifications

Emerging Writers

- Instead of posting the images on a digital program, post each image on a large sheet of chart paper and have students do a gallery walk with a partner to record supporting evidence on the poster.
- Have students draw a picture of what they think the character might look like instead of using stock photos.
- Try this activity using the picture book *The Gruffalo* by Julia Donaldson so students can practice using textual evidence with images.

Proficient Writers

- Have students develop their compositions into an oral presentation, such as a commercial, and have them present to the class.

- Divide students into groups and have them create visual representations of all the story elements.
- Take a popular novel that has already been developed into a movie. Have students attack or defend the casting.
- Have students locate possible images for the lesson instead of the teacher providing them.

See It Sample

Cast the Character: Miss Lana

- I would cast Marilyn Monroe as Miss Lana. She is beautiful and glamorous.

- Textual Evidence from Three Times Lucky
- Wears wigs
- Dresses in costume
- Is glamorous
- Loving and compassionate
- Looks likes a movie star
- Is a good cook
- Hard worker

DO THIS! NOT THAT!

The idea for this lesson started with a cricket and a cookbook. I had just finished teaching a unit on informational texts and used an article I found in a science magazine on harvesting crickets for consumption (they are high in protein). The students in the class were particularly interested in the cricket section because of its text features and layout. It included a nutrition table, an image that was to scale of a cricket, and a brief how-to passage that explained steps for growing your own crickets. That same evening, I was reading *Eat This, Not That* and *Cook This, Not That* by David Zincsenko and Matt Goulding which highlights healthier substitutions for popular meals. While reading, I noticed that the layout of the cookbook and the cricket text from my lesson had some of the same text features. In fact, they included how-to sections, nutritional information, and images all on one page. Using both of those texts as a guide, my students created their own writings that merged both persuasion and informational into one genre. That coupled with the brief and succinct nature of the composition made for a successful writing lesson.

Focus Genre: Persuasive/Informational

Target Grade Level: 3–5

Standards

Develop a topic with facts, definitions, or details.

Apply a wide range of strategies to comprehend, interpret, evaluate, and appreciate texts.

Write informative texts to examine a topic and coney ideas and information.

Write persuasive compositions with supporting evidence to convey a position or opinion.

Anchor Texts

Eat This, Not That by David Zinczenko and Matt Goulding

Cook This, Not That by David Zinczenko and Matt Goulding

The Boy Who Harnessed the Wind: Picture Book Edition by William Kamkwamba and Bryan Mealer

Jayden's Impossible Garden by Melina Mangal

Harlem Grown: How One Big Idea Transformed a Neighborhood by Tony Hillery

The Mess That We Made by Michelle Lord

We Are Water Protectors by Carole Lindstrom

One Plastic Bag: Isatou Ceesay and the Recycling Women of Gambia by Miranda Paul

Materials

- Notecards
- Sticky notes
- Do This! Not That! template (p. 262)

Teach It

1. Begin by talking to students about some activities or hobbies they might enjoy. These could include sports, video gaming, reading, etc.
2. Share with the class something that you enjoy doing, a book or movie you like, or another related idea.
3. Start off by saying, "I'd rather ________ than ________." It is likely that students will naturally ask you why, but if they do not, volunteer your reasoning. Make a list of reasons why you enjoy one activity over the other.
4. Show students a sample page from the cookbooks listed in the anchor text list.
5. Ask students to write down anything they notice about the sample on a sticky note.
6. Discuss their noticings as a class.
7. Explain to students that they are going to write about a topic of their own choosing in the same format as the mentor texts.
8. Begin by drawing a picture or locating an image that connects to the topic. (Remember that cricket example from earlier? Having an image or figure that is related to your topic adds another helpful text feature.)
9. Using the mentor text as an example and the list of reasons you provided for your sentence in Step 3, start drafting your writing. Use the Do This! Not That! template (p. 262) for reference, if needed.
10. Have students brainstorm their own topic. Then have them make a list of their reasons connected to their chosen topic.
11. Distribute a notecard to each student.
12. Have students draw a picture that is related to their topic on the unlined side of the notecard.
13. Using the Do This! Not That! template or the teacher sample, provide students time to draft their own writings.

Try It

- Try this when you want students to merge the persuasive and informational genre into one writing.
- Use this as a way for students to include related images or drawings that connect to the topic.
- Try this when you want students to apply compare and contrast components in one writing activity.

Extensions

- Locate concepts or topics specific to your discipline that have two opposing sides or multiple views and have students conduct research on the two sides of the topic (e.g., In science, you can connect this to energy alternatives and environmental issues.)
- Use this activity as a potential hook for an extended writing on a related topic.
- Connect this to historical figures, approaches to math-related problems, for character comparisons, and more.

Modifications

Emerging Writers

- Instead of having students write complete sentences on their notecards, have them use bullets to include specific details about their topic.
- Use this as a review for class read alouds and have students complete their notecard on a book they'd like to read again. (Read this, not that!)
- Have students work with a partner to complete the activity.

Proficient Writers

- Instead of using a notecard, have students create a PowerPoint or Google slide for a digital version.
- Have students incorporate additional text features in their writings including text boxes, little known facts, diagrams, and captions.
- Compile the notecards into a class book on a specific overarching topic.

See It Sample

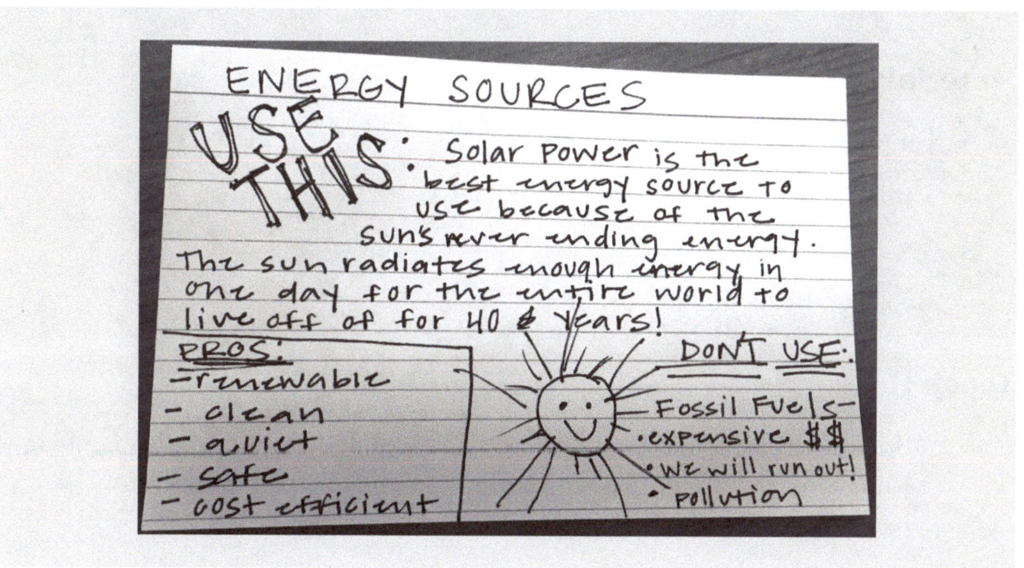

Photo by Alfred Cain

BOOK IN A BOX

Book reports are so yesterday, but they do offer opportunities to evaluate students' comprehension and practice the skill of summary. While traditional book reports have the tendency to be a little boring, a Book in a Box allows students to demonstrate mastery of the same standards and skills, but in a more creative manner. Plus, since some students might be nervous about speaking in front of their peers, much like the Story Bags, this strategy allows them to use physical objects, which can serve as reminders of key parts of a book and also provide them with a distraction that can help offset their nerves.

Focus Genre: Persuasive/Informational

Target Grade Level: K–5

Standards

Develop a composition with a beginning, middle, and end.

Write persuasive compositions with supporting evidence to convey a position or opinion.

Apply a wide range of strategies to comprehend, interpret, evaluate, and appreciate texts.

Anchor Texts

Any text works for this lesson. In fact, most often students will have their own individual anchor text, since this lesson is meant as a way to write and share their own personal reading interests.

Materials

- Empty shoe boxes
- Various physical objects based on the book
- 5 × 7 Notecards
- Book in a Box template (p. 263)

Teach It

1. Prior to teaching this lesson, choose a book that the entire class is familiar with. This might be a popular class read aloud or a novel the entire class has read.

2. Locate five objects that could be connected to the book and place them in a shoe box or similar size box. For example, if I utilized Sheila Turnage's book, *Three Times Lucky*, here are some items I might include. Each of these objects represents a key detail in the novel and could be used to retell the story.
    - Message in a bottle (The main character sends these to her missing mother.)
    - Wig (Miss Lana wears a different wig every day.)
    - Crime scene tape (Someone commits a crime in the novel.)
    - A lavender paint strip (Dale's brother's name is lavender.)
    - A menu (The café is the main setting of the story.)

A few days' prior to this lesson, you might ask students for suggestions of items that might be connected or related to this popular book. This can help get them thinking about objects that are connected to the story, but also help you as you create one for the class as a model.

3. Begin by telling the class that you have a great book you want to tell them about, but don't reveal the title of the book yet. Share the items with the class. As you show the students each item, explain how it is connected to the book.
4. Explain how each of the objects used helps you retell the story and create a summary about what had been read.
5. Tell students that for this activity, they are going to choose a book that they have read and create their own Book in a Box to share. Remind students that since the books they are using may not have been read by everyone, they are going to use this activity not just to summarize their story but also persuade others to read it.
6. Provide students with the Book in a Box template (p. 263).
7. Have students choose the book they want to use. Once they have selected their book, have them locate five items that are connected to their book.
8. Distribute a notecard to each student. Have them make a list of their objects along with a reason why each object was selected.
9. Have students close with three reasons why someone should read the book they are profiling.
10. Share with the class.

Try It

- Try this as a way to integrate oral presentations into your teaching.
- Use this as a more engaging way to assess students' reading comprehension and the skill of summary.
- Use this during assessment-heavy months, around holidays, or when students need a fun break from a traditional assessment.

Extensions

- Have students use their Books in a Box for the creation of a class curated exhibit hall of literature. Students display their objects and a brief written summary around the classroom for other students, parents or caregivers, or community members to view.
- Have students expand the bulleted list of examples and justifications into a fully involved paragraph or written composition.
- Extend this to other subject areas and incorporate the research genre as well for different concepts and units in other disciplines.

Modifications

Emerging Writers

- Reduce the number of objects required or have sample props that students might choose from when creating their own boxes.
- Have students work with a partner to create a collaborative product.
- Instead of using objects, have students draw pictures or use sample images for a Book Poster.

Proficient Writers

- Using only the objects, have students attempt to guess the genre or title simply based on the objects listed or displayed.
- Have students write an extended explanation of each chosen artifact or object.
- Use this activity as a springboard for a debate between students over which book should be read first.

See It Sample

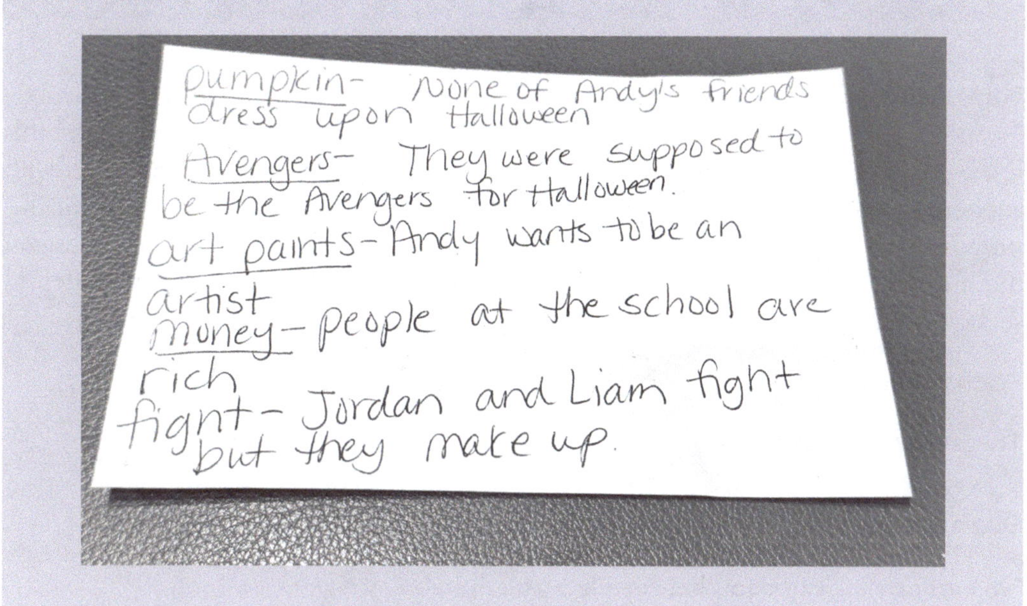

Source: Easel image from iStock.com/Liudmila Chernetska; jack-o-lantern image from iStock.com/nickylarson974; arguing image from iStock.com/mediaphotos; superhero image from iStock.com/Lana_Stem; money image from iStock.com/alfexe

PAINT STRIP PERSUASION

Formulating an opinion is only one part of persuasive writing. The next step involves locating and positioning details and evidence that support your position. In this lesson, we focus on formulating an opinion, but taking that opinion a step further with supporting evidence that supports your position. Paint strips work beautifully for this purpose because they make it easy to quantify how much evidence is needed based on the number of blocks on the strip. Students can also separate and organize different sections of their writings by color-coding the paint strips.

Focus Genre: Persuasive

Target Grade Level: K–5

Standards

Determine the distinction between fact and opinion.

Write persuasive compositions with supporting evidence to convey a position or opinion.

Anchor Texts

Don't Let the Pigeon Drive the Bus! by Mo Willems

Can I Have a Stegosaurus, Mom? Can I? by Lois G. Grambling

LaRue for Mayor: Letters From the Campaign Trail by Mark Teague

The True Story of the Three Little Pigs by Jon Scieszka

Can I Be Your Dog? by Troy Cummings

Give Bees a Chance by Bethany Barton

Don't Feed the Bear by Kathleen Doherty

The Big Bed by Bunmi Laditan

Escargot by Dashka Slater

Dr. Coo and the Pigeon Protest by Sarah Hampson

Materials

- Different colored paint strips in different configurations (three block, four block, etc.)
- Chart paper

Teach It

1. Begin by reading one of the mentor texts from the list.
2. As a recap of the reading, have students recall information from the text related directly to the opinion or position. Ask them to share what reasons or evidence they remember from the book that supports that opinion or position.
3. Create a practice opinion or related position. Make sure that you use something that the students are familiar with so that they can provide sample evidence.
4. Ask students to give reasons or evidence that support this opinion and record their ideas on chart paper.
5. Brainstorm with students some topics they might write about. These might include an argument for a new pet, extra recess, a video game, etc.
6. Explain to students that they will be writing about their own topic using paint strips to help them collect their reasons.
7. Have them begin by writing their opinion or position at the top of the paint strip.
8. Explain that the number of blocks in the paint strip is how many pieces of evidence or reasons they should provide.
9. Once students have completed their paint strips, have them share their opinions and reasons with the class.

Try It

- Try this when you want students to use a list format to collect reasons or evidence that supports their opinion.
- Use this when you want students to practice locating evidence as support for a position.
- Try this as a modification for the Post-It® Persuasion (p. 188).

Extensions

- Use this for research writing in other disciplines like science or social studies. Have students collect evidence from their sources that supports their position.
- Use this for teaching comparison and contrast lessons or for work with opposing positions or sides.
- Have students use their material for oral class debates.

Modifications

Emerging Writers

- Create a set of ready-made opinion or position cards and evidence cards. Have students pick an opinion and then look through the provided evidence for items that support their statement.
- Have students draw pictures on the paint strip spaces instead of writing words and sentences.
- Have students practice sorting opinions and evidence so that students can distinguish the differences between the two.

Proficient Writers

- Challenge students to use different sources to support and elaborate upon their reasons. (This would be a great way to integrate citation of sources.)
- Use this to start working on the genre of argument and encourage students to find evidence that supports the counter argument.
- Have students take each reason they drafted on their initial paint strip and then transfer each of those reasons to a new paint strip. For example, if they originally had a three-block paint strip with three reasons, they would now get three new three-block paint strips. Extend the writing by instructing students to give more examples and evidence that supports each individual reason so they have a multiparagraph composition.

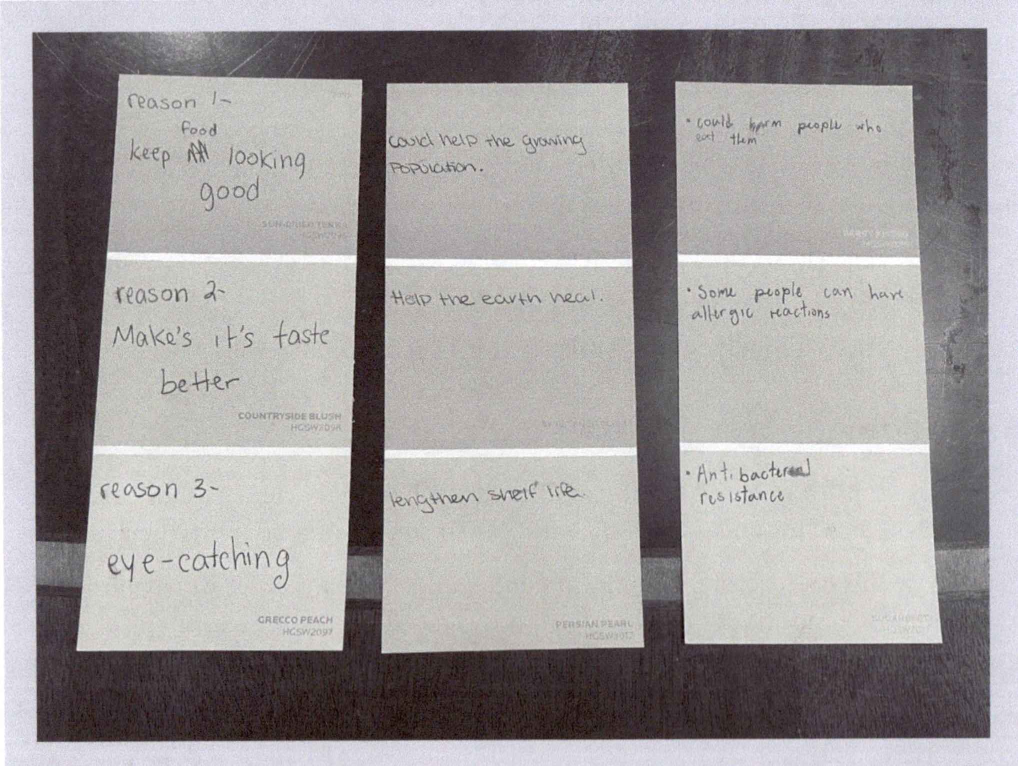

See It Sample

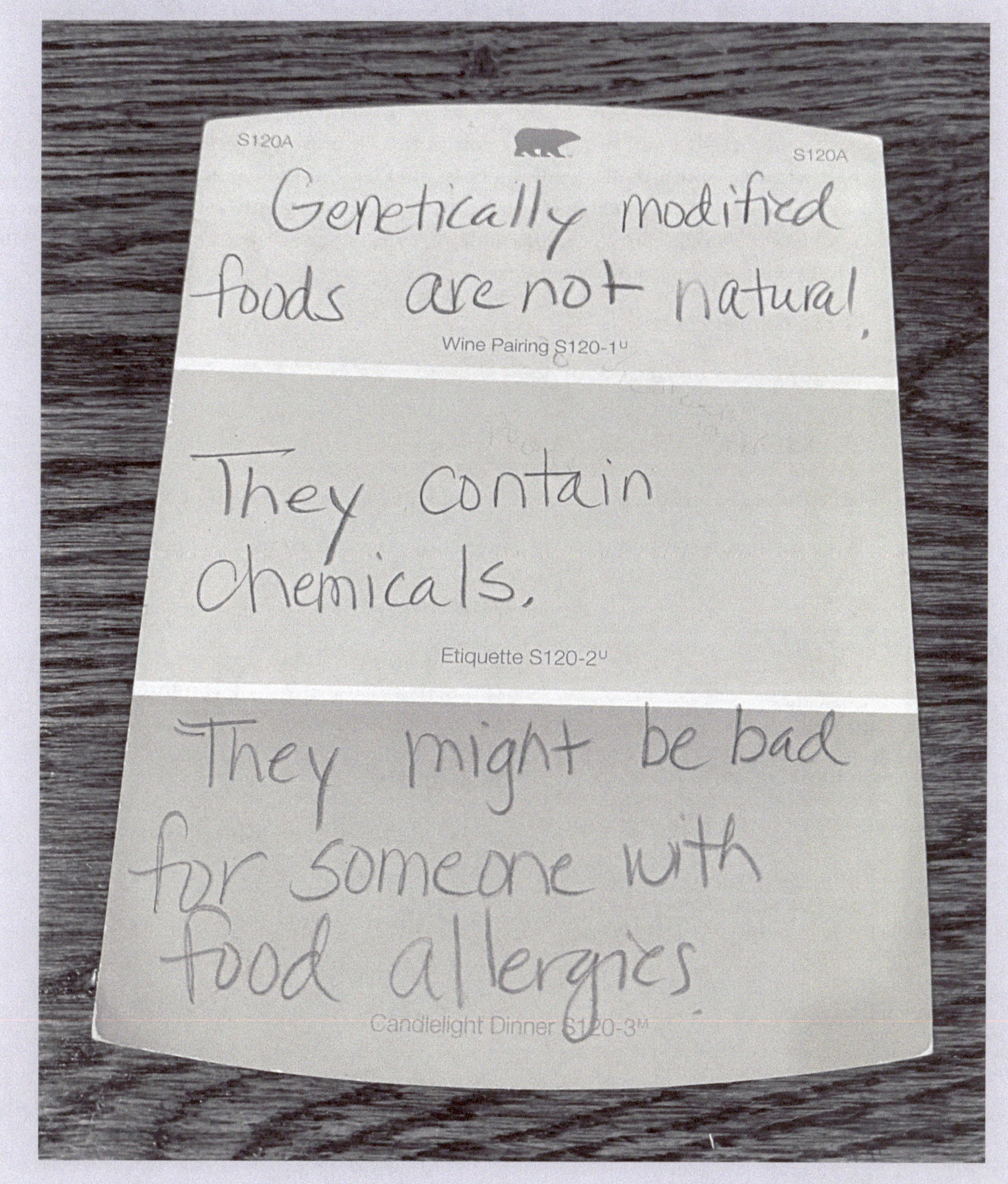

STOPLIGHT SUPPORT

Sometimes students have difficulty determining if the evidence they included is not only credible, but also needed and on topic. In some instances, students might use weak evidence that can negatively contribute to the overall message and purpose of their writing. With this strategy, students categorize evidence and reasons that they might use in their writing. Because we use colors commonly associated with movement (red = stop; green = go), this strategy offers an easy way to remember what constitutes good and on-topic evidence.

Focus Genre: Persuasive

Target Grade Level: 3–5

Standards

Determine the distinction between strong and weak textual evidence and support.

Write persuasive compositions with supporting evidence to convey a position or opinion.

Quick Tip!

Most often when I teach this lesson, I use an informational text and we use facts from the book to categorize and sort based on statements or topics. However, you could use a narrative story and have students categorize evidence about the setting, characters, or problem.

Depending on students' readiness levels you can choose how many blocks you want the paint strip to include. I often start with the four-block layout.

Stop & Think

Depending on your mentor text or example you use, this part may shift. For example, if you are using a story, you might have students draft an opinion about the story and then look for evidence that supports it. You may also focus on characters, setting, etc. If using an informational text, you might have students locate facts that support a statement or position.

Anchor Texts

For this lesson, anchor texts are helpful, and you can certainly use any book you think would work for the purposes of this lesson.

Materials

- Red and green paint strips
- Sticky notes
- Chart paper
- Stoplight Support template (p. 264)

Teach It

1. Before class, display two sheets of chart paper. Title one sheet of chart paper Red Light Evidence and the other Green Light Evidence.
2. Remind students of the material that you will be focusing on in the lesson.
3. Have students use sticky notes to record evidence on the topic being studied. Students should write one piece of evidence per sticky note. (Based on class size or readiness level, determine how many pieces of evidence you want each student to provide.)

4. Spread the sticky notes created by the class out on the ground in a pile. Have students crowd around the pile.
5. Take two examples from the pile of sticky notes. (One should be weak evidence and one should be strong.) Discuss these qualities with the students.
6. Explain that strong evidence is green light evidence and weak evidence is red light evidence.
7. Place the sticky notes on the appropriate chart paper.
8. Have students circulate the room and pick up random pieces of evidence that their classmates have written.
9. Have students read the evidence chosen and place it on the chart paper where they think it belongs. In this case, red light evidence examples are those that are not on topic, are weak and loosely defined, or include extraneous details that do not serve as quality pieces of evidence. Green light evidence are those examples that include relevant information; have strong, well-thought-out reasoning; and are directly tied to the phenomenon in need of evidence.
10. Once all evidence is placed on the chart papers, discuss the results with the class.
11. Provide students with another sample topic or statement and provide them with a green and red paint strip or the Stoplight Support template on page 264.
12. Have them follow the same sticky note process at their desks working with a partner to collect the appropriate evidence for the appropriate category.
13. Once students are done gathering and sorting evidence, have them share their results with the class.

Try It

- Use this when you want students to practice gathering evidence for topic support.
- Try this when you want students to categorize facts based on their relevance and connections to the central topic.
- Use this as way to encourage collaboration in the classroom and partner writing.

Extensions

- Use this same strategy for generating strong leads and opening sentences or clincher sentences and tight conclusions.
- Try this strategy for peer editing and conferencing. Have students list the strong characteristics of the writing on green paint strips and the weak parts on the red ones.

Modifications

Emerging Writers

- Instead of using paint strips, have students write any evidence on sticky notes or notecards and then sort it based on strong versus weak examples.
- Do this in a collaborative manner much like the Yesterday I Had the . . . lesson (p. 57) where each student contributes one reason to the paint strip and then swaps with a neighbor.

Proficient Writers

- Have students use this strategy when drafting evidence to support an argument. Students could complete this activity for each source they use.
- Instead of strong and weak evidence, use this strategy to categorize credible and uncredible sources.
- Have students complete a similar lesson individually or with a partner using the Stoplight Support template (p. 264).

See It Sample

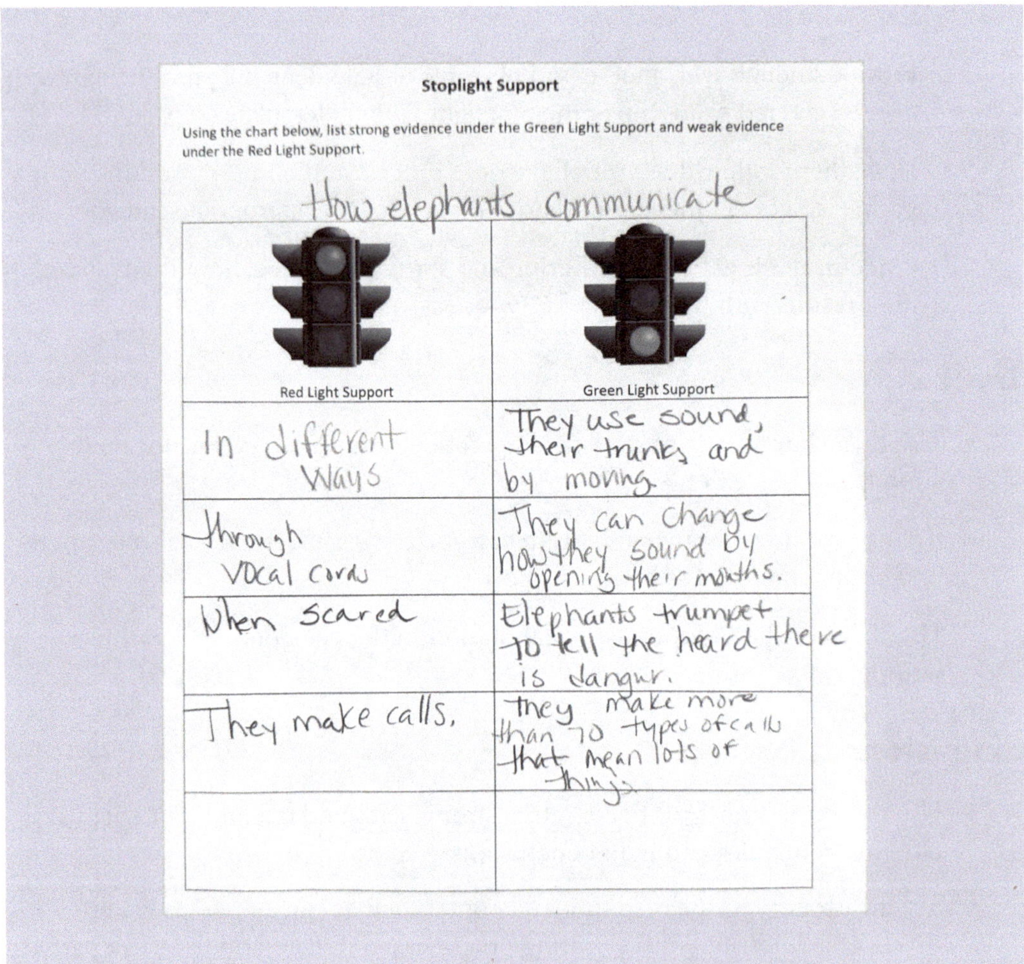

Stoplight Support

Using the chart below, list strong evidence under the Green Light Support and weak evidence under the Red Light Support.

How elephants communicate

Red Light Support	Green Light Support
In different Ways	They use sound, their trunks and by moving.
Through vocal cords	They can change how they sound by opening their mouths.
When scared	Elephants trumpet to tell the heard there is dangur.
They make calls.	they make more than 70 types of calls that mean lots of things

WALK OUT SONGS

All of my children are competitive swimmers, so I log countless hours in the stands at swim meets during the year. At championship meets where there are preliminaries and finals, the top seed in finals gets to choose a walk out song, which is played when the swimmers walk to the blocks.

Sitting in the stands, I began to think of ways to use this idea in my classroom. My first thoughts went to boxing matches, where boxers enter the ring with their entourage while a specific song, typically one that is upbeat, high intensity, and energetic is played. Boxers enter the ring to songs like Survivor's "Eye of the Tiger," Kanye West's "Stronger," and AC/DC's "Thunderstruck."

Walk out songs should have a certain level of intensity and should in some way, connect to the character or individual doing the walking. Knowing that songs can elicit certain moods and that lyrics can be used as evidence of that mood and character connections, the Walk Out Songs lesson addresses several academic elements in the classroom, all while offering yet another opportunity for students to play around with writing. Plus, it also involves some persuasive tactics, as students have to justify and defend their choices based on the evidence.

Focus Genre: Narrative/Persuasive

Target Grade Level: K–5

Standards

Write persuasive compositions with supporting evidence to convey a position or opinion.

Apply a wide range of strategies to comprehend, interpret, evaluate, and appreciate texts.

Anchor Texts

In this lesson, the anchor text are the song lyrics chosen.

Materials

- Sticky notes
- Paint strips
- Paper
- Copies of lyrics for songs used
- Walk Out Song template (p. 265)

The songs should vary based on the class and grade level. I often start by playing a song that I might connect to a character and then start a class discussion. I also share clips of sports figures and celebrities walking out on stage or to the arena and we discuss the song choices and mood.

Teach It

1. To get students ready for this activity, provide them a list of the sports figures or celebrities. Ask students to generate a list of character traits about each of the figures that will be shown before you show the clip. (You can do this as a whole-class activity, with a partner, or individually.) This can activate prior knowledge and get them thinking about who the person is before they watch the walk out. Make sure they are familiar with the individuals in order to complete this part.

2. Show students clips of the different sports figures or celebrities from Step 1 entering an arena or sports field with a walk out song. Check out walk out video clips for boxers, basketball teams, swimmers, football teams, or other sports figures for ideas.

3. Have students jot down noticings on a sheet of paper about each character and their chosen song.

4. Return to the discussion about the characters and figures. Talk about these traits and how they are reinforced or highlighted in the choice of walkout music. (This can be done in pairs or in small groups as well.)

5. Distribute the lyrics to the songs used in the walkouts. Have students work in small groups to highlight the lyrics that best match the character traits they identified in the class discussion. (It works best to give each group a specific figure or celebrity and lyrics for that one walk out song.)

Worried about students picking inappropriate songs? I often have a binder or list of samples that could be used that I know are age appropriate.

6. Have students share their ideas with the class.

7. Using this lesson as a frame, have students choose their own personal walk out song. Have them make a list of their character traits and then find a song that they'd like to use as their walk out song.

8. Use the Walk Out Song template (p. 265) for students to match their qualities and character traits to the chosen lyrics.

9. Have students share their choice of walk out song along with their supporting evidence for their choice with the class.

Walk Out Song	
Song I chose: "Nobody's Fool" by Kenny Loggins	
Character Traits/Adjectives That Describe Me (one trait per box)	**Song Lyrics That Support**
Determined	"I'm going all the way" "Don't care how long it takes"
Pressure does not bother me Successful	"You can turn up the heat" "Don't care how long it takes" "I'm going all the way"
Intelligent	"I may not look so smart, but I'm nobody's fool"
Quick on my feet	"Got to learn to be on the ball"

Try It

- Try this as a fresh idea for character and persuasive writing.
- Use this when you want students to practice the skill of textual evidence through the integration of song lyrics in their writing.
- Use this strategy as a way to capitalize on student interest by allowing them to bring in their personal song choices.

Extensions

- Revisit this idea throughout the year and have students complete a "Me Playlist" with songs that best illustrate who they are as a person.
- Have students write an extended piece utilizing the lyrics as justification for their choice of song. Here, students explain the lyric connections with their own personal character traits in paragraph form.
- Show students a character that they are familiar with. Play a sampling of songs and have students choose the most appropriate choice based on the character's traits. Have students justify and explain their choices.
- Play a song and have students determine which character from a provided list would best match with the song.

Modifications

Emerging Writers

- Assign students a partner and have them choose a walk out song for their classmate.
- Have a song bank already available for students to choose from for their walk out song. (Use this modification if you are concerned about inappropriate

lyrics, want to save time with searching, or if filters and security at your school prevent students from downloading music on campus.)

- Use walk out songs as a reward. Each week, choose a student who will share their walk out song that the class will exit to at the end of the school day.
- Play three sample songs for the class and have students vote on which song should be used for a character in a literary work.

Proficient Writers

- Have students generate a playlist for a character from a novel, a historical figure, or a classmate. Challenge students to guess the character simply based on the songs.
- Provide students with two sample songs and have them make an argument for the best choice based on the subject chosen.

See It Sample

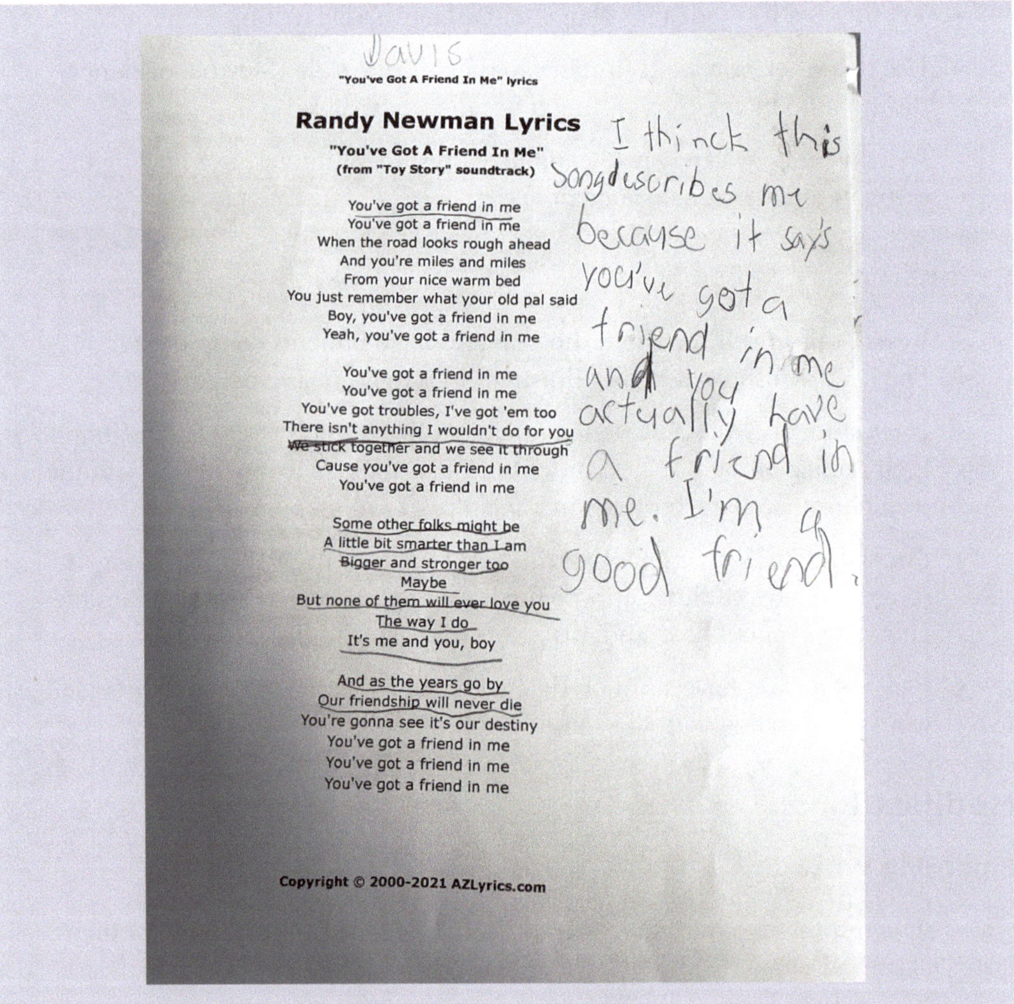

Davis

"You've Got A Friend In Me" lyrics

Randy Newman Lyrics

"You've Got A Friend In Me"
(from "Toy Story" soundtrack)

You've got a friend in me
You've got a friend in me
When the road looks rough ahead
And you're miles and miles
From your nice warm bed
You just remember what your old pal said
Boy, you've got a friend in me
Yeah, you've got a friend in me

You've got a friend in me
You've got a friend in me
You've got troubles, I've got 'em too
There isn't anything I wouldn't do for you
We stick together and we see it through
Cause you've got a friend in me
You've got a friend in me

Some other folks might be
A little bit smarter than I am
Bigger and stronger too
Maybe
But none of them will ever love you
The way I do
It's me and you, boy

And as the years go by
Our friendship will never die
You're gonna see it's our destiny
You've got a friend in me
You've got a friend in me
You've got a friend in me

Copyright © 2000-2021 AZLyrics.com

I thinck this song describes me because it says you've got a friend in me and you actually have a friend in me. I'm a good friend.

Photo by Alfred Cain

Chapter 7

THE MEASURE OF SUCCESS

Every experienced teacher knows that even with the best strategies, materials, administrative support, and parent involvement, sometimes things simply don't work. In fact, it is often when the teacher expects a lesson or strategy to go off without a hitch that the wheels fall off the wagon.

Getting students engaged in reading and writing is certainly a main focus for literacy educators, but there are also other components that must be considered as well. Developing lessons that build on each other and help students become stronger readers and writers also requires strategic and purposeful planning when it comes to assessment. Managing classroom routines is also paramount for success.

While there are going to be times when it seems as though someone is pulling the rug out from you as you try to teach, how we address these challenges can help us improve our instruction and build learning opportunities for all students. Establishing routines, while remaining flexible in our class schedule when the unexpected happens can improve our students' experiences as well as help us navigate the predictable unpredictability of classroom teaching.

This chapter focuses on a few ways in which teachers can not only establish the routines and practices necessary for effective reading and writing instruction, but also implement effective progress monitoring, assessment and feedback methods, and ways in which students might engage in and take part in these processes as well.

The Motivational Factor

No matter what age we are, we all struggle at some point with motivation, especially when we are faced with a task we do not like or do not have the experience to complete. Nothing makes me shut down faster than to be dragged into a task that I don't feel is valuable or has purpose or relevance. I need to know the "why" behind a task before I can invest in the completion, and in some cases, our students are no different.

One of my favorite qualities of early-grades literacy instruction is that in most cases, our youngest learners have not developed strong attitudes toward reading and writing just yet. This certainly isn't the case with middle grades and secondary learners as those students have years of experience in schools that can affect their opinions and attitudes about literacy. Often, this is not the case with younger learners. For example, I was once in a kindergarten class reading Norton Juster's *The Hello, Goodbye Window*. There's a place in that picture book where the narrator explains that he can play with anything in the kitchen except what's in the cabinet under the kitchen sink because it can make him sick. When I paused my reading to ask, "What could be in the cabinet that might make you sick?" one student yelled out, "Roaches!" Now, that was not the answer I was looking for, but what stood out to me is that that student was not afraid of taking a risk and sharing his thoughts. For some older students, getting them to feel comfortable sharing their ideas and thoughts can be more challenging, since some are afraid that their responses are incorrect. (The fear of being wrong is a real thing—it is actually called *atelophobia*!) Because their school experiences are limited, younger students don't always feel this way and are often more willing to share their ideas than their older counterparts. Thus, motivating students to share and discuss their readings and writings is sometimes a little easier.

However, one challenge for teachers in the early grades is experience and ability to write proficiently. Since many are emerging readers and writers, teachers often spend time spelling words, writing out exemplars, encouraging students, and answering questions over and over again. Part of this is due simply to the lack of experience students have in the areas of reading and writing. But the only way we ever get better at something is through practice, so it is important to give students daily opportunities to practice reading and writing.

So how do we motivate our classroom of writers? For starters, utilizing books and writing activities that capitalize on student interest is huge. Do your students like to learn about strange animals? Find books, articles, or video clips on unusual animals to share in class. Contact a zoo, local veterinarian clinic, or wildlife association and ask if one of their experts would video chat with your class. Then have your students draft sample interview questions to ask the class guest. After the class visit, have students write a thank you note to the visitor. In this quick idea, we've capitalized on student interest, completed some research, drafted sample questions with a specific purpose, and practiced the genre of letter writing.

Do your students love Taylor Swift? Are they learning to read? Use the lyric feed when playing a song in your favorite music app (of course, choose a grade-level appropriate song) and have students read or sing along with the lyrics as you display them. Or print the lyrics and have students track the print as they follow along with the words.

Source: iStock.com/hapabapa

Have any athletes in your class? Gamers? Use those experiences and knowledge to help build lessons around those interests and strengths. For example, if you have students who play a video game like Fortnite, use their knowledge of maps when they annotate other maps for social studies lessons. Instead of having them draft biographies of historical figures, have them write about their favorite athlete, actor, or singer. There are ways to teach the required standards that not only meets the academic needs of your class, but also builds on their personal and home literacies as well.

Meeting Students Where They Are

When I work with teachers, I often hear concerns about reading and writing readiness level and how this translates into classroom instruction. Elementary teachers know it is not unusual to have students in your classroom who are learning letter–sound relationships while others are reading chapter books. This can make lesson planning and classroom instruction a bit challenging to say the least! One way to easily address this is to use a variety of leveled texts in your instruction. This can allow you to teach essentially the same lesson but utilize reading materials that are "just right" for the students, which can help improve comprehension and their performance on writing tasks.

Another possibility is to locate a variety of texts on several grade levels or that are written in different formats. For example, one student might better understand an infographic due to the structure and nature of its composition rather than an extended passage that does not utilize images or figures. In fact, when working with teachers across grade levels, I often choose a topic and then locate a variety of sources, digital included, that are centered on that topic. Not only can it help make a topic more accessible for students, but it also allows them to see how different texts are structured which can assist them when reading a variety of text types across disciplines and on standardized assessments.

Another easy way to meet students where they are is through the integration of read alouds. Have you ever noticed that your students can understand, discuss, and engage with material that is read aloud even if it is above their independent reading level? Reading aloud to students is an easy way to model fluency, introduce new vocabulary, and expose students to different genres. Don't discount picture books with upper elementary kids either! In fact, I read picture books to my grown teachers—there's no age limit. Similarly, chapter books can be used with primary students as well, just make sure they are books that have short chapters like Katherine Applegate's *The One and Only Ivan*, Betty G. Birney's *The World According to Humphrey*, or Patrick Skene Catling's *The Chocolate Touch*. Chapter books written in verse or even biographies like the *Who Were . . . ?* series are excellent options for read aloud.

And while read alouds and teacher-led engagements can certainly expose students to multiple genres and authors, times for students to make genre choices independently is important as well. Here is a super easy way for students to take ownership of their own reading choices: Use a book pass. Here is how it works:

- Provide students with the Book Pass template (p. 266).
- Give students a stack of books to sift through.
- As students look at a specific book, they record the information on their template and then make any comments regarding their opinions and reactions to the book.
- Pass books around about half a dozen times.
- Once students have completed their template, they now have a list of books from a variety of genres that they may choose to check out in the library.

In short, using a book pass helps students see a variety of books from multiple authors and a variety of genres, which they may choose to check out at a later date. In fact, it offers them one more chance to interact with multiple books across several genres and authors. In this situation, exposure is the key. No more getting to the library and wandering around without any direction. Now, students have a list of books that they might choose to check out when they head to the library.

Other ideas include Book Tastings, where a student who has read a book offers a brief overview of the story and shares this with students. Book Tastings are set up so that students can rotate through stations and hear the highlights of a book before moving on to the next. Think about it like an appetizer sampling you see on restaurant menus. You get a sample of each book and then based on your reaction to the sample, you decide if you want to try out the entire text. Book Speed Dates work well too. Students spend 2 to 4 minutes telling the high points of their books before they move on to a new partner or "date" to share their talking points. Regardless of how you choose to do this, each of the strategies listed here address the important component of getting students exposed to multiple genres and authors. While these suggestions might seem like they are more reading focused, good writers read. Thus providing students with opportunities to engage with multiple genres, writing styles, and authors can help them become more skilled and proficient writers.

The reality is that students, and adults alike for that matter, are only going to get better at something when they have ample time for practice. Thus, students are not going to become better readers or writers if they don't read and write on a daily basis. It is that simple: they have to read and write daily. While the type of reading and writing they do each day might look different, it is imperative that some type be practiced daily. Plus, this can help students get their much-needed experience with a variety or genres and text structures, which can help them fill their literacy passports.

Literacy Passports

When I think about writing and how students gain proficiency at a variety of writing tasks, it really is less about the genre and structure and more about *experiencing* writing. For some students, their experience with certain types of writing are a one-and-done, and in fact, many standard sets and pacing guides are set up so that is exactly what happens. Persuasive writing? Check. Narrative writing? Check. The problem with this is that teaching writing genre by genre, and then moving on to the next one, only allows students limited experiences. How many of you have standards sets or pacing guides that focus on a particular genre for each nine weeks? Now, that certainly is not a bad approach because it *does* ensure that students at least get exposed to a variety of genres, but it limits their depth and understanding of the subtle nuances of each genre. Consider a schedule like this:

- First nine weeks (personal narrative)
- Second nine weeks (expository)
- Third nine weeks (persuasive)
- Fourth nine weeks (personal narrative)

With a model like this, students focus on one particular genre for each quarter and then move on to an entirely different genre for the next nine weeks. As a result, these genres become compartmentalized and exist in silos, thus giving students limited experiences with each. Once the first nine weeks is over, many students won't experience a specific genre again until later in the year if they ever *do* experience it again. This can be problematic for a few reasons. For one, it creates the belief that different genres of writing always exist in their own vacuums. Yet, it is not at all uncommon to see components of the persuasive genre show up in personal narratives. Similarly, components of arguments can also be informational as well. When teaching genres in silos, it can nurture the belief that all genres are bounded sets that do not merge and exist as black and white, not grey. However, genres and stylistic components can merge and bleed over and in fact, acknowledging these qualities can help students develop a deeper and more thorough understanding of writing. This often creates stronger and more engaging writing.

Here's where a literacy passport can come in handy: Let's say that I have never traveled to Paris, France, before. On my first trip there, I will probably see the real "touristy" places that everyone sees when they go to Paris for the first time. You would probably go to the Eiffel Tower, the Louvre, and Moulin Rouge. After visiting on this first trip, you get your first stamp in your passport for a visit to Paris, France. You can check France off on your "Places to Visit" list since you now have evidence that you have visited. Once. Now imagine that you return to Paris on several occasions and as a result have multiple stamps in your passport.

While you might return to those first three landmarks, since you have checked off the "must see" places, you might now venture off onto side streets and try out local bakeries for pastries. Stop in a quaint gift shop and buy a trinket or head into a local bistro for a cup of coffee. You see, returning to a place that you have visited before and often, allows you to explore new areas, shops, and dining. While you may return to the Eiffel Tower each time you head back to Paris, it is likely that you will venture out into places that only those who live in Paris or are frequent visitors know about. In other words, you have developed a deeper understanding of this place. You know it

because you have visited it on multiple occasions, during different seasons, and with different traveling partners. Thus, your experience with Paris is different than someone who has only visited once. Plus, when you spend an extended time in a location, that prolonged engagement offers its own benefits because your longer visit allows you the luxury of lingering. Ask yourself, how often do we allow students to linger along the pages of a book or with the words they write?

How does that relate to writing? First off, many students only have a few stamps on their literacy passports. For example, they might have one persuasive stamp, one personal narrative stamp, and one expository stamp on their literacy passports. In other words, it would be the same as going to Paris, France, one time and only seeing those three landmarks that everyone sees. Then going to Australia and only visiting the Sydney Opera House and the Outback before heading off to Egypt to see the pyramids. In each of these examples, the travelers are barely brushing the surface of the wonders of each country. The same holds true for only visiting the persuasive genre once for nine weeks. Sure, you learn that in order to persuade someone you have to state your position and provide evidence that gets your reader to side with you, but that is it. Only visiting that genre once doesn't allow students the opportunity to get to know the subtle nuances of persuasive writing, like for example, how the use of carefully crafted dialogue might help convince your reader, or how opening with a vignette or quote can serve as an effective hook. You see, those qualities are only experienced when you return often and on a regular basis, for a variety of purposes and topics. Similarly, returning to the same stories for repeated readings often allows readers to notice details and events that were overlooked the first time. While repeated readings can certainly improve comprehension, it can also help further the overall enjoyment of reading. There are books I have read dozens of times, and each time, there is something I notice that was missed prior. Why, because I am allowed to linger and not simply pass through.

Even more concerning though are those students who have blank literacy passports because they haven't had the opportunities to see the writing world. Sadly, many students haven't had the opportunity to truly engage with the craft of writing in their academic settings. And they are missing out on the wonders of the writing world.

In order for students to truly understand how a particular genre of writing *functions* they must visit and revisit it often over an extended time for a variety of purposes, audiences, and about a number of topics. It is not enough for students to write an argumentative essay and then move on. They really need to experience the genre of argument in multiple content areas, utilize it for short and extended writing pieces, and craft arguments on a variety of topics. When this happens, students are essentially visiting argument over and over again, thus gaining multiple literacy passport stamps and developing a more sophisticated and thorough understanding of the genre instead of a simple surface level, drive-by approach.

When planning writing engagements and experiences to help students fill their literacy passports, consider the following:

- Is this the student's first experience with this genre? If so, you need to hit the high points or the main attractions first.
- Who is the intended audience?
- How much time are you able to devote to this writing task?
- When will students see this again?
- What other writing genres or components of author's craft are closely related to this genre?
- What types of supports will students need to successfully complete this type of writing?
- Do I really need to grade this? Can you get the information needed through a more informal method of assessment?

Considering these bullet points can help plan writing engagements that are purposeful and effective in today's busy classroom because they help focus the lessons on the end game. Ask yourself, "What is my endgame?"

Stop & Think

I am not saying that you should *tell* students that a writing task won't be graded; I am simply asking you to consider whether or not *you* need to formally grade it or if you can get the information needed through a more informal method.

Feedback and Assessment

As students write, the nature and frequency of feedback and assessment is incredibly important. When I was teaching middle school, I observed one of my students copying an essay over onto a clean sheet of paper for her language arts class. When I asked her what she was doing, she informed me that she was writing her final draft. Final draft? How? There were no comments or suggestions written on her rough draft and what she was writing on the fancy lined paper was exactly the same as what was written on the other paper. I inquired further about how and what she was doing, and when I found out that there had been no conversation between her and her teacher nor had the teacher read her paper, I asked, "So are you writing the same thing again on this new paper?" Her response? "Yep."

Now, let me be clear. As a writing teacher I certainly do not read every single sentence or composition that my students write. I don't have the time, and nor do you. However, I have to read enough of it that I can offer them feedback and suggestions in order for me to assess their writing effectively. Otherwise, how do they determine what needs to be changed or addressed? Giving feedback does not have to be a daunting process, and in fact, when completed in small bursts, it can be beneficial for the students and the teacher.

How should feedback look? That depends on the type of writing and on the student. Sometimes, feedback might simply be delivered as an affirmative statement regarding a student's word choice, or a comment about how they utilized dialogue when writing about their characters. While you might not sit down and have an extended conversation with every student, every day, providing some type of feedback, written or oral, daily, can help improve a student's writing performance.

Sometimes students might not know exactly how to give feedback to their peers because they do not have much experience doing so. Correspondingly, some students might struggle with what to do when they receive feedback. This is one of the reasons why it is so important for students to have as much experience giving and receiving feedback as possible. In addition, feedback should be actionable with specifics regarding how and what to address. Below are a few suggested revisions one might make to the feedback provided. By giving students a specific example that is actionable, it can make revision much easier.

Instead of . . .	Try this . . .
Tell me more about your characters.	What about adding some dialogue between characters?
More description needed	What about adding a few adjectives to describe your characters or the setting?
Lots of short, choppy sentences	What about combining some of these shorter sentences? For example, . . .
Sentence fragment	What type of punctuation could be added to complete this sentence?

Aside from offering actionable feedback, it is important for teachers to determine the focus of a specific piece of writing. Most rubrics have an overwhelming amount of material for assessment, which can be difficult for students to grasp. Determining the focus for a writing composition can help students know what they need to attend to. For example, instead of asking students to focus on organization, vivid vocabulary, effective hooks and leads, clincher sentences, and character development in one composition, you might choose to focus on organization and vivid vocabulary. The more narrow focus can make it easier for students to complete the task and not get overwhelmed with feedback on multiple components of the writing.

Along with actionable feedback items, there are several quick feedback strategies that can be employed. One easy way to incorporate feedback into your writing instruction and plans is to use a strategy known as Three Pluses and a Wish. For this feedback strategy, you list three items that are positive about the writing and then one item you wish they had done.

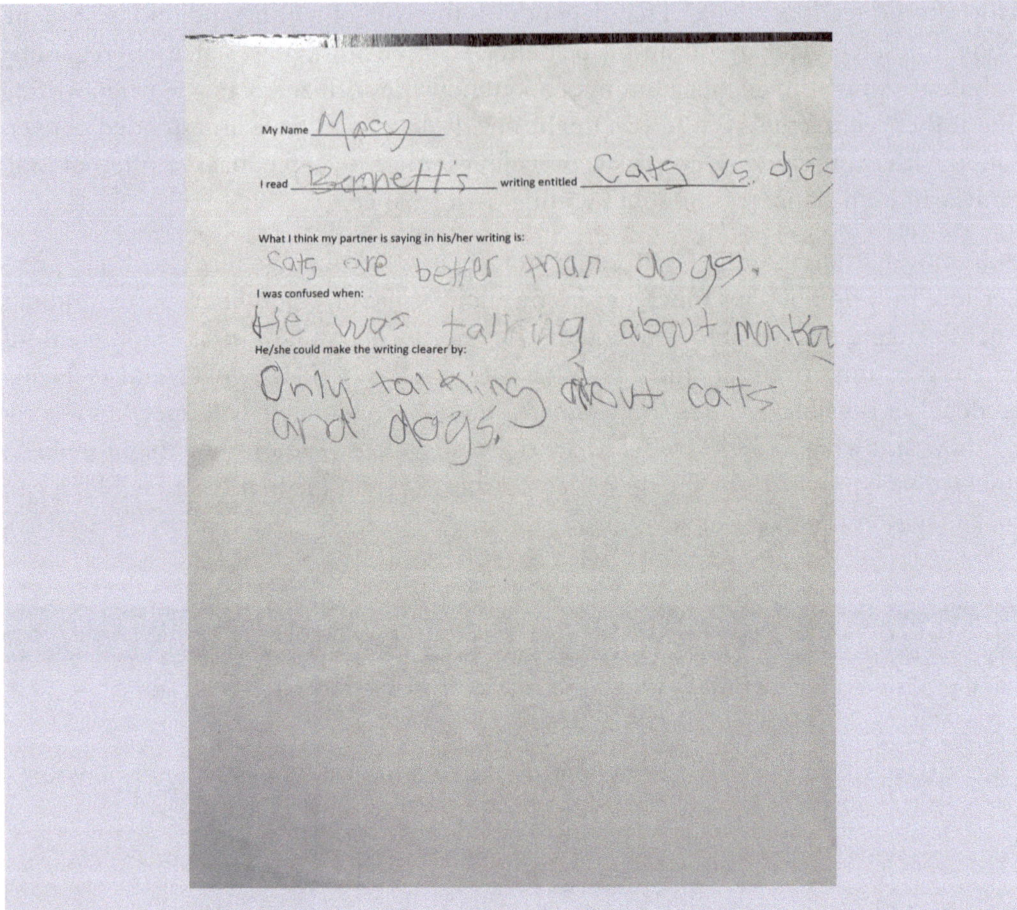

My Name Macy

I read Bennett's writing entitled Cats vs. dogs

What I think my partner is saying in his/her writing is:

Cats are better than dogs.

I was confused when:

He was talking about monke

He/she could make the writing clearer by:

Only talking about cats and dogs.

For emerging writers, you might consider revising it to One Plus and a Wish. This particular strategy works well because it allows students to give both positive and constructive feedback. Plus, it gives the writer a tangible item to address, which can help writers begin the sometimes intimidating task of revision.

Another feedback strategy is the implementation and use of feedback cards. I often use paint strips for this strategy as I have found that I can create different genre-specific feedback prompts and questions on paint strips.

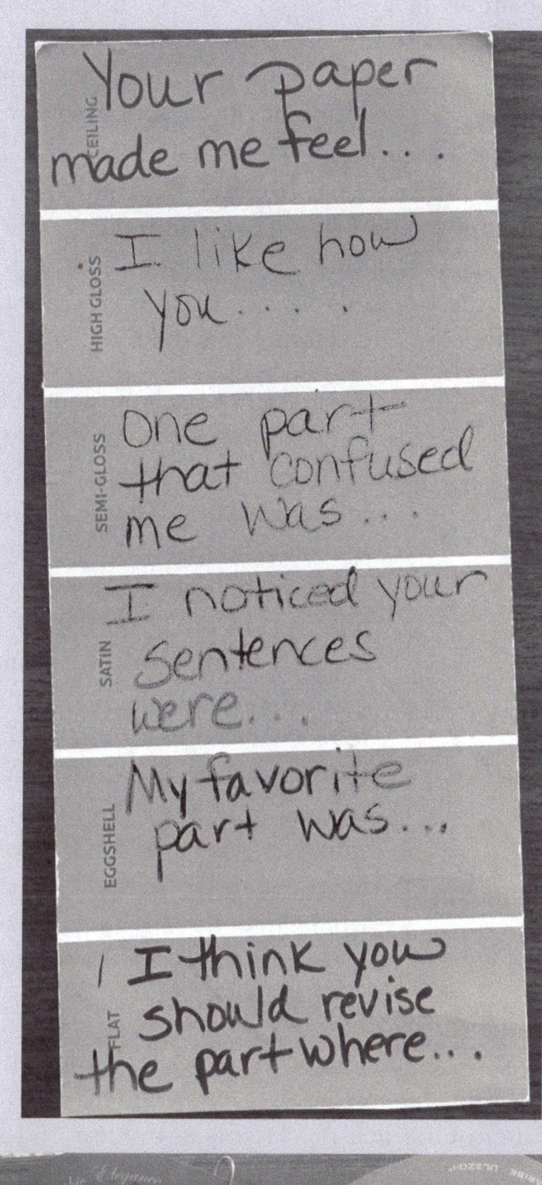
Your paper made me feel...
CEILING
I like how you....
HIGH GLOSS
One part that confused me was...
SEMI-GLOSS
I noticed your sentences were...
SATIN
My favorite part was...
EGGSHELL
I think you should revise the part where...
FLAT

All my sentences have end punctuation.
My sentences begin with capital letters.
conclusion sentence.
topic sentence.
DARKEST GRAPE

To do this, the teacher simply makes a list of some possible feedback starter prompts or sentences that students can use when working with a peer. Having several choices can help students decide what is the most appropriate feedback to include based on the paper they are reading. You can also modify this to incorporate a self-reflection component by creating specific prompts and questions geared to a specific learner. I like to include these cards on craft rings because students can switch out cards that they have mastered or add new ones that are genre or topic specific. Another easy way to give feedback to students is by using sticky notes to write comments about their compositions. Sometimes these comments are suggestions or questions, whereas other times they might be simple corrections or positive statements.

> **Stop & Think**
>
> Incidentally, I never write directly on a student's paper. That can get a little cluttered for some students and I have found that using sticky notes allows a student to move that feedback around, which is especially important when they are correcting an area in their paper or taking up a teacher's suggestion. Plus, you can color code your comments. For example, green sticky notes might be used for grammar suggestions, blue might be used for questions about the writing, etc.

If you find yourself pressed for time or have a large number of students, you might integrate feedback into your instruction by involving the entire class in the process. One way to do this is through the use of a strategy called Speed Write. With this strategy, students meet with a partner for a short time, read a small portion of their partner's writing and then move on to another partner after 5 to 7 minutes. Using this format, students are able to receive feedback from multiple peers in a short time. Plus, because they are only responsible for reading a small portion of their partner's writing, valuable class time isn't spent reading an entire lengthy writing. In addition, students can choose what part of their writing they want their partner to focus on, which can foster agency and autonomy.

Just like other aspects of writing, giving and receiving feedback should be practiced and implemented on a regular basis. Modeling appropriate strategies and showing students how they can respond to each other's writings in a variety of modalities can help them embrace the feedback process and build stronger and more confident writers.

While feedback certainly can improve a student's writing, it also serves as an informal assessment method. Many times, assessment is relegated to formal measures, typically occurring at the end of the process and focuses on the final product. For some students, that may be too late for them to make any adjustments or respond and revise. While formal and culminating assessments are certainly important and necessary, the need for frequent informal assessments that are administered throughout the completion of a task can have better results. Don't wait until the completion of a writing assignment to assess; instead build in opportunities for assessment throughout the process. These might be quick checks for daily grades or opportunities for assessment at a few points during a longer process.

Having students write daily in some form or fashion can provide you with additional opportunities for assessment. This can be helpful for some students who may miss a component on the culminating assessment, lose a portion of their writing (my students always did), or have an off-assessment day where their grade might not accurately reflect their skill. Here's a real-world example of what I'm talking about:

A while back, I attended my girls' first long course swim meet of the season. During this meet, several of the swimmers on our team competed in the 200-meter butterfly. While several of our swimmers completed this race successfully, many did not. A few were disqualified for illegal strokes, and two swimmers made it to the 100-meter mark and got out of the pool. In this example, part of their ability to complete this strenuous task was directly related to the training they received that prepared them for this difficult race. Those who successfully finished the race were most often the ones who had trained for it in practice, executed drills that were extended and high intensity, and integrated training days that allowed their bodies to recover from a grueling practice routine. Those were the successful swimmers, the ones who were able to finish, disqualified or not. Notice that the disqualified swimmers are included in the group of successful swimmers. Why? They completed the task, and that should count for something, right?

Now what about those kids who got out of the pool in the middle of the race. After 100 meters, they threw in the towel. Is there no hope for them to be successful in the 200-meter fly? Of course not, but what it does mean is that they need to train for it and be ready to perform this high intensity race that requires a sophisticated cocktail of strength, stamina, technique, and mental preparation. They must take part in training that helps them get to the end goal of completing that race. This might mean focusing on completing the 100-meter fly at their next few meets, and then moving to the 200 meter. Progressive training can help their performance by building strength, experience, and confidence.

Here's something else worth noting. One of the swimmers was disqualified at the very end of the 200 fly for taking three freestyle pulls before he finished the race. He subsequently climbed out of the pool and threw up on deck. He finished, legal or not. There was no doubt that kid had given it his all even though he got a DQ. He saw the task through to the end.

Now, I have thought a lot about that one kid's race. He successfully completed 195 meters of the butterfly, but on the last 5 meters, he deviated from the requirements of that race, and as a result, nothing he did in the 195 meters prior counted. Nothing. One hundred ninety-five meters of crushing physicality was erased by three quick freestyle pulls.

How does this compare to writing, you might ask? What about our students who do work on four out of five days, but do not perform on the fifth, which happens to be an assessment day? Do they get credit for the work they completed those four days? Sometimes, yes. Most often, no. Like Collin, the swimmer who swam 195 meters of fly and then did three freestyle pulls, all their effort on those prior days often is erased by one assessment, one grade. So as writing teachers, how do we make those other 195 meters count?

This story reminds me of how important it is for teachers to incorporate multiple opportunities for assessment to capture a more accurate and comprehensive picture of a student's academic performance. By assessing students often and using a variety of tools and methods, we can help make certain that our students' assessments reflect their actual skills and mastery. For young students, sometimes breaking a larger skill into small components and offering feedback on the individual sub skills that compromise the larger skill can help our writers gain confidence in their literacy skills. Plus, by breaking larger skills down into smaller more manageable units, it makes it easier to assess learners at different levels. Some students may master different sub skills at different rates, however, for the teacher, it makes lesson planning, monitoring, and assessing more manageable.

Goal-Setting

When we begin a new workout or weight loss regime, we often start by setting goals. Instruction is no different. While you may have goals that are based on the standards required for a specific grade level, those are not the only goals to keep in mind. Sometimes goals are written in "I can" statements like these:

- I can describe how characters develop and interact.
- I can use descriptive language.
- I can write a complete sentence.
- I can determine the meaning of words and phrases used in the text.
- I can determine the meaning of words and phrases used in the text including common figures of speech.
- I can write an information piece that includes a topic, facts, and an ending.

Those are directly tied to academic standards and goals, but what if we involved our students in the creation of their own writing goals? They might look a little different. For example, students might say

- I will write letters to my grandma every month.
- I will draw my own comic strip with characters and dialogue.
- I will learn how to spell *their*, *there*, and *they're*.

Do you see how those goals are different? The difference exists in the fact that they are individual and catered directly to the student who is writing them. The goals I listed earlier are blanket, one-size-fits-all goals that do not take into account the individual. The individualized goals still utilize standards-based skills and competencies, but they include something that blanket goal statements don't: the student as the individual learner. Having students create their own goals, in consultation with their teachers or classmates, can help ensure that students have a vested interest in their educational goals and aspirations. Plus, it can help students begin to take an active role in their education and help them function as active partners in their educational experiences.

Aside from individual student goals, consider having students draft class goals related to literacy. What types of writings do they want to learn? What kinds of writing engagements do they enjoy the most? What questions or research might they conduct?

Having the class collaborate to create goals for the whole group can help build community and a shared effort into a common goal. Plus, these class goals can offer students opportunities to encourage their classmates, revise their goals based on changes that occur during the year, and monitor their progress as individuals and a collective. For you as the teacher, these become one more tangible example of progress. To keep track of these, you might list these class goals in a specific place in your classroom so that students and visitors to your class can track the progress toward the goal. Revisit these goals on a regular basis so that adjustments can be made or new goals can be constructed once the original ones are achieved.

Help Students Help Themselves

For many of our writers, developing confidence in letter formation, idea generation, spelling, reading and writing takes time. If you think about our youngest writers, they are learning a myriad material in a short amount of time. As an adult who has a lot of experience reading and writing, when you sit down to draft a piece of writing, much of what you do when you begin to compose comes fairly easily and with a degree of automaticity. While idea generation might be difficult, or organization, it is likely that you are not consciously asking yourself which words to capitalize, where end punctuation goes, what side of the paper you start your writing on, or how big a space to leave between words. Now think about our youngest writers. Many of them have to think about those very items. Imagine a primary student who begins to write a composition. They might have to decide or actively think or remember the following:

- What end punctuation do I use?
- How do I spell . . . ?
- Do I start writing on the right or left of the paper?
- How big should my space be?
- Is this word capitalized?

Do you see how they may be navigating a myriad questions and uncertainties about the basic structure which makes the other literacy skills that may be the focus of the composition, an afterthought. However, there are definitely some measures teachers can take that might help students as they begin to navigate their own writings.

For one, make certain students know that there are places in the classroom where material is posted that they might use for their writings. Many primary and upper elementary classrooms have charts, posters, and words displayed on the walls. However, do your students know that they should and can use these for assistance when writing? I bet some students haven't paid direct attention to all these pieces of print on display. Here are some easy tips for drawing their attention to these displays:

- During whole group instruction, reference charts and posted material on the walls for students to view and use for answering questions.
- Instead of immediately spelling a word for a student, ask them where they might look in the classroom to find that word.

- For charts and posters that you want students to use and reference when writing, make sure they are posted at eye level for your students. Charts and displays that are in your classroom as district or school requirements should be displayed up high because they are not meant for the students to use. Any chart you want students to reference should be posted at the student's eye level.
- Consider creating a Velcro word wall. This works well because you attach words to the wall using Velcro which means students can physically remove a word, take it to their seats, copy it in their writing composition and then put it back on the wall.
- Don't buy ready-made posters. Use blank chart paper and make class-created charts based on the specific needs of your class.

Stop & Think

Think about the cereal aisle in the grocery store. Where are all the sugary cereals displayed? At eye level for children. Where is the shredded wheat and granola? On the top shelf because they are marketed for adults, not kids.

Having students pay attention to the words in the room can aid them in learning how to help themselves by locating and using the resources around them.

While those ideas above are meant to assist the entire class, creating individual notes or "cheat sheets" for students can be beneficial too. For example, if a student has trouble spelling the words *too*, *to*, and *two*, I might have them record these on a paint strip with the definitions. That way, when they are writing, they can simply take out the paint strip and use it as a reminder of the proper spelling. When writing across disciplines, I might have students use notecards or a paint strip to record discipline specific vocabulary to use in their writings. If they don't know the definition, having the word on a list won't help them, but if they are stuck on spelling, those notecards can help them utilize the appropriate vocabulary that they know without worrying about spelling. Plus, when incorporating simple ideas like this, it makes the educational experience much more individualized.

The First Step Is . . .

While teaching writing might seem overwhelming, it actually can be a joyous experience. The first step in getting started involves simply picking up the pencil and putting down that first letter. Giving students the place and space to pick up that pencil is just as important. By building a nurturing classroom environment where students feel safe to share their words and ideas, teachers can help their classroom of writers grow and flourish.

Vicki Jamieson, author of *Rollergirl* and *When Stars are Scattered*, once told a group of teachers, "Everyone has a story; the only difference is that writers write them down." That one sentence has stayed with me because it posits that we all can be writers *if* we get the words on the page and write our stories down. While our students might be novice writers in some ways, they are full of ideas and stories to tell; they simply need encouragement and practice so that they can grow into capable and confident writers. Opportunities to read, write, and reflect provide students with the ability to express themselves and develop their own voices. That's why writing should start from the beginning. What will your students write today?

APPENDIX

The Rest of the Story

Visit the companion website at
https://companion.corwin.com/courses/writefromthebeginning
for downloadable versions of these resources.

We All Saw a ____________________.

Use the box below to draw a picture of what you saw.

We all saw a ____________________

____

____

____

I Saw a ________________________________.

Use the box below to draw a picture of what you saw.

I saw a ________________________________

____

____

____

Six-Room Image Poem

Image/Object Choose an image/object to focus on for this activity. Write down a description of the image/object.	**Light** Refer back to the item chosen in box one. Think about how the light shines on the item. Are there shadows? Is there a bright light or is it dimly lit?
Sound What sounds are associated with this image/object? What you do you hear? What sounds are made?	**Questions** What questions do you have about this image/object?
Feelings List any feelings associated with the image/object.	**Repeated Words** Look over the previous five boxes for any repeated words used. List them in this box.

After filling in each of the boxes, look back over the template and pull out words and phrases that could be used to write a poem about your image. You do not have to use every example from the template. You can add words and phrases as needed.

Source: Adapted from Georgia Heard's *Awakening the Heart*

Heart Map

Fill in this heart map with things in your life that you love. You might include the following:

- People you care about
- Places you love to visit
- Things you love to do
- Some of your favorite memories
- Favorite hobbies, foods, colors, movies, etc.

Everyday Writing

Did you know that our everyday lives often are great places to look for writing ideas? Think about the places you go on a regular basis or the activities or hobbies you enjoy. Make a list of those places, activities, or hobbies. Then record specific details about that idea. Consider where you are, who you are with, what is said, how you feel, etc.

Everyday Activities	Details and Descriptions

I Am From . . .

I am from . . .
Family
Favorites
Traditions
Friends
Hobbies
Other ideas

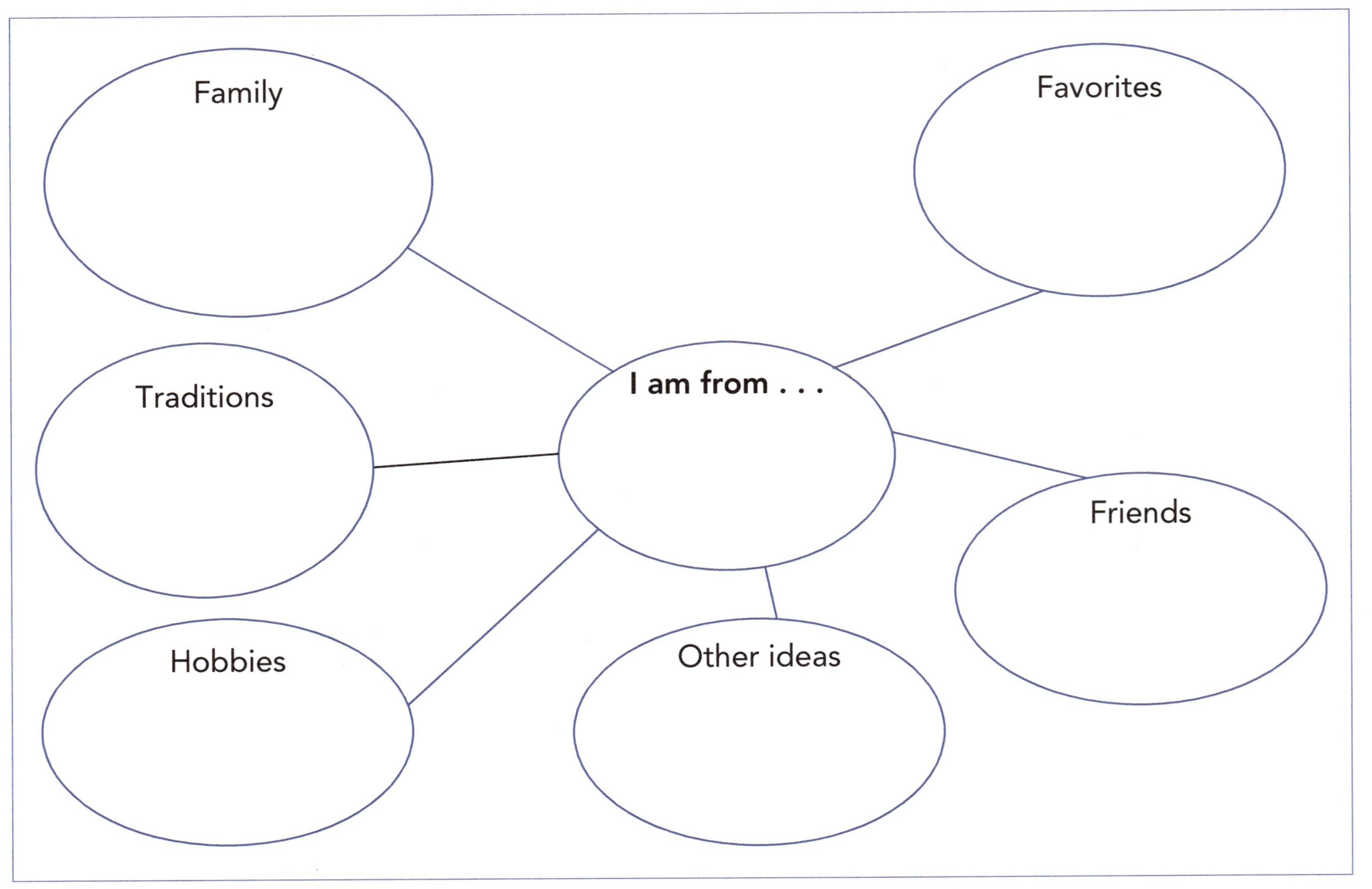

I Am From . . . Part 2

Use the box below to draw a picture of where you are from.

I am from

____

____

____

____

Yesterday I Had the . . .

Color	Items That Are This Color	Adjectives to Describe This Color	Moods Associated With This Color

Sentences for Stretching

I like dogs.

I play Fortnite.

That movie was good.

Playing video games is fun.

Summer vacation was awesome.

That girl is pretty.

She is in sixth grade.

He is mean.

We play outside at recess.

I like pizza.

I don't eat vegetables.

I like fruit.

That book is my favorite.

I go to football practice,

My sister goes to school.

My teacher is nice.

He likes cats.

I do not like chores.

Let's go to swim practice.

We won the race.

NVA^2

Nouns	Verbs	Adjectives

NVA²

Nouns	Verbs	Adjectives	Adverbs

Sensory Writing

Record details from the read aloud that appeal to the different senses.

Title of Book	Sight
Smell	Taste
Touch	Hear

Character Props

Character Chosen ______________________________

Character Traits

Prop	Justification	Textual Evidence (if applicable)

Numbers and Me

Put your name **in** the center. Include numbers that are related to you in the big box surrounding your name. You might include number of pets, siblings, your age, what grade you are in, etc.

Your Name

Animal Problems

Use the box below to draw a picture of your animal.

My animal is a ____.

It has a problem. The problem is ______________________________

____

____

____

I Bet You Didn't Know . . .

The ____

I bet you didn't know ____________________________________

____

____

____

____

Body Biography

Using the template attached, create a Body Biography of a character. Include the following:

The Heart: What does your character love the most? Who do they love? What matters the most to your character?

Quotations: What are some of your character's most memorable quotes? What items did they say that were most important? Include these in speech bubbles near the character's head.

Background: In the area around the body template, include information about the setting, other characters with whom your character spends time, any important events that occurred, etc. Draw and/or write these in the spaces around the body.

Hands: Include four adjectives that describe your character and record them on the hands.

Thoughts: What are your character's thoughts and ideas? What might they think about based upon their role in the story. Include these in thought bubbles near the character's head.

Arms and Legs: Include four major events from the story and record them on the arms and legs. (Write one event on one body part. For example, Event 1 is written on one arm. Event 2 is written on the other arm.)

Feet: Include two of your favorite details about your character from the story.

iStock.com/Oink Oink

Body Biography Checklist

Using bulletin board paper, create a Body Biography of a character. Begin by drawing a large outline of a body. Using this body outline as your template, include the following:

The Heart: What does your character love the most? Who do they love? What matters the most to your character?

Quotations: What are some of your character's most memorable quotes? What items did they say that were most important? Include these in speech bubbles near the character's head.

Background: In the area around the body template, include information about the setting, other characters with whom your character spends time, any important events that occurred, etc. Draw and/or write these in the spaces around the body.

Hands: Include four adjectives that describe your character and record them on the hands.

Thoughts: What are your character's thoughts and ideas? What might they think about based upon their role in the story. Include these in thought bubbles near the character's head.

Arms and legs: Include four major events from the story and record them on the arms and legs. (Write one event on one body part. For example, Event 1 is written on one arm. Event 2 is written on the other arm.)

Feet: Include two of your favorite details about your character from the story.

Would You Rather?

Would you rather be a ________________________ or a ________________________?

I would rather be a ____________ because __________________________________

____.

Text Mapping Slips

General Text Mapping Slip

1. Highlight the title and subtitles.
2. Put a box around the graphics, side bars, and illustrations.
3. Choose a word from the text. Use an address label to write a definition for the word and stick it on the article.
4. Change the subheadings to hashtags or questions.
5. Create a question for the chapter. Draw an arrow to the place in the text where you can find the answer.

Focusing on Text Features Slip

1. Highlight the title and subtitles.
2. Put a box around the graphics, side bars, and illustrations.
3. Circle any captions.
4. Change the subheadings to hashtags or questions.
5. Highlight any bold printed words.

Focusing on Comprehension Text Map Slip

1. Choose an image from the text. Write a new caption for it.
2. Choose a word from the text. Use an address label to write a definition for the word and stick it on the article.
3. Change the subheadings to hashtags or questions.
4. Create a question for the selection of the text. Write the question on a sticky note or notecard. Draw an arrow to the place in the text that answers the question.
5. Find a website that can be used for information on this topic. Write the web address on a sticky note or address label and stick it on the text.
6. Replace one of the images, diagrams, or figures with your own image.

Who Would Win?

A ______________________________ or a ______________________________?

The ____

would win because ______________________________________

____.

Whose Line Is It?

Quotes/Lines From Characters	The Character Who Said This Is . . .	I Know This Because . . .

Musical Voice

Song Title	Noticings *(mood, feeling, tempo, etc.)*

Character Playlist

Song and Artist	Justification for Inclusion

Novel Playlist

Song and Artist	Justification for Inclusion

Character Partner Poem

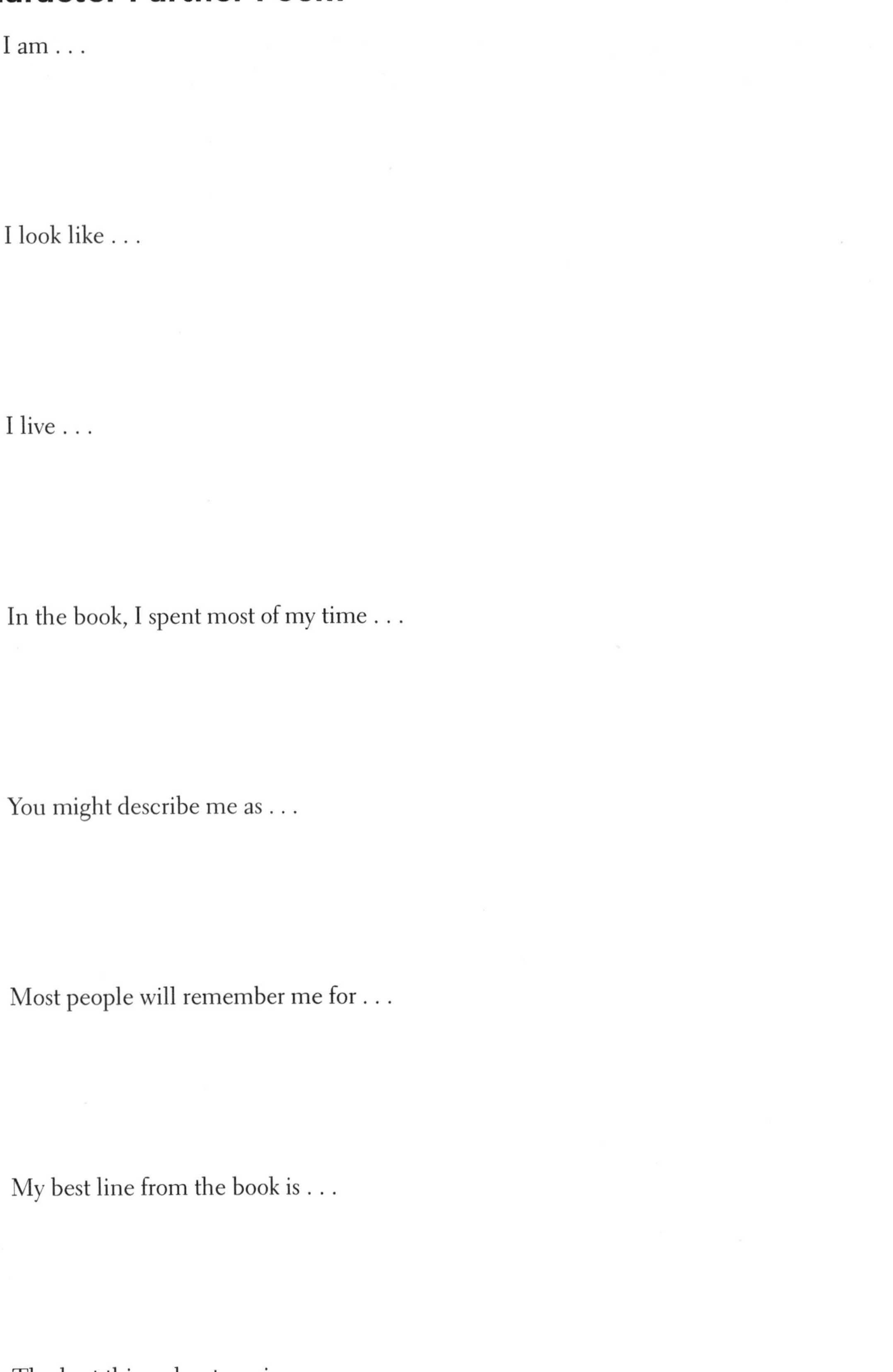

I am . . .

I look like . . .

I live . . .

In the book, I spent most of my time . . .

You might describe me as . . .

Most people will remember me for . . .

My best line from the book is . . .

The best thing about me is . . .

Name Writing Organizer

Version 1

First Name
Middle Name
Last Name

Name Writing Organizer

Version 2

First Name
Nick Name
Last Name

Name Writing Organizer

Version 3

First Name

Middle Name

Last Name (Hyphenated)	

Do This! Not That!

Do This!

Not That!

Book in a Box

Book Chosen ______________________________

Item	Justification	Textual Evidence (if applicable)

Stoplight Support

Using the chart below, list strong evidence under the Green Light Support and weak evidence under the Red Light Support. *See the companion website for a color version of this form.*

Red Light Support	Green Light Support

Stop light image source: iStock.com/Faisal Faisal

Walk Out Song

Song I Chose ______________________________

Character Traits/Adjectives That Describe Me (one trait per box)	Song Lyrics That Support

Book Pass

Title of Book	Author	My Thoughts/ Comments	Plan to Read

REFERENCES

Aram, D., & Levin, I. (2001). Mother-child joint writing in low SES: Sociocultural factors, maternal mediation and emergent literacy. *Cognitive Development, 16*(3), 831–852. https://doi.org/10.1016/S0885-2014(01)00067-3

Burgess, S. R., Hecht, S. A., & Lonigan, C. J. (2002). Relations of the home literacy environment (HLE) to the development of reading-related abilities: A one-year longitudinal study. *Reading Research Quarterly*, 37(4), 408–426. http://www.jstor.org/stable/748260

Freire, P., & Macedo, D. (1987). *Literacy: Reading the word and the world.* Bergin & Garvey.

Harper, R. (2017). *Content-area writing that rocks (and Works)*! Shell Education.

Harper, R. (2021). *Write now and write on: 37 strategies for authentic daily writing in every content area*. Corwin.

Harper, R. (2023). *Writing workouts: Strategies to build students' writing skills, stamina, and success*. Corwin.

Kumpulainen, K., Sairanen, H., & Nordström, A. (2020). Young children's digital literacy practices in the sociocultural contexts of their homes. *Journal of Early Childhood Literacy*, 20(3), 472–499. https://doi.org/10.1177/1468798420925116

Marsh, J., Hannon, P., Lewis, M., & Ritchie, L. (2017). Young children's initiation into family literacy practices in the digital age. *Journal of Early Childhood Research, 15*(1), 47–60. https://doi.org/10.1177/1476718X15582095

Puranik, C., Phillips, B., Lonigan, C., & Gibson, E. (2018). Home literacy practices and preschool children's emergent writing skills: An initial investigation. *Early Childhood Research Quarterly, 42*, 228–238. https://doi.org/10.1016/j.ecresq.2017.10.004

Rosenwald, G. C., & Ochberg, R. L. (Eds.). (1992). *Storied lives: The cultural politics of self-understanding*. Yale University Press.

Sénéchal, M., & LeFevre, J. A. (2002). Parental involvement in the development of children's reading skill: A five-year longitudinal study. *Child Development*, 73(2), 445–460. https://doi.org/10.1111/1467-8624.00417

Sénéchal, M., Lefevre, J. A., Thomas, E. M., & Daley, K. E. (1998). Differential effects of home literacy experiences on the development of oral and written language. *Reading Research Quarterly*, 33, 96–116. https://doi.org/10.1598/RRQ.33.1.5

Skibbe, L., Bindman, S., Hindman, A., Aram, D., & Morrison, F. (2013). Longitudinal relations between parental writing support and preschoolers' language and literacy skills. *Reading Research Quarterly*, 48(4), 387–401. https://doi.org/10.1002/rrq.55

Tovani, C. (2000). *I read it, but I don't get it: Comprehension strategies for adolescent readers*. Stenhouse.

Wang, A. (2021). *Watercress*. Neal Porter Books.

White, E. B. (1952). *Charlotte's web*. Harper & Brothers.

Yagoda, B. (2005). *The sound on the page: Style and voice in writing*. Harper Perennial.

INDEX

Helping educators make the greatest impact

CORWIN HAS ONE MISSION: to enhance education through intentional professional learning.

We build long-term relationships with our authors, educators, clients, and associations who partner with us to develop and continuously improve the best evidence-based practices that establish and support lifelong learning.

Zeitfracht Medien GmbH
Ferdinand-Jühlke-Straße 7
99095 Erfurt, Deutschland
produktsicherheit@kolibri360.de